Advance Praise

"Who are stakeholders? Where does innovation come from? What are the latest business trends? How has Huawei HMS managed to succeed? I believe that you will find the answers to these questions, and many more, by reading this book – it provides insight into the unique value of the Huawei HMS ecosystem.

Huawei has opened up all of its chip-device-cloud capabilities to developers via HMS Core, so that they can develop, grow and monetize, fostering innovation and spurring success on a new scale. This book provides important knowledge on the development history of Huawei's HMS ecosystem, and the open APIs and capabilities in HMS Core that have helped make app development seamlessly efficient. You can look forward to envisioning the realization and evolution of this truly independent ecosystem."

– Xiangyu Chen, co-founder and CEO of iDreamSky

"Huawei is a leader in the user device and 5G sector, having earned widespread global acclaim for its mobile phones. With the goal of nurturing digital innovation in the 5G era, HUAWEI Developers and HMS Core expert teams have managed to distill their years of device and cloud expertise into this book.

It aims to assist global developers with quickly building mobile apps, and seeks to enlist them in jointly building the HMS ecosystem. It is by working together that we can enrich society at large, and share the benefits with all. In view of this, I'd highly recommend this book, to help you with establishing a closer relationship with your users."

– Honghao Wang, CMO of 58.com

"As a close partner of Huawei, Qunar was one of the early adopters of Huawei HMS Core. Tourism is an industry with a long fulfillment chain, and a wide range of service links, including preparation, reservation, transportation, accommodation, sightseeing, and community. Each of these can be powered by HMS capabilities. With Awareness Kit, our users are able to book more cost-effective travel products, while traveling in a more thoughtful and intelligent way. Account Kit and Push Kit improve user experience and reduce our operational costs. As the HMS ecosystem continues to evolve, each innovation will be made even easier to implement. More and more developers will choose to partner with us with the shared goal of providing more efficient and intelligent products and services for users around the globe."

– Xiaojie Huang, CMO of Qunar

"In today's globalized world, every innovation should be encouraged. Developers are no longer just isolated individuals. Instead we are closely linked, and the emergence of HMS Core opens up decades of Huawei's accumulated technical prowess to all, under an ideal of: Tech for All and Tech for Good. This book introduces the HMS ecosystem and its technologies from multiple dimensions – ecosystem development, technical architecture, and support systems, so that developers can familiarize themselves with it, and ultimately become part of it."

– Xueliang Zhan, tech lead of Xiao Hongshu

Partnering with HMS: A Guide for App Developers

Partnering with HMS:
A Guide for App
Developers

Xihai Wang
Yue Wang
Hailiang Wu

CRC Press
Taylor & Francis Group
Boca Raton London New York

CRC Press is an imprint of the
Taylor & Francis Group, an **informa** business

HZ BOOKS
华章科技

First edition published 2022
by CRC Press
6000 Broken Sound Parkway NW, Suite 300, Boca Raton, FL 33487-2742

and by CRC Press
2 Park Square, Milton Park, Abingdon, Oxon, OX14 4RN

Library of Congress Cataloging-in-Publication Data
Names: Wang, Xihai, 1980- author. | Wang, Yue, 1977- author. |
Wu, Hailiang, 1983- author.
Title: Partnering with HMS : a guide for app developers / Xihai Wang,
Yue Wang, Hailiang Wu.
Description: First edition. | Boca Raton : CRC Press, 2022. | Includes
bibliographical references. | Summary: "This is the first book to
introduce the Huawei Mobile Services (HMS) ecosystem. It gives
developers a basic understanding of the ecosystem and how to leverage
kit and tool capabilities to make their apps better"— Provided by
publisher.
Identifiers: LCCN 2021013053 (print) | LCCN 2021013054 (ebook) |
ISBN 9781032073934 (hbk) | ISBN 9781032073941 (pbk) |
ISBN 9781003206699 (ebk)
Subjects: LCSH: Mobile computing. | Application software—Development. |
Hua wei ji shu you xian gong si.
Classification: LCC QA76.59 .W35 2022 (print) | LCC QA76.59 (ebook) |
DDC 005.25—dc23
LC record available at https://lccn.loc.gov/2021013053
LC ebook record available at https://lccn.loc.gov/2021013054

ISBN: 978-1-032-07393-4 (hbk)
ISBN: 978-1-032-07394-1 (pbk)
ISBN: 978-1-003-20669-9 (ebk)

DOI: 10.1201/9781003206699

Typeset in Minion
by codeMantra

Contents

Foreword I

We at Huawei have been under siege of US crackdowns since May 16, 2019, but we've managed to overcome. Huawei is not the only one affected – our customers and consumers were also hurt. We are doing our best to fix things, and like repairing a plane riddled with bullet holes, we've spent the past year working to staying aloft and grown stronger in the process.

We do know that building an ecosystem is an arduous undertaking, and since real progress doesn't happen overnight, we are ready for the long road ahead. It's now become clear that a truly global Huawei Mobile Services (HMS) ecosystem is in our midst. In the face of this year of unprecedented change, we have made remarkable progress toward our goals. In 10 short months, HMS Core has ventured into uncharted territory, filling in significant gaps in the existing app development capabilities, by pursuing groundbreaking innovation and open capabilities.

By December 2020, the HMS ecosystem was already serving more than 700 million Huawei end users around the world – with 120,000 apps having been integrated with HMS Core – and 2.3 million registered Huawei developers having been brought into the fold. We strive to integrate localized services into the HMS ecosystem to provide better services for consumers around the world. It is an ecosystem designed to excel in a truly sustainable way.

The all-intelligent Internet of Everything (IoE) has turned digital services into a literally trillion-dollar market, which is now entirely up for grabs. New services and apps seem to come and go at a breathtaking pace, and thus, it has never been more important for the provision of services to be diversified and made equitable rather than monopolized by a single country or company. We at Huawei are committed to building the world's third major smart device paradigm – an all-new HMS ecosystem, originating in China but serving the globe, and a breath of fresh air for developers, service providers, and consumers alike.

We believe that over the next 30 years, our world will become intelligent in seemingly inconceivable ways: Everyday objects will be able to sense, connect with, and even perceive their surroundings. Huawei's Consumer Business Group runs long term under a strategy of the HUAWEI Seamless AI Life in the hope of working more closely with developers and partners from around the world, to continuously build up an open, win-win HMS ecosystem, thus making this lofty vision a reality, for the benefit of all. We hope that digital innovation can take root, sprout, and grow into a big tree in the ecosystem soil, whose fruits can be enjoyed by all in the future. To achieve this goal, we will strive toward the following commitments:

Giving each idea the space and support it needs to grow into a viable reality. A full-scale IoE can only be achieved when small and medium-sized enterprises are involved, innovating from the ground up to accelerate the digitalization of the physical world. We know that innovators need and want support from a platform that can give them open and comprehensive capabilities. With that support, they'll be able to focus on creation and skill building. Huawei has created a trailblazing streamlined Cloud-Pipe-Device-Chip architecture, to power networks, devices, and apps, facilitating the construction of a full-fledged ecosystem. Huawei has made its capabilities fully and constantly open through HMS Core, in the understanding that every new innovation brings us one step closer to a fully connected future.

Ensuring that each product and service will reach end users, with newfound ease. Future-oriented innovation ultimately aims to serve society with intelligent digital services. One of the unique values of our ecosystem is how it bridges the gap between users and the underlying technology that powers their lives. Huawei's Consumer Business Group and its carrier partners have hundreds of millions of users around the world. The mobile phone and other all-scenario devices are intertwined with every facet of daily life, from smart homes, to smart travel, to e-commerce. The ubiquitous connectivity of the HMS ecosystem means that our partners and developers can make their digital services available to literally billions of users in the blink of an eye.

Cultivating talent on a global scale. Huawei has proposed its pioneering TECH4ALL Digital Inclusion Initiative, in order to address the lack of opportunity and patchwork growth in the mobile development field.

At a time in which we are more connected than ever, it's important that no one gets left behind. In building the HMS ecosystem, launching the billion-dollar Shining Star Program, and carrying out localized developer activities, we hope to spur growth and innovation across the board, in every corner of the globe, helping small and medium-sized enterprises gain a foothold, support economic growth, and empower digital sovereignty. This is how Huawei can continue to serve global consumers with innovative digital services and create greater value to society.

To help more developers and users understand and join Huawei's HMS ecosystem, we have planned a series of books on the HMS ecosystem. In the book, we share many of the crucial technologies behind HMS, as well as best practices and experiences that developers, technology enthusiasts, and ecosystem partners are sure to find invaluable.

We hope you find this book as enriching and rewarding to read as we expect, and appreciate any and all feedback.

Ping'an Zhang
President, Huawei Consumer Cloud Service Department

Foreword II

A S A FORMER DEVELOPER, I'm thrilled to see this book published. Perhaps it is my knowledge from experience that a product needs to go through some hard times before it is ready for use. In addition to product development, developers also need to know how to acquire users and monetize a product after it is developed. This is the textbook we developers have been looking for.

Huawei HMS 5.0 was released globally and greatly optimized to improve user experience for developers. We believe that HUAWEI Developers will grow in its ranks, and this book will give each developer a panorama of the HMS ecosystem and illustrated tutorials to integrate HMS Core kits. The authors have applied their years of firsthand technical experience to help demonstrate how the open capabilities in HMS Core can be put into practice.

Huawei's Consumer Business Group has hundreds of millions of users around the world, and each of these users enjoys quicker access to innovation, thanks to Huawei's all-scenario devices. Developers can count on this book as a guide for how to use HMS Core open capabilities and toolkits, and a means to build apps and acquire paid users with optimal efficiency.

Twenty years of the mobile Internet have created even more developers of the mobile app, and many apps have been inspired by HMS Core. By December 2020, 2.3 million of them registered on HUAWEI Developers, with over 120,000 apps integrated with HMS Core.

Kwai is one of such apps. We started with the goal of linking ordinary people in new ways, and we have succeeded in connecting hundreds of millions of users and enriching lives through the promise of technology.

We expect more developers and more innovative apps to join the HMS ecosystem!

Yixiao Cheng
Founder, Kwai

Foreword III

BRINGING SERVICES ONLINE AND endowing them with intelligent attributes are the major trends in our ongoing mobile Internet era. We have seen countless services brought online, countless people connected to networks, and countless lives improved. In this era, the enablement provided by a platform is indispensable for incubating developers who are longing to succeed in innovations. This book signals an indication that Huawei is ready to team up with developers to get prepared for the blossoming of digital services.

As one of many beneficiaries of the HMS ecosystem, Himalaya serves more than 35 million users through Huawei's products and services. Huawei has accelerated the popularity of Himalaya by making it accessible in most life scenarios, locations, and devices.

The world around us is changing constantly and dramatically, but the one constant is that globalization is here to stay. We believe that with Huawei HMS support, Chinese developers can reach people in other countries and regions more effectively, acquire users more quickly, and achieve success more widely. We also believe that thanks to this ecosystem, the journey will be smoother, inspiration will become real and life-changing, and more of humanity can enjoy digital services.

Jianjun Yu
CEO, Himalaya

Preface

WHAT INSPIRED THIS BOOK?

The year 2020 marks two decades of the mobile Internet era that China has undergone, and in June of this year, Huawei released HMS 5.0, just five months after having released HMS 4.0, one of many transformative events that, just like 2G toward 4G, the mobile Internet has undergone in the past two decades. Developers of mobile apps came forward and created a digital wonderland of sorts that accelerated the development of the industry and ecosystems. With 5G at our doorstep, what will the future mobile world look like? How do we connect all these devices? How do we provide users with services that are both good and versatile? These are the concerns shared by every person participating in ecosystem development.

According to a HUAWEI Developers report in December 2020, Huawei has 2.3 million registered developers worldwide, and more than 120,000 apps have been integrated with HMS Core. Behind this rapid growth is our very own HMS ecosystem, built to reflect our confidence and commitment to a successful business model for developers and their apps. The earliest iterations of HMS had few basic capabilities, a stark contrast to the most recent HMS 5.0, which boasts over 50 open capabilities and an architecture that has been optimized over and over again to best serve developers. Instead of settling for technical documentation, a developer curious about HMS would benefit from the systematic and thorough coverage of ecosystem concepts a book can provide. We – HUAWEI Developers, HMS Research and Development (R&D), and Consumer Cloud Services – thus came together to co-write this book on the HMS ecosystem, *Partnering with HMS: A Guide for App Developers.*

We've spent years on the technology. We understand how our ecosystem started and grew. Now, we've distilled what we know to help developers Develop, Grow, and Monetize with us. Here, you get detailed instructions on how you can use HMS open capabilities to develop quality apps, acquire users, and effectively monetize your hard work. You'll also get a detailed look at how Huawei HMS came to be, the business model and value chain that underpins the entire ecosystem, as well as the privacy compliance framework, which is so crucial to all operations. It is our hope you will join us in learning, understanding, and partnering with us in the HMS ecosystem. Let's keep it open, secure, and win-win.

WHAT'S IN STORE IN THIS BOOK?

This is the first book to introduce the Huawei HMS ecosystem. It gives developers a basic understanding of the ecosystem and how to leverage kit and tool capabilities to make their apps better.

We at the HMS ecosystem R&D department strive to give you a book that is easy-to-follow and comprehensive, with informative sample code.

WHO IS THIS BOOK INTENDED FOR?

- Engineers working in mobile app design, development, and testing
- Product, operations, and marketing practitioners in mobile app ecosystems
- Advocates for the mobile app ecosystem
- Promoters, practitioners, and potential participants who are interested in the development of mobile app ecosystems
- Instructors and students in related university courses

WHAT'S THE BEST WAY TO READ THIS BOOK?

Here is a breakdown of the 12 chapters:

Chapters 1 and 2 delve into the development timeline of the HMS Core ecosystem, as well as its overall architecture and methods for integrating it, a bird's-eye view that will be relevant to anyone interested in creating mobile apps.

Chapters 3–11 are quick start guides for kit integration and practical environment setup, detailing the functions and principles behind each kit.

By showing you how to integrate kits, we explain in detail Account Kit, IAP, Push Kit, Location Kit, Map Kit, Site Kit, Safety Detect, and FIDO. Learn how to quickly integrate the open capabilities found in each HMS Core kit.

Chapter 12 introduces the app testing solution offered by Huawei and releasing apps on AppGallery. Experience what it's like to test your app on different phone models and release your app on AppGallery.

Appendix lists prominent developer services provided by the ecosystem, such as Customer Service, HUAWEI Forum, and Codelabs, as well as training and incentive programs.

If you are experienced at developing mobile apps, this book will be an excellent companion reference. If you're starting from scratch, learning some Android basics will prove useful.

The HMS ecosystem features the HUAWEI DevEco Studio. Since you are likely to be more familiar with Android Studio, we have used it in examples. Choose either that or HUAWEI DevEco Studio to help you build your app.

Screenshots in this book may differ from the software interface, depending on the latest version.

YOUR SUPPORT

Despite our best efforts, errors and inaccuracies are inevitable with a project of this magnitude. Please email any comments or suggestions to devConnect@huawei.com, or contact us through @HUAWEI Developers (Weibo or WeChat accounts). Your feedback is essential to helping us grow and improve.

Acknowledgments

THIS BOOK IS JOINTLY written by HUAWEI Developers and HMS R&D. Management and consultants of the Consumer Cloud Service Department of Huawei have offered much guidance, support, and encouragement. Editors of the Taylor & Francis Group have provided strict and meticulous correction. I would like to thank you all for your love of this book and your hard work!

Below is the list of people involved with writing, reviewing, and translating this book:

Authors: Xihai Wang, Yue Wang, Hailiang Wu

Co-authors: Bin Chen, Chun Cui, Deli Tong, Fangjing Shi, Gao Pan, Jiegou Yan, Juntao Lv, Weilong Hou, Xiang Han, Xiao Jiang, Xinyu Weng, Yi Zhu, Yingying Zhang, Yue Zong, Yunfang Yang, Yusheng Zhong, Ziliang Zhai

Technical reviewers: Dafang Cao, Deqian Liu, Xiaojia Liao, Xiaomei Zhang, Xinyue Zhang, Yuanyang Liu, Zhihong Wang

Translators: Chunmei Chen, Deborah Siew Ming Chin, Haiqiang He, Hongxia Ma, Jing Ni, Ling Mei, Miao Zhang, Nathanael Schneider, Qi Chen, Rongrong Liu, Wuqian Zhou, Xu Yan, Yang Wang, Yuchuan Xie, Zhenzhen Qin

Special Thanks
Special thanks are owed to Aiqin Guo, Gaofeng Li, Lan Peng, Ran Liu, Xingchang Deng, Yawei Zang, Yinjia Gao, and other Huawei consumer business consultants for their valuable input.

Finally, thank you all for your support!

Xihai Wang

Authors

Xihai Wang is the founder of the HMS ecosystem and chief judge for DIGIX competitions run by the Huawei Consumer Cloud Service. Devoted to the software field for more than 15 years, he has recently focused on promoting open HMS capabilities and working with global developers to build an all-scenario smart ecosystem.

Yue Wang is the co-founder and advocate for the Quick App Alliance. He has nearly two decades of experience in developing and delivering major management software, distributed middleware, and platforms in the telecommunications field. This international field has benefited from many of his patent articles and grants. His core work is now dedicated to building open HMS Core capabilities while helping global developers succeed in the market.

Hailiang Wu is the chief lecturer for the HDD and HMS courses. Building on 10 years of experience in software development and architecture design, he now advocates for open HMS capabilities and the HMS ecosystem on a global stage, including technical support for global developers.

CHAPTER 1

Overview of the HMS Ecosystem

1.1 THE RISE OF MOBILE APP ECOSYSTEMS

Let's go back two decades and re-witness the rapid development of the mobile Internet in China and its catalysis of the unprecedented prosperity of today's mobile app market.

1.1.1 Development of the Mobile Internet

The soaring development of the mobile Internet can be attributed to the regeneration of the mobile network communications infrastructure. To overcome the limitations of 2G mobile phones on data speeds, the mobile Internet was born around 2000 from among simple Wireless App Protocol (WAP) applications. The WAP translated HTML information on webpages into Wireless Markup Language (WML) and displayed such content on mobile devices, providing users with access to company WAP sites on WAP-compatible browsers. Carriers in China were among the first to employ WAP for mobile applications. China Mobile, the largest carrier in China, launched the Monternet services at the end of 2000 to provide multimedia messaging (MMS) and games. KONGZHONG and a range of other service providers soon emerged in response. Users began to enjoy mobile Internet services through MMS and Internet browsing.

Since 2007, Internet browsing became much more enjoyable, thanks to the 3G mobile network. Major Internet companies were eager to gain a foothold in

DOI: 10.1201/9781003206699-1

1

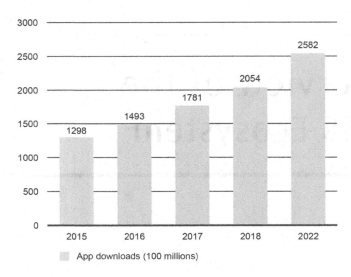

FIGURE 1.1   Global downloads of mobile apps from 2015 to 2018, and projected global downloads in 2022.

the mobile market and began transforming their business models and incorporating mobile devices, in order to stay relevant. Since 2012, the ubiquity of smartphones with touchscreens has spurred rampant demand for mobile Internet access, which in furtherance has driven the need for mobile apps.

Driven by the growth in smartphone usage and concurrent app trend, developers around the world were enthusiastic in their pursuit of innovation. By 2020, over five million apps had been released on app stores around the world, to the point that there's now an app for seemingly every purpose: from every conceivable form of entertainment, to every mode of travel, and so much more. Apps have reshaped the way we live, work, and interact with the world around us, and are now indispensable in every facet of daily life. Figure 1.1 shows the growth in global app downloads from 2015 to 2018 and projections for 2022.

1.1.2 History of Mobile App Ecosystems

We've seen that mobile apps are a market that is big today and bigger tomorrow. At this scale, we hear of ecosystems. The concept of a business ecosystem first appeared in an article published by the *Harvard Business Review* in May 1993, referring to an economic community formed by organizations and individuals that affect and are affected by each other.

Members of a business ecosystem include suppliers, users, and other stakeholders. Ecosystem leaders guide members to reorient their investments, find mutually supportive roles, and move toward a shared vision.

Similarly, a mobile app ecosystem consists of developers, users, and a platform that connects them. So why become an ecosystem in the first place? Developers are motivated by faster, more cost-effective ways to monetize their products, users are always on the lookout for better experience and services, whereas the ecosystem platform provides all-round support for developers and a rich array of apps for users, meeting everyone's needs. The three together thus form a close and intertwined relation with each other as a whole.

Let's learn about the three stages of growing a mobile app ecosystem.

1. Building a distribution platform to establish an initiative

At the early stage of mobile app development, users faced a number of challenges. They couldn't find the apps they wanted without hassle. They might have downloaded a risky app. Some apps were just too complicated to download and install. Neither the process nor the experience was friendly to casual users, and there was widespread demand for more secure and convenient alternatives.

Developers were similarly challenged. They had to release their apps on numerous websites, a process that was inefficient and required constant maintenance. The sheer number of third-party websites and user portals meant that it was harder for developers to promote their apps and encourage users to sign up. Developers would also benefit substantially from a streamlined distribution channel, as it would reduce costs and help with acquiring new users.

A unified distribution platform satisfied both demands, so smart device vendors built their own – Apple with App Store, Google with Google Play, and Huawei with AppGallery. Thanks to these platforms, developers get their apps efficiently distributed, while users enjoy a one-stop shop to search for, install, and upgrade the apps they need.

So long as developers create quality apps, they will be able to acquire more users and earn more money. Apps on distribution platforms reach a larger user base more quickly, who, in turn, enjoy a better experience getting and using such apps. The app distribution platforms were the precursors to the mobile app ecosystem, as shown in Figure 1.2.

FIGURE 1.2   Initial stages of a mobile app ecosystem.

2. Providing support at all levels to develop the ecosystem

As these ecosystems grew, so did the number and types of apps available. Unfortunately, not all these apps stood out. Developers must beat the homogeneous competition with truly innovative ideas, and they must make an app both well and quickly. How could they overcome this dual challenge? Even preparations are complex – factors such as server resources, technical breakthroughs, R&D labor costs, business models, and security and privacy all need to be fully considered. This means that developers have to spend a considerable amount of time and money on research and development before they can begin working toward their goals. In the ever-changing mobile Internet market, the length of the R&D cycle determines the success of a product. A shorter development cycle and lower costs mean that a developer can focus their attention on standing out – building something that is both novel and commercially viable. Their ideal would be an ecosystem platform with basic capabilities for app development, tools to facilitate efficient delivery, and platforms for technical innovation.

To be successful at this stage, an ecosystem platform has to attract more developers and host as many apps as necessary to fulfill user demand. Two problems need to be resolved: One is how to provide competitive capabilities to attract more developers, and the other is how to optimize user experience of apps on their devices so that more users can be attracted to their ecosystem, growing the developer's user base. In this way, the developer and the platform form a mutually symbiotic relationship.

An ideal ecosystem platform provides all-round support for developers by leveraging the advantages of its existing assets. This entails the provision of basic capabilities for app development, abundant resources for promotion and incentives, and technical support in key domains. This support helps developers compete in the market, which, in turn, drives a healthy ecosystem. That's why each ecosystem platform endeavors to provide as many open capabilities and services as it can to help developers develop apps more efficiently and support quick app release, so as to establish its own competitiveness in the ecosystem.

Let's take a look at how major ecosystem platforms have opened up. In terms of app development, SDKs for hardware and software provide basic capabilities such as location, maps, cloud storage, digital rights protection, and gaming. In terms of efficiency improvement, new tools and languages – such as Apple's Xcode and Swift, Google's Android Studio, and Huawei's DevEco Studio – have boosted developer productivity and output quality to new heights. These platforms also provide the latest technology, in the form of AR, VR, and AI, to ensure that developers stay relevant regardless of their field. By being so open and supportive, platforms enrich their apps, give their users a better experience, and strengthen the mutual dependence they have with their developers.

3. Promoting deeper integration into a community with a shared future

As of May 2020, more than five million mobile apps have been created, a far cry from the early days of the mobile Internet when scarcity ruled. An ecosystem is no longer just about how many apps it has – it has become more discerning, removing apps with poor user experience from its app store. Platforms now care more about growing better apps so their developers can profit. These ecosystems have evolved in multiple ways:

First, they offer refined capabilities to help developers operate their apps better. The Analytics capabilities provided by Google Firebase and Huawei HMS Core give developers insight into users and user behavior and enable better responsiveness and strategic adjustment.

Second, they have introduced new ways of access, making it easier for apps to reach users through diversified interaction modes and for developers to harness traffic and monetization opportunities.

Apple's Siri helps users find the apps they want via voice interactions. HUAWEI Assistant opens frequently used apps with a single touch, to ensure that users enjoy intelligent features and timely messaging in every scenario.

The types of apps that are accessible to users also continue to evolve. A typical example is Huawei's quick app, a new, installation-free app paradigm, which spares developers from having to spend more to drive downloads and updates, saving both them and their users' time when joining the ecosystem and effort when promoting their apps.

Due to these trends and others, today's app ecosystems must focus on developer enablement, and developers likewise, need to be highly attentive to the ecosystem, in order to build cutting-edge apps. This partnership ensures that the ecosystem functions as a close community with a shared future and facilitates that a smarter future, in which devices and content are seamlessly interlinked by a rich array of apps and portals, is within reach.

1.1.3 Value Distribution of Mobile App Ecosystems

Like other commercial forces, a mobile app ecosystem is subject to the principles of supply and demand. Demand comes from consumers – or users – who want convenience and diverse services and are willing to pay for a better experience. On the supply side are developers, who build and operate apps in order to make money from them.

Since smart devices are what connect developers and users, vendors form the key linchpin in the ecosystem. Apple is one such vendor, as is Google, which occupies a comparable role, due to its control over the Android system. As shown in Figure 1.3, the value chain of a mobile ecosystem can be divided into three parts.

In such an ecosystem, how do developers and smart device vendors monetize their businesses?

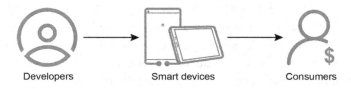

Developers　　　　　Smart devices　　　　　Consumers

FIGURE 1.3　Value chain of a mobile app ecosystem.

1. Developer Profit Model

    Developers make money mainly through either or both:

    a. Ads: offering services to consumers for free to entice more visitors and displaying advertisements to garner revenue.

    b. Paid services: charging consumers for services to garner revenue, via either in-app purchases or access to the app itself.

    When using ads as shown in Figure 1.4, developers earn ad revenue. Google provides an SDK for developers to display ads pushed by Google Ads. Ads have evolved alongside mobile app ecosystems, with the emergence of third-party providers and monitoring platforms. Developers thus must grow their user base while relying on the ad platform to monetize this traffic for them and share the income therefrom with them.

    The importance of ads as a profit model is clear. For example, a weather app helps its users prepare for their trip anytime. Developing and maintaining such an app require server space, which incurs substantial costs, yet the app itself is free to use. The developer behind the app can cover these costs and earn a profit by displaying splash and banner ads, which bring in substantial revenue even at a minimal user base.

    By contrast, the paid services model involves premium apps that users are willing to pay for, as shown in Figure 1.5. This profit model requires an online payment infrastructure, and emerging payment platforms at home and abroad have made it easier than ever for users to purchase paid services. Developers of paid services only need to focus on quality, relying on payment platforms to charge user fees. And payment platforms get a share from this. Both Apple and Google

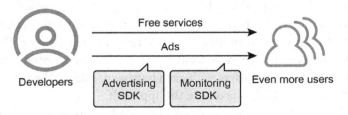

FIGURE 1.4   Business logic behind ad revenue.

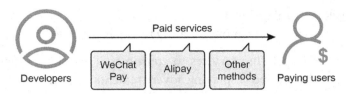

FIGURE 1.5   Business logic behind paid service revenue.

have launched their own payment SDKs to help developers monetize their apps faster.

For example, an early childhood education app that features text, image, and audio content may be so enriching and educational that parents are willing to pay for it, ensuring that there is a significant user base for the app, through which the developer earns money.

Developers have diversified the way they make money, increasingly mixing and matching between the two business models as they see fit. For example, developers who stick to ads might offer an ad-free experience for paid members. Developers who prefer paid services might offer free services with ads as an incentive to entice more users. Video services offer ad-free streaming of paid movies, while rolling ads for free users.

2. Vendor Profit Model

In addition to relying on hardware sales, smart device vendors acting the role of an ecosystem platform earn from their mobile app ecosystems. They mostly adopt two business models. The first one is native apps. Apps that come preinstalled on devices vendors sell are a source of ad revenue, while apps the user can pay for also bring in money, as shown in Figure 1.6.

For instance, a smart device vendor might preinstall its own video player at the top of the home screen. By offering movies and TV shows, the vendor can earn ad money from non-members and subscription money from members. While similar to other OTT video apps in providing video content for profit, such vendor-provided video apps acquire users with each hardware sale, so the vendor does not need to spend to promote the app itself.

For vendors, there is also another model – as an app distributor over their device operating system. On the app market preinstalled

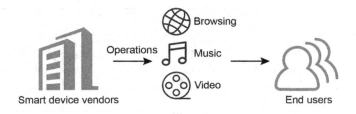

FIGURE 1.6   Profit model for smart device vendors (1).

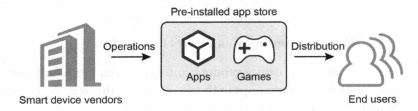

FIGURE 1.7   Profit model for smart device vendors (2).

on their devices, vendors provide promotional resources to developers to market their apps. In return, these vendors earn from this promotion. They also share in the revenue that developers receive from the exposure and subsequent paid users. Apple's App Store is the only app market available on Apple devices, and thus the only way for developers to reach Apple device users. Developers have to promote their apps on App Store, and they may need to share their revenue with Apple, if they would like to provide paid apps for Apple users. Likewise with Android, developers have to promote ads and may have to share revenue on either Google Play or a similar vendor store to reach Android users. Figure 1.7 illustrates this second business model for vendors.

In China, vendor app stores require that apps pass compatibility and security tests to ensure that they can run on most mainstream device models. This means that users have peace of mind when downloading and installing apps, which, in turn, makes them more inclined to use a vendor app store. By releasing and promoting their apps on these stores, developers are able to boost app downloads. In turn, vendors increase profitability, both by operations and revenue sharing. Developers of game apps and other types of paid apps

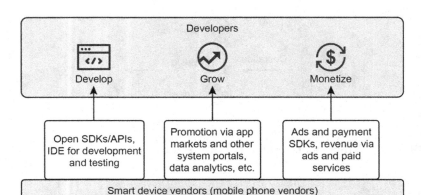

FIGURE 1.8   Business community with a shared future.

share revenue with device vendors, and device vendors offer promi-nent positions for their apps in the app stores. In this way, developers benefit from more visibility on the app stores as well.

Today's app ecosystems have become increasingly intricate: evolv-ing from a simple app distribution model to that in which the devel-oper is supported throughout the entire lifecycle of app development. This new model is illustrated in Figure 1.8.

Since vendors are no longer just app distributors, they now offer an array of APIs, SDKs, and tools to improve developer efficiency. They open up a world of software and hardware capabilities for a favorable environment for product innovation that attracts more developers to be part of their ecosystem.

To grow apps, vendors offer resources for promotion in their app markets and system portals. Because the smartphone is the closest point of contact, it can be indispensable as a tool for attracting users without undermining user experience. Thanks to robust system capabilities, vendors give developers a holistic data analysis system, with more multidimensional data to better analyze operations and attract more users.

To monetize apps, vendors offer payment functions as win-win operations with developers. Resource slots are allocated based on revenue sharing so developers don't need to spend on attracting traf-fic and revenue. Also, vendors give developers access via SDKs to their advertising systems so that developers can display in-app ads and thus get revenue from vendors. Thanks to the vendor's brand reputation and quality control capabilities, developers can benefit from higher-quality ads and advertisers. In this way, an acclaimed vendor's ad SDK can help developers earn more revenue, while maintaining high-end user experience.

These symbiotic relationships indicate that the business of smart device vendors and app developers is seamlessly interlinked, with both highly invested in maintaining a dynamic and sustainable app development ecosystem for the future.

1.2 THE HISTORY OF THE HMS ECOSYSTEM

This section provides a glimpse into how Huawei's device business and cloud services developed, as well as the origins and development of the HMS ecosystem.

1.2.1 Huawei's Device Business and Cloud Services

In 2003, Huawei established its mobile phone division, which was then known as Huawei Device, with the goal of tapping into a flourishing device market. The first seven years saw Huawei focus its efforts on fixed wireless terminals and data card services. However, the company's experience as an original design manufacturer (ODM) at this time helped it accumulate expertise in the mobile phone field. In 2004, Huawei exhibited China's first-ever WCDMA mobile phone at the 3GSM Conference in Cannes, France, and in 2009, unveiled its first Android smartphone at the Mobile World Congress (MWC).

The year 2012 marked a significant strategy shift for Huawei's device business: from an ODM to a dedicated smartphone brand in its own right, from low-end mobile phones to mid-range and high-end smartphones, and from carrier resale to the open market. Leveraging its strength in industrialized systems gained from years of experience in the communications sector, Huawei's consumer business[1] has won over consumers by equipping devices with standout battery life, calling quality, and mobile photography capabilities, as well as inventive Android software optimizations. Huawei gained a foothold as a top-three global smartphone brand (by market share) from 2015 and vaulted into second place in 2018. Huawei has offered abundant cloud services to serve its massive user base in its commitment to upgrading user experience and sharing success with developers. Monthly active users (MAUs) of Huawei smart devices exceeded 700 million in December 2020. This enormous user base lays the groundwork for HMS ecosystem development.

With the emergence of cloud services, a result of the ubiquitous mobile Internet, Huawei expanded its service scope in 2015, to encompass the following four categories of consumer cloud services:

1. Basic cloud services: Account Kit, ROM upgrade services, etc.

2. User-facing services: AppGallery, GameCenter, HiLives, HiCare, Wallet, etc.

3. Content operations services: Music, Video, Reader, etc.

4. Open platform services: end-to-end developer tools that support Huawei's mobile app ecosystem.

An ever-growing number of today's users now enjoy access to convenient cloud services, a trend accentuated by the rise of new technologies, such as AI and 5G. They would prefer to interact with their devices on an intelligent basis, across all usage scenarios, and regard their smartphone as the primary point of access. Huawei believes that a close, mutually beneficial partnership with developers is critical to prosperity. It balances experience and innovation in propelling its cloud services. Thanks to a rapidly growing user base, user activity, and average revenue per user (ARPU) of Huawei smartphones, developers have increasingly made Huawei's open HMS capabilities as their framework of choice for mobile app developing, spurring the growth and evolution of the HMS ecosystem at large.

1.2.2 Emergence of an HMS Ecosystem

Every Huawei smartphone, even the earliest models, comes equipped with both AppGallery and Account Kit. The services in the HMS ecosystem are designed to enrich our lives, and Account Kit was first. Let's start there in our walk through the HMS journey.

Back at the beginning of 2011, Huawei phone users proposed a Find My Phone function for the Emotion User Interface (EMUI)[2]: An

Internet-connected phone would report its location and other information to the Huawei cloud service platform. Someone who lost their phone could sign in to the cloud website and find, call, lock, and erase it, quickly and easily.

When fulfilling this urgent demand for the Find My Phone function, Huawei's R&D team immediately found the going got tough. A user needs to authorize the reporting of their phone's location, not to mention searching for and locking the phone. Without a unified account system for Huawei phones, Find My Phone wouldn't happen. Given these demands, the team decided to prioritize the development of Account Kit: launching it in mid-2011 to mobile services such as Find Device and Cloud. By 2013, Account Kit had already garnered more than 20 million active users, even more remarkable considering that initially it was not made accessible to developers.

In 2012, Huawei's smartphone business set sail, with high-end smartphone innovation as anchor. As the third-largest global smartphone manufacturer by the end of that year, Huawei joined hands with developers. Some game developers, in particular, eagerly eyed Account Kit, as a point of entry to Huawei's enormous user base. In response, Huawei launched the first open HMS Core Account SDK the following year. By integrating the Account Kit SDK, developers would enjoy access to the kit's sign-in and authorization functions, sparing them the need to devote time or money to developing account systems or account/password management and verification functions of their own. Account Kit served as a bridge connecting developer apps to Huawei phones and has since been integrated with third-party apps and evolved into the base of the HMS ecosystem, indispensable to a wide range of Huawei-developed apps, including Video, Music, Reader, and Themes.

In-App Purchases (IAP) is another service that has been accessible to developers for a long time. In 2011, mobile Internet services – mobile payment in particular – started to take hold in China, and e-payment channels, like Alipay, WeChat, and UnionPay, became everyday services. At the same time, game developers had grown frustrated at the need to integrate multiple payment SDKs and manage the fallout of a patchwork, inconsistent user experience.

Developers preferred an in-app purchase service that would converge the major mobile payment channels. Huawei fulfilled this need in 2012 and more than 20 content providers (CPs) integrated the SDK into their apps within the first week of its launch.

IAP now powers an impressive array of payment methods: HUAWEI Pay, HUAWEI Points, phone top-ups, and many others, enabling developers to manage the pricing of virtual offerings. IAP has proved critical to facilitating app monetization and served tens of thousands of developers – as a key part of the HMS ecosystem – across 177 countries and regions, as of 2019.

Growing in tandem with mobile app development, Push Kit was also crucial in the infancy of the HMS ecosystem. Apple had created its Apple Push Notification service (APNs) for iOS app developers, at an early stage, as an inclusive push solution at the heart of mobile app operations and promotions. Google soon followed suit with its closed-source Android Cloud to Device Messaging (C2DM), made available beginning with Android 2.2. Unfortunately, Android app developers in China were unable to access the completely free and open push services prior to 2012.

In 2011 and 2012, China experienced an explosion in smartphone sales and the widespread proliferation of mobile apps – with over 400,000 apps being released on Android, and 20,000 to 30,000 apps being released every week. Due to the limitations of push services in China, large app developers set up their own push servers, while numerous smaller developers had no choice but to depend on the available paid services and experienced lengthy notification-related delays and low arrival rates. Power consumption and device security-related concerns made the publicly accessible push services far from ideal.

As Huawei Device swept the smartphone market in 2011, it leaned on its strength as a manufacturer to develop a dedicated push notification service for its products. To ensure the service was stable, reliable, efficient in real time, and accessible to developers, Huawei invited them to participate in beta testing for its first push SDK in late 2011. Huawei's push service demonstrated a higher delivery rate and smaller delays than the other push services available on the market. The first official version of Push Kit was launched in early 2012 and garnered over one million active users within three months. By the end of 2012, that figure had surpassed 10 million.

With its 500 million MAUs, Push Kit is among the most popular HMS services widely used by developers around the world, supporting messaging to web and iOS apps as well. It facilitates the sending of millions of messages per second and tens of billions per day.

Although Account Kit, Push Kit, and IAP have all proved fundamental to the HMS ecosystem, they were all developed along separate tracks. This parallel development model proved problematic when Game Service, Analytics Kit, and other capabilities were also made publicly available, beginning in 2013. Thus in 2015, the HMS team restructured all open capabilities and extracted their shared components into HMS Core, a framework which enables lightweight SDKs to be provided for specific capabilities.

That effort led to smaller SDKs, faster integration, and more convenient HMS Core updates. The new architecture fully unlocked the potential of the HMS ecosystem, inspiring the rollout of new capabilities. By August 2019, the HMS ecosystem had grown to encompass 51 open capabilities and services, serving millions of developers in more than 170 countries and regions. Figure 1.9 illustrates the HMS architecture before and after the reconstruction.

January 15, 2020 marked the global release of HMS Core 4.0. This suite of HMS open capabilities was the star at Huawei's Consumer Business Product and Strategy Virtual Launch. HMS Core 4.0 responded to developer demand with new capabilities: Machine Learning (ML) Kit, Scan Kit, Nearby Service, Safety Detect, Location Kit, WisePlay DRM, and Map

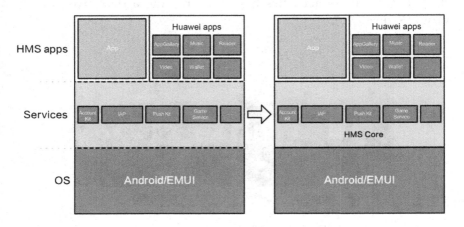

FIGURE 1.9   HMS architecture reconstruction.

Kit. System and chip-level capabilities, such as Camera Engine, AR, VR, and HiAI, served as a perfect complement, giving the HMS ecosystem a new level of all-round versatility. By April 2020, the HMS ecosystem had grown to include 90 capabilities and services, and 53 of them available outside of the Chinese mainland. By harnessing the boundless potential of chip-device-cloud capabilities, HMS has given developers the tools they need to pursue digital innovation.

1.2.3 The HMS Ecosystem Today

As the HMS ecosystem continues to grow on a global scale, Huawei remains as committed as ever to expanding its reach and connecting with more developers. Developers who join the HMS ecosystem can flourish by following a four-step process: know, learn, participate, and monetize, and Huawei supports developers at every step on their journey.

In 2018, HUAWEI Developers[3] debuted the HUAWEI Developer Day (HDD)[4] event series, which involves open exchange between developers and Huawei teams on the latest mobile device technologies, product features, HMS open capabilities, and other knowledge of interest, also serving as an important channel for feedback on the HMS ecosystem. By 2020, HDDs have been held in more than a dozen cities across China, including Beijing, Shanghai, Guangzhou, Chengdu, and Dalian. Nearly 10,000 developers have participated in the offline salons, technical exchanges, open classes, and onsite codelabs, and live streams from these activities have garnered more than five million views (Figure 1.10).

Beijing   Nanjing

FIGURE 1.10   Past HDD events in China.

Portugal   Malaysia

FIGURE 1.11   Past HDD events outside of China.

HDDs have also proved to be a hit around the world, having thus far been held in France, Spain, Poland, Russia, and Portugal (in Europe); India, Malaysia, Thailand, and the Philippines (in the Asia Pacific region); the United Arab Emirates, Egypt, Saudi Arabia, and South Africa (in the MEA region); and Mexico, Colombia, Peru, Brazil, and Costa Rica (in Latin America). Regardless of where an HDD event takes place, it is sure to attract passionate local developers, and yield productive dialog (Figure 1.11).

Huawei launched its Shining-Star Program in 2017 with the aim of inspiring global developers to join the HMS ecosystem and, by 2019, had increased the awards granted through the initiative from around US$143 million to US$1 billion. The program has been well-received and, as of May 2020, had shed light on the work of more than 300 partners and developers, following 21 rounds of selection. Shining-Star Program apps reach far throughout the HMS ecosystem (Figure 1.12).

Photo 1   Photo 2

FIGURE 1.12   Past Shining-Star Program events. Photo 1: Shining-Star Program Launch; Photo 2: HUAWEI Developer Day.

For student developers, Huawei has launched the HUAWEI Student Developers (HSD) program. Aimed at outstanding developers who express interest in releasing HMS Core–integrated apps outside of China, Huawei offers additional incentives. The Shining-Star Program has thus far nurtured the development of more than 10,000 innovative apps. The presence of so many talented developers and outstanding apps has attracted more developers to the HMS ecosystem, helping it expand into a bona fide global presence.

However, developer enablement activities and incentives are by no means all that the HMS ecosystem offers developers. Thanks to the sheer size of Huawei's user base, HMS can help drive traffic to developers' apps. In 2019 alone, Huawei shipped over 240 million smartphones, and MAUs on Huawei devices exceeded 700 million. The numbers speak for themselves and are summarized below (Figure 1.13).

With so many successful HMS apps and traffic streams now available, developers can tap into new markets and succeed on a scale they could hardly imagine just years ago.

Thanks to its multifaceted approach and developer-centric initiatives, the HMS ecosystem is expanding its developer and app bases at an unprecedented rate. By December 2020, it had 2.3 million registered developers around the world, a 77% increase over the previous year. The number of registered developers outside of China soared to 300,000, a staggering 199% year-on-year increase. More than 120,000 apps integrated HMS open capabilities, including more than 21,000 new apps outside of China, vaulting HMS into its position as the third-largest mobile app ecosystem.

FIGURE 1.13 Popular cloud services in 2020.

1.3 HMS ECOSYSTEM ARCHITECTURE

This section describes what are the open capabilities built into the HMS ecosystem, as well as how the privacy compliance framework is designed to protect users.

1.3.1 Architecture Behind HMS Open Capabilities

Huawei provides HMS Core – a broad array of chip-device-cloud capabilities – within the framework of an open ecosystem, giving you the tools to pursue groundbreaking innovation. This all-sensing, all-connected, and ubiquitously intelligent ecosystem endows hardware with unprecedented capabilities and enriches the lives of users with all-scenario digital services.

The HMS open framework consists of two layers: the HMS Apps and the HMS Core & Connect. The HMS Core & Connect layer is further divided into the HMS Connect layer and the HMS Core layer, as shown in Figure 1.14.

1. HMS Apps layer

    HMS ecosystem apps fall into two categories: Huawei apps (self-developed by Huawei), and developer apps (contributed by developers around the world). These apps provide digital services for users via Huawei devices.

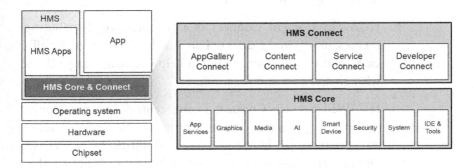

FIGURE 1.14   Architecture of the HMS ecosystem.

a. HMS apps are usually preinstalled in EMUI. Noteworthy examples include: HUAWEI AppGallery, HUAWEI Browser, HUAWEI Cloud, HUAWEI Assistant, HUAWEI Video, and HUAWEI Reader.

b. Developer apps are released on HUAWEI AppGallery. They run the gamut of app categories: games, entertainment, social, multimedia, business, news & reading, shopping, finance, education, health & fitness, and lifestyle and convenience. These apps have greatly enriched the HMS ecosystem.

2. HMS Connect layer

This layer provides end-to-end management capabilities for app operations personnel, from HMS access to app monetization, allowing them to manage developers, apps, content, and services with newfound ease.

a. HUAWEI AppGallery Connect provides one-stop services throughout the lifecycle of an app: from innovation and development, through distribution and operations, to operating performance analysis. Taking advantage of Huawei's long-term expertise in globalization, quality assurance, security, and project management, it helps developers to acquire more users and gain revenue with easier app development and O&M, better version quality, and wide-ranging distribution and operations services.

b. HUAWEI Content Connect is a platform for distributing themes, music, and videos to Huawei-developed apps. Its efficient, end-to-end operations can help you reach target users with greater ease and precision.

c. HUAWEI Service Connect is the central hub for atomic services, aggregating traffic from 1+8+N devices across all scenarios. It harnesses AI capabilities to power an all-encompassing integration and distribution solution that needs to be implemented only once.

d. HUAWEI Developer Connect, an official partner platform of HUAWEI Consumer, is committed to fostering your development, testing, promotion, and monetization, helping you build experience in innovation and a user base in smart devices.

3. HMS Core layer

This layer provides open capabilities and tools for the following fields:

a. **App Services:** a suite of app capabilities, such as Account Kit for simple, secure, and quick sign-in and authorization functions.

b. **Media:** encompasses Camera Engine, which comes equipped with a range of efficient features, such as ultra-wide angle, Portrait mode, HDR, background blur, and Super Night mode, designed to enrich apps with cutting-edge photography and videography.

c. **Graphics:** aggregates image processing capabilities. One of them is the AR Engine, with core algorithms integrated into basic AR tracking (motion, environment, body, and face), allowing apps to bridge the virtual and real worlds.

d. **System:** opens system-level capabilities such as Nearby Service, which allows devices to easily discover nearby devices and set up communication with them using Bluetooth or Wi-Fi. Nearby Connection and Nearby Message also enable devices in proximity to communicate.

e. **AI:** includes capabilities that make building AI apps easier and efficient. One of them is ML Kit for diversified, industry-leading machine learning.

f. **Security:** incorporates Fast Identity Online (FIDO) – a highly-entrusted biometric authentication and online identity verification solution, which allows you to provide secure and easy-to-use password-free authentication for users.

g. **Smart Device:** provides a range of capabilities that are designed for smart devices. For example, HiCar connects mobile devices to vehicles, and brings out the best in each, even when connecting to multiple devices. This ensures that smart device functions can now be implemented in vehicles.

8. **IDE&Tools:** handy utilities for wide-ranging open capabilities.

   a. HMS Toolkit, an IDE plug-in, provides all the tools for creation, coding and conversion, debugging, testing, and release of HMS Core-integrated apps.

   b. DevEco Studio is a HUAWEI Consumer IDE that eases you into the HMS ecosystem's open capabilities. Its comprehensive functions include project management, coding, compilation, building, emulation, and debugging.

In defining these layers, we've laid out how HMS Core can serve as your one-stop solution for efficient development, rapid growth, and flexible monetization.

1.3.2 HMS Privacy Compliance Framework

In 1995, the EU formulated the *Data Protection Directive* (Directive 95/46/EC) to protect the personal data of its citizens. Seven years later, it announced *plans for data protection reform* with the *General Data Protection Regulation (GDPR)* draft.

The GDPR was approved on April 14, 2016, and became enforceable beginning May 25, 2018. The legal concepts and basic principles of personal data protection in the GDPR are well recognized worldwide. Argentina, New Zealand, Canada, Japan, Brazil, Turkey, and China have all referred to it when formulating or amending their own legislation. Governments now attach greater importance to privacy protection, with stricter laws and harsher punishments for violation.

We at Huawei have established independent privacy and security teams worldwide to research and enforce privacy and security protection throughout our product lifecycles. We implement privacy protection from the Generally Accepted Privacy Principles (GAPP) to the GDPR, both of which join the local laws of each country and region as the foundation of Huawei's privacy compliance framework. The parts of the framework are shown here in Figure 1.15.

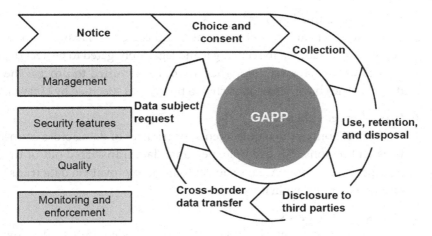

FIGURE 1.15   Huawei's global privacy compliance framework.

1. Notice

Before collecting any personal data, Huawei will notify users of the following information: (1) type of data to be collected; (2) data processing purposes and methods; (3) rights of the data subject, or user; and (4) Huawei's measures to protect the data.

2. Choice and consent

Personal data will only be collected with the user's consent, written authorization, or other lawful grounds, and a record of such consent or authorization will be retained. Huawei permits users to opt-out or withdraw their consent.

3. Collection

Huawei collects only as much data as is required for relevant and necessary purposes.

4. Use, retention, and disposal

Huawei will only process, use, and retain the information it collects as specified in the notice to users. We maintain the accuracy, integrity, and relevance of the data we process. Robust protection mechanisms safeguard data from being stolen, misused, abused, or leaked.

5. Disclosure to third parties

The suppliers and business partners authorized by Huawei to process data are qualified in securing it and legally obligated to protect the data as well as Huawei does. They are only permitted to process the data that they have been contracted to process, as specified by Huawei.

6. Cross-border data transfer

Huawei honors the requirements for transfer of data across countries and regions. For example, personal data transferred out of the European Economic Area is subject to prior approval via data transfer agreement or explicit user consent.

7. Data subject requests

As a data controller, Huawei permits users to view, update, destroy, or transfer their personal data as they see fit.

Huawei considers cyber security and privacy protection its highest priorities, and thus places them at the heart of HMS. Along with improving user experience, HMS is committed to building a brand trusted to protect you and your information online.

So far, we've had a look back at the birth of mobile app ecosystems and a refresher on the business models and development history of mainstream players in the ecosystem. As a force to be reckoned with in the mobile app ecosystem, HMS is growing rapidly, and we welcome you in. Join us as we learn to integrate HMS and become a successful business partner in the next few chapters.

1.4 SUMMARY

This chapter reviews how the mobile app ecosystem flourishes in the world, as well as how HMS emerged and develops. In the following chapters, we will walk you through the technical framework of the HMS ecosystem and provide you with step-by-step guidance on how to integrate HMS Core capabilities.

NOTES

1 In 2014, Huawei Device was renamed Huawei Consumer Business Group (BG) for the purpose of better external communications.
2 EMUI is an Android-based custom user interface developed by Huawei for its mobile devices.

3 HUAWEI Developers (https://developer.huawei.com/consumer/en/) is a platform dedicated to pooling and coordinating development resources across the value chain, by working with developers, to craft an optimal experience for Huawei device users. It serves as a one-stop platform for developers of Huawei device-based apps, assisting them with development, testing, distribution, and monetization, while also fostering innovation across the board.

4 HDD is a channel built on HUAWEI Developers that enables Huawei teams to better communicate with developers. It focuses on sharing knowledge on the latest technologies and forms of mobile devices, industry trends, and open capabilities and services on Huawei devices. It facilitates the joint efforts of Huawei and developers to create an optimal smart experience for hundreds of millions of Huawei device users.

CHAPTER 2

HMS Core

2.1 WHAT DOES HMS CORE OFFER?

HMS Core solidly backs you up through your app's journey, from Develop to Grow and to Monetize. Develop kits make app development faster and at a higher quality; Grow kits expand your user base with fine-grained operations; Monetize kits help you get paid with easier payment and greater user engagement. Figure 2.1 is the big picture of what HMS Core can offer you:

HMS Core is constantly growing. To stay up to date with the latest information, you can visit the HUAWEI Developers official website, at https://developer.huawei.com/consumer/en/.

2.1.1 Develop: Creating Premium Apps Quickly and Cost-Effectively

Now, we'll introduce some of the most popular HMS Core capabilities.

2.1.1.1 Account Kit

Users can be turned off by a tedious registration process. However, an app needs to know its users to offer individualized services. If the question is how to balance user experience and user acquisition, Account Kit is the answer.

Compliant with industry protocols including OAuth 2.0 and OpenID Connect, Account Kit provides easy, secure authorization and sign-in. Once your app has Account Kit integrated, your users can sign in using their HUAWEI IDs with just one tap for authorization. See Figure 2.2 to know how this process works.

DOI: 10.1201/9781003206699-2

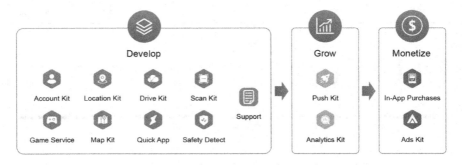

FIGURE 2.1   Framework of HMS Core open capabilities.

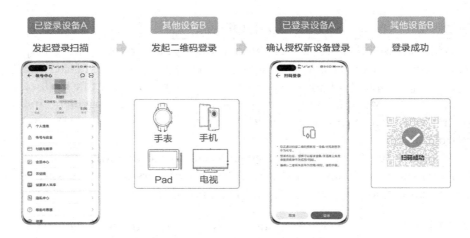

FIGURE 2.2   Example of Account Kit in practice.

1. If a user once signed in via a HUAWEI ID opens your app, they will be automatically signed in with their HUAWEI ID – with no authorization required. Easier and faster sign-ins mean lower churn.

2. Account Kit uses two-factor authentication (2FA) and encrypts data across the entire transmission process, safeguarding account security under global privacy standards.

3. By integrating Account Kit, your app will gain direct access to the vast HUAWEI ID user base, encompassing users of all types of Huawei devices, including smartphones, tablets, smart screens, and head units.

2.1.1.2 FIDO

Identity verification during sign-in or payment helps bolster the security of an account or financial transaction. Traditionally, this was accomplished with password-protected access; however, passwords are prone to being leaked or forgotten. Today's users demand fast and secure identity verification – something that HUAWEI FIDO has made an everyday reality.

The service has two core features: online identity verification (FIDO2) and local biometric authentication (BioAuthn). Figure 2.3 illustrates how FIDO2 looks in practice.

2.1.1.3 Map Kit, Site Kit, and Location Kit

These kits are indispensable for e-commerce, express delivery, travel, social networking, etc. For example, a shopping app with Location Kit and

FIGURE 2.3   FIDO 3D face and fingerprint authentication.

Map Kit integrated lets users quickly add auto-located addresses as their delivery addresses, and a travel app with Site Kit integrated helps users find and discover destinations and nearby hotels and restaurants.

Map Kit, Site Kit, and Location Kit make implementing these features easier than ever. Map Kit and Site Kit both work on map data. Map Kit provides display, drawing, interaction, customization, and route planning. Site Kit provides place-related data to connect your users with their surroundings, via the nearby place search, keyword search, place detail search, and geocoding functions. Location Kit triangulates Global Navigation Satellite System (GNSS), Wi-Fi, and base station signals to obtain accurate locations that can then be used for fused location, activity identification, and geofencing purposes.

Figure 2.4 shows three scenarios of kit collaboration:

Scenario 1: Site Kit uses data from Location Kit to search for nearby places.

Scenario 2: Map Kit uses data from Location Kit to plan routes.

Scenario 3: Map Kit uses Points of Interest (POIs) from Site Kit to draw maps.

Just like these examples, mix and match the kit functions to suit your needs.

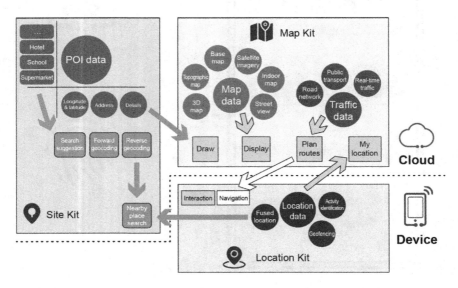

FIGURE 2.4   Collaboration among Map Kit, Site Kit, and Location Kit.

2.1.1.4 Safety Detect

App users want the best, but they also want the safest. They want to know if devices running the apps are vulnerable, apps could be infected by viruses, or apps are prone to privacy leaks upon attacks.

Therefore, app developers must prioritize safeguarding user data to the greatest possible extent.

That is where Safety Detect comes into the picture. As a multidimensional security detection service, it encompasses system integrity check (SysIntegrity), app security check (AppsCheck), malicious URL check (URLCheck), and fake user detection (UserDetect). Figure 2.5 shows you how Safety Detect does this in practice.

2.1.2 Grow: Targeting and Engaging with More Users

Generally speaking, daily app operations require developers to push real-time messages, with the goal of both retaining existing users as well as acquiring new users. However, this is easier said than done. Reaching a large user base in a short amount of time is a challenging proposition. Pushing messages to users with specific attributes, or to specific audience in a dynamic way, is even more difficult.

Let's take a look at how Push Kit addresses these challenges.

1. Push Kit has proven capable of sending tens of billions of messages per day, thanks to the presence of Huawei data centers in more than 200 countries and regions.

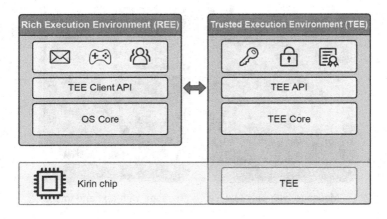

FIGURE 2.5   Safety Detect.

2. The system-level message channel ensures that an EMUI device can receive and display push messages via Push Kit, even if your app is not launched. The device informs the Push Kit server that the message has been received, and the server then sends a real-time receipt to your app.

3. Push Kit can send messages to a specific audience by tag, topic, scenario, and geofence, while also supporting multidimensional data analysis. Figure 2.6 provides two examples of messages from Push Kit.

2.1.3 Monetize: Expanding Your Global Reach with Multiple Channels

Seeing our app adopted is already rewarding enough, and earning money from it – whether it's from ads or paid services – is like the icing on the cake. Paid services require the availability of in-app payment methods, such as payment cards and Direct Carrier Billing (DCB). However, equipping your app with multiple methods will cost you much time and money. HUAWEI IAP is here to change that.

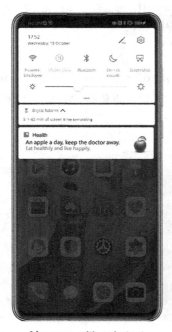 

Message with only text   Message with text and image

FIGURE 2.6   Messages from Push Kit.

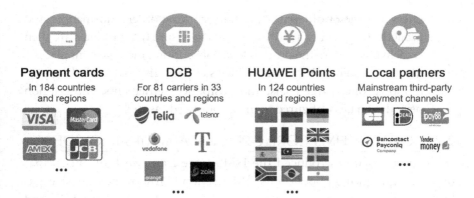

FIGURE 2.7   Mainstream global payment methods.

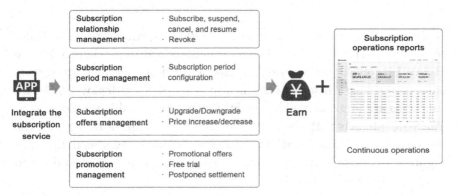

FIGURE 2.8   IAP management capabilities.

1. IAP serves global users by offering access to a myriad of mainstream payment methods, including payment cards, DCB, HUAWEI Points, and third-party payment channels, as shown in Figure 2.7. It supports payment cards in 184 countries and regions, DCB for 81 carriers in 33 countries and regions, and HUAWEI Points in 124 countries and regions. IAP has also partnered with prominent third-party payment providers such as iPay88, Yandex Money, and iDeal.

2. Other IAP functions include product management, order management, and subscription management, as shown in Figure 2.8. Product management supports automatic pricing in local currencies (170+ countries and regions) for products at 195 price tiers, as well as product information display in more than 70 different languages. Order management

offers a range of different APIs for recording order information, and proactively querying abnormal orders to ensure that products are then re-delivered before the order is lost. Subscription management places a diverse menu of subscription policies at your disposal, including promotional offers, free trials, and postponed settlements. Subscription periods can be configured to meet your needs as well.

2.2 HOW ARE HMS CORE OPEN CAPABILITIES PROVIDED?

In Section 2.1, we introduced the HMS Core framework of open capabilities, highlighting popular kits. This section will show how these capabilities are open to you, currently through two ways: HMS Core SDK and cloud-based RESTful APIs.

2.2.1 HMS Core SDK

HMS Core SDK can be divided into the following two parts: cloud functions and device functions. Cloud functions are implemented by the HUAWEI Developers website, Huawei OAuth server, and kit servers (such as the Map Kit server on which map services are deployed). Device functions are implemented by the HMS Core SDK and HMS Core APK. The SDK interacts with the APK in order for it to communicate with the device OS (e.g., Huawei EMUI) and Huawei cloud servers, as outlined in Figure 2.9. To use HMS Core open capabilities, all you need to do is to integrate the HMS Core SDK.

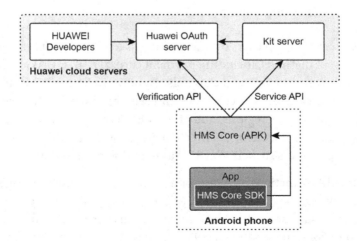

FIGURE 2.9   Opening up capabilities via the HMS Core SDK.

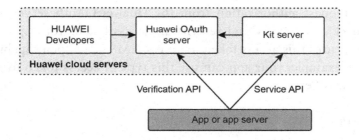

FIGURE 2.10 Opening up capabilities via RESTful APIs.

2.2.2 RESTful APIs

HMS Core open capabilities are also available through RESTful APIs on clouds. See Figure 2.10 to check how RESTful APIs provide access to these capabilities.

RESTful API implementation is a supplement to HMS Core SDK implementation. You can choose to implement whichever, depending on your needs.

Before calling HMS Core capabilities, you'll need to make sure that you have obtained the necessary credentials and use them only as authorized to ensure user data and system security.

2.3 HOW ARE INTEGRATIONS AUTHORIZED?

Section 2.2 detailed how HMS Core capabilities are opened to developers. Now, we'll introduce what authorizations you will need and how they are granted.

Our open capabilities are only accessible to your app with the required credential. Create it first on HUAWEI Developers: an API key, OAuth client ID, or service account.

1. API key: used for accessing public resources of HMS Core open capabilities, such as geographic location data of Map Kit.

2. OAuth client ID: used for accessing user-authorized resources. To do this, your app obtains an access token, once authorized, from the Huawei OAuth server. Your app can then use this access token to access Drive Kit and Health Kit, for instance.

3. Service account: used for connecting your app server to the HMS Core kit server. Your app server provides a JSON Web Token (JWT)

to request authorization from the Huawei OAuth server, which checks its validity and returns an access token. Your app server then uses this access token to access HMS Core open capabilities. For example, your app can use this type of access token to access Nearby Service.

2.3.1 API Key

2.3.1.1 How to Obtain

Access the HUAWEI Developers console to create an API key, as shown in Figure 2.11.

2.3.1.2 How to Use

URL-encode your API key and use the generated string to replace *{URL Encoded API Key}*.

API call request format:

```
URL? key={URL Encoded API Key}
```

(a)

(b)

FIGURE 2.11   Creating an API key.

Check the kit server URL and input the necessary parameters, as described in the API reference. Below is an example:

```
https://oauth-api.cloud.huawei.com/v1/demo/indexes?key
=CV3X1%2FJG7mdNZm0319puvwPAktmfw1aj8XvBb6sm696MqoW57eh
nUC
```

2.3.1.3 How to Interact

In Figure 2.12, an app uses an API key to access a kit server via a RESTful API.

The process works as follows:

1. The app or its server accesses the kit server using the API key.

2. The kit server sends a request to the Huawei OAuth server to verify the API key.

3. If the API key is valid, the kit server provides the requested resources.

2.3.2 OAuth Client ID

2.3.2.1 How to Obtain

OAuth 2.0 is the industry-standard protocol for authorization – a streamlined method for mobile, desktop, and web apps to access resources authorized by users. Under this protocol, an access token is generated as a credential upon user authorization, which your app then uses for access. OAuth 2.0 provides four methods for obtaining access tokens: Authorization Code, Client Credentials, Resource Owner Credentials, and Implicit. HMS Core uses the first two of these methods.

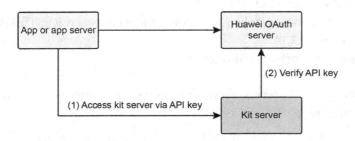

FIGURE 2.12 Accessing the kit server using an API key.

FIGURE 2.13   Creating an OAuth client ID.

Before requesting an access token from the Huawei OAuth server, sign in to the HUAWEI Developers console and create an OAuth client ID. You'll then get a client ID and a secret. See Figure 2.13.

In Authorization Code mode, your app will use the client ID and secret to obtain the access token. In Client Credentials mode, the access token is obtained without user authorization but works only for access to public resources.

For more information about OAuth 2.0, please visit https://oauth.net/2/.

2.3.2.2 How to Interact

An app uses an access token to access a kit server via a RESTful API, as shown in Figure 2.14.

The process works as follows:

1. The app or its server obtains an access token after being authorized by the user.

2. The app or its server uses the token to access the kit server through the RESTful API.

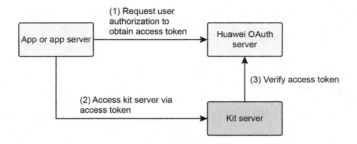

FIGURE 2.14   Accessing the kit server using an access token.

3. The kit server requests that the Huawei OAuth server verifies the token.

4. If the token is valid, the kit server provides the requested resources.

2.3.3 Service Account

2.3.3.1 How to Obtain

To enable interactions between your app server and an HMS Core kit server, first create a service account on the HUAWEI Developers console. Download the JSON file you obtained when creating the account and use it to make a JWT, the credential actually used for server-to-server interactions. See Figure 2.15.

A JWT consists of three parts separated by dots (.): header, payload, and signature. To create the signature, take the header and payload and sign them using the SHA256withRSA algorithm. For more information about JWT, please visit https://jwt.io/introduction/.

Now, we'll create a JWT header. See Table 2.1 for the format.

JSON header example:

```
{
"kid":"c60c27b8f2f34e9bac2b07c852f1800e",
"typ":"JWT",
"alg":"RS256"
}
```

Base64-encoded JSON header:

eyJraWQiOiJjNjBjMjdiOGYyZjM0ZTliYWMyYjA3Yzg1MmYxODAw
ZSIsInR5cCI6IkpXVCIsImFsZyI6IlJTMjU2In0

Next, let's generate a JWT payload as described in Table 2.2.

FIGURE 2.15   Creating a service account.

TABLE 2.1   JWT Header

Parameter	Value
kid	The **key_id** in your service account's JSON file.
typ	Always **JWT**.
alg	Always **RS256**.

TABLE 2.2   JWT Payload

Parameter	Value
iss	The **sub_account** in your service account's JSON file.
aud	Always **https://oauth-login.cloud.huawei.com/oauth2/v3/token**.
iat	UTC timestamp when a JWT is signed, that is, the number of seconds counting from 1970-01-01 00:00:00 (UTC) to the signing time.
exp	UTC timestamp when a JWT expires, that is, the **iat** plus 3600.

JSON payload example:

```
{
"aud": "https://oauth-login.cloud.huawei.
com/oauth2/v3/token",
"iss": "300125961",
"exp": 1581410664,
"iat": 1581407064
}
```

Base64-encoded JSON payload:

eyJhdWQiOiJodHRwczovL29hdXRoLWxvZ2luLmNsb3VkLmh1YXdlaS5
5jb20vb2F1dGgyL3YzL3Rva2VuIiwiaXNzIjoiMzAwMTI1OTYxIiwi
ZXhwIjoxNTgxNDEwNjY0LCJpYXQiOjE1ODE0MDcwNjR9

Finally, let's create a JWT signature. Take the Base64-encoded header and payload separated by a dot (.), and sign that with SHA256withRSA using the private key[1] in your service account's JSON file.

```
JWT signature=SHA256withRSA (base64UrlEncode(header) +
"." +base64UrlEncode(payload), private_key);
```

2.3.3.2 How to Use

Send the JWT in the **Authorization** header of an HTTP request using the **Bearer** schema.

```
Authorization: Bearer JWT
```

There must be a space between **Bearer** and **JWT**.

An HTTP request should look like the following:

```
GET /v1/demo/indexes HTTP/1.1
Authorization:Bearer eyJraWQiOiIx---xxx.eyJhdWQiOiJod
HR---xxx.QRodgXa2xeXSt4Gp---xxx
Host: oauth-api.cloud.huawei.com
```

2.3.3.3 How to Interact

Figure 2.16 shows how an app server uses an access token that is obtained through a JWT to access a kit server.

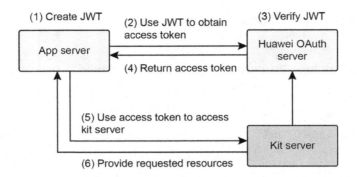

FIGURE 2.16   Accessing the kit server using an access token.

The process works as follows:

1. A JWT is created using the service account's JSON file.

2. The app server requests authorization to the Huawei OAuth server using the JWT.

3. The Huawei OAuth server checks whether the JWT is valid.

4. If it is valid, the Huawei OAuth server returns an access token.

5. The app server uses the access token to request access to resources.

6. The kit server provides the requested resources.

NOTE

1 Not stored by Huawei. You'll need to maintain its security on your own.

CHAPTER 3

Quick Start

3.1 REGISTRATION AND IDENTITY VERIFICATION

Let's start with how to register a HUAWEI Developers account and complete identity verification.

3.1.1 Registering an Account

Visit HUAWEI Developers at https://developer.huawei.com/consumer/en/ and click **Sign up** in the upper right corner, as shown in Figure 3.1. On the page that is displayed, register a HUAWEI ID with either your phone number or email address. Here we'll use an email address for registration, as indicated in Figure 3.2. Fill in all of the required information and click **REGISTER.**

Read the **HUAWEI ID Privacy Notice and Terms & Conditions** carefully. Under the terms, some of your personal data will be collected, but it will only be used for the purposes of analytics and service improvement. Huawei pledges to comply with all applicable laws and regulations, as well as security and privacy policies, in protecting your personal data. If you wish to accept the terms in the agreement, click **Agree**, as shown in Figure 3.3.

3.1.2 Verifying Your Identity

After registration, you'll need to prove that you are who you claim to be. To do so, use the HUAWEI ID you registered to sign in to HUAWEI Developers and click **Console** in the upper right corner or click **Identity verification** in your personal account information, as shown in Figure 3.4.

DOI: 10.1201/9781003206699-3

FIGURE 3.1   Signing up.

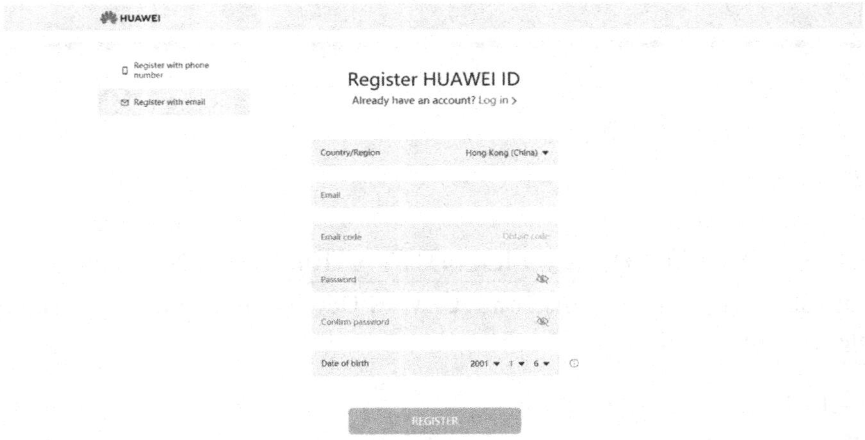

FIGURE 3.2   Registering with an email address.

Choose to verify yourself as an individual developer or enterprise developer. To verify as an individual developer, click **Next** under **Individual**, as shown in Figure 3.5.

Fill in your identity information, especially the parameters marked with an asterisk, as shown in Figure 3.6.

Upload your identity documents, which are a bank document plus an ID card, passport, or any other supporting documents such as a driver's license. Figure 3.7 shows how to upload the documents, as well as which document combinations are accepted.

Read both the **Statement About HUAWEI Developer and Privacy** and **HUAWEI Developer Service Agreement** to make sure you confirm the agreements and click **Submit**, as shown in Figure 3.8. Huawei will review your application and email you the results as soon as possible.

The process described above is for registering as an individual developer. To register as an enterprise developer, you'll need a Data Universal

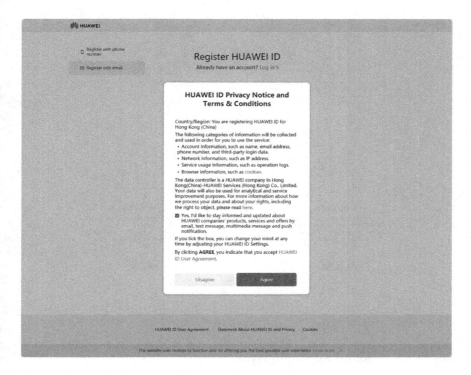

FIGURE 3.3   Privacy statement.

Numbering System (DUNS) number or business license. For more details, please refer to the identity verification guide at https://developer. huawei.com/consumer/en/doc/start/atpopb-0000001062836624.

FIGURE 3.4   Initiating identity verification.

FIGURE 3.5   Selecting a developer type.

FIGURE 3.6   Filling in the identity information.

FIGURE 3.7   Uploading identity documents.

FIGURE 3.8   Submitting information for review.

Once your identity verification application has been approved, you'll be an officially registered Huawei developer.

3.2 SETTING UP A DEVELOPMENT ENVIRONMENT

Now that you're a Huawei developer, you're ready to integrate HMS Core open capabilities. But before we get started, let's first set up an Android development environment, using our knowledge of Android basics. To get tasks done, we will need:

- JDK 1.8 or later

- Android SDK 21 or later

- Android Studio 3.5.3 or later

- A Huawei phone running HMS Core (APK) 4.0.0.300 or later

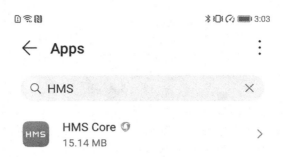

FIGURE 3.9 Apps screen.

To learn how to download and install the latest versions of JDK, Android SDK, and Android Studio, please consult with Java and Android support.

To find out if your HMS Core (APK) is the latest, go to **Settings > Apps > Apps** on your phone and search for HMS Core, as shown in Figure 3.9.

Then, touch the name to display the app details, as illustrated in Figure 3.10. If the version is earlier than 4.0.0.300, you'll need to download and install the latest version from HUAWEI AppGallery.

3.3 CREATING AN APP PROJECT

Now that we have our development environment, let's create an Android project. Throughout this book, we'll use an app named Pet Store as an example, to illustrate how we create a project for it and integrate Account Kit, IAP, Push Kit, and other essential services.

3.3.1 App Functions

Pet Store has been designed with the following functions:

- Account registration: lets users register a user name and password.

- Sign-in: lets users sign in to the app with their user name and password, fingerprint, or via a third-party account.

- Personal center settings: lets users access their personal center, set a delivery address, and register a fingerprint for sign-in.

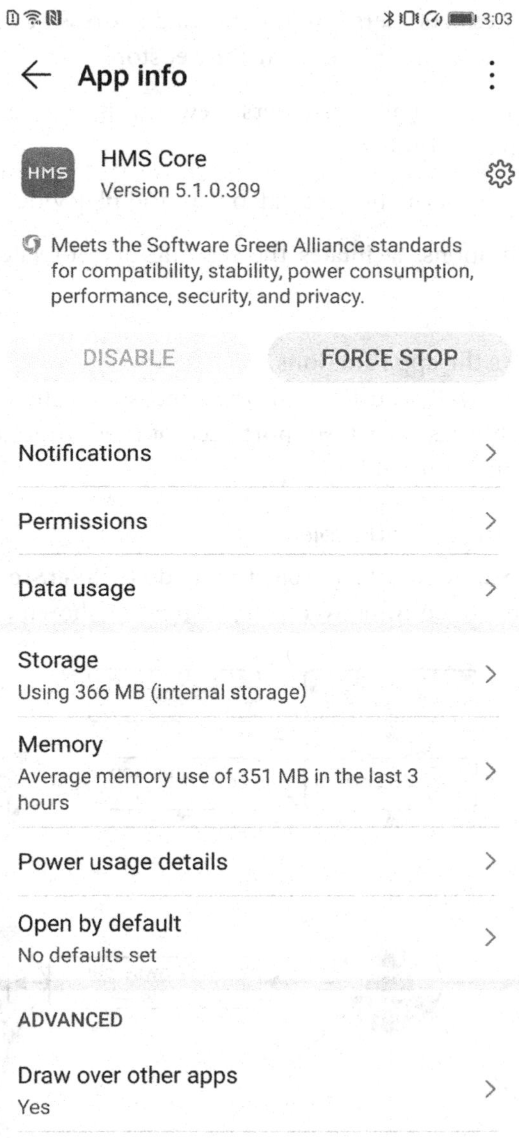

FIGURE 3.10   HMS Core app information screen.

- Nearby stores: lets users find the detailed address of a pet store, get a route there, and find places near the pet store.

- Membership purchase: lets users view and purchase products, and review purchase orders.

- Pet videos: lets users browse video lists and play videos.

- Push notifications: facilitates the sending of pet-related messages to users.

Figure 3.11 shows the app functions.

This book will walk you through the process of integrating different HMS Core capabilities, which support each of these functions. Now, let's get started building our Pet Store app.

3.3.2 Creating an Android Project

Open Android Studio, create a project named **HMSPetStoreApp**, and set the package name to **com.huawei.hmspetstore**, as shown in Figure 3.12.

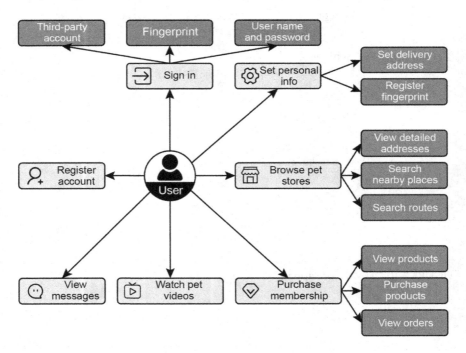

FIGURE 3.11   Pet Store app functions.

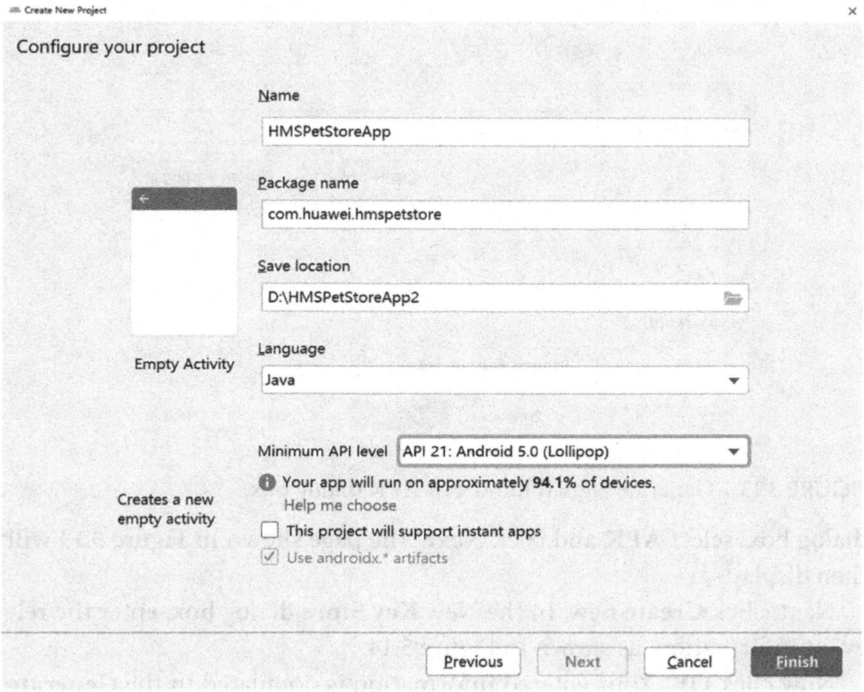

FIGURE 3.12   Creating a project for the Pet Store app.

Click **Next** to retain the default settings until the project has been created.

3.3.3 Creating a Keystore File

Android requires that all APKs be digitally signed with a certificate before they are installed on a device or updated. These certificates are stored in a keystore file. To generate

---

NOTICE

1. Use the package name you have.
2. Based on the SDKs to be integrated and the devices supported by your app, set **Minimum API level** by referring to required Android versions for different kits and features, which are available at https://developer.huawei.com/consumer/en/doc/development/-HMSCore-Guides/emui-version-dependent-0000001050042515.

---

this file, use either Android Studio or the keytool utility installed with JDK. Here we'll use Android Studio. In the Android Studio navigation bar, go to **Build > Generate Signed APK**. In the **Generate Signed Bundle or APK**

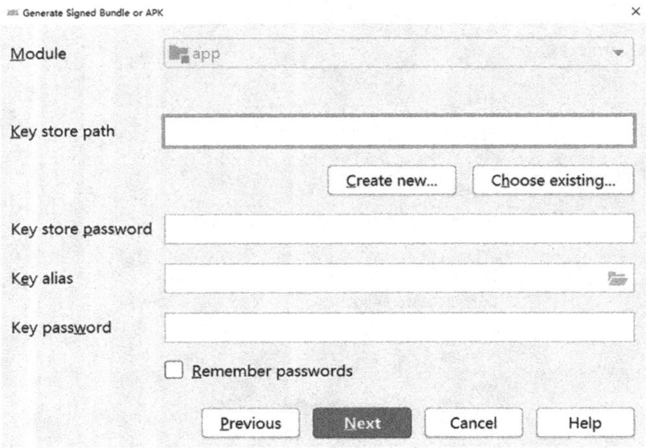

FIGURE 3.13   Generate Signed Bundle or APK dialog box.

dialog box, select **APK** and click **Next**. The page shown in Figure 3.13 will then display.

Next, click **Create new**. In the **New Key Store** dialog box, enter the relevant information, as shown in Figure 3.14.

Now click **OK**. Your entered information is populated in the **Generate Signed Bundle or APK** dialog box, as shown in Figure 3.15.

Click **Next** once you have confirmed that the information is correct. Then, set **Build Variants** to **release** and **Signature Versions** to **V2 (Full APK Signature)**, as shown in Figure 3.16.

We have now successfully created a keystore file. Click **Finish**, and the generated keystore file **HMSPetStoreApp.jks** will appear in the **app** directory. You'll need it to sign all subsequent updates to your app, so it's important to keep this file secure.

3.3.4 Configuring Signing in Gradle

Now that we already have a keystore file, we can edit the **build.gradle** file in **app** with the keystore information. To do so, add the following snippet to the **android** block:

```
signingConfigs {
  config {
    storeFile file("HMSPetStoreApp.jks")
    storePassword "hms_petstore"
    keyAlias "key0"
```

FIGURE 3.14 Entering the required information.

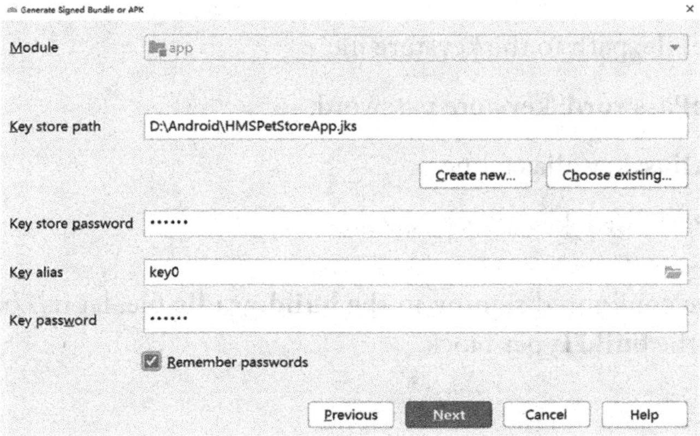

FIGURE 3.15 Populating keystore information.

FIGURE 3.16   Setting Build Variants and Signature Versions.

```
    keyPassword "hms_petstore"
    v2SigningEnabled true
  }
}
```

In this snippet, the new block **signingConfigs** in **android** contains the **config** block, and **config** contains the following keystore information:

- **storeFile**: path to the keystore file.

- **storePassword**: keystore password.

- **keyAlias**: key alias name.

- **keyPassword**: key alias password.

As we have configured signing in the **build.gradle** file, let us continue to configure the **buildTypes** block.

```
buildTypes {
  debug {
```

```
      minifyEnabled false
      proguardFiles getDefaultProguardFile('proguard-
android-optimize.txt'),
        'proguard-rules.pro'
      signingConfig signingConfigs.config
    }
  release {
      minifyEnabled false
      proguardFiles getDefaultProguardFile('proguard-
android-optimize.txt'),
        'proguard-rules.pro'
      signingConfig signingConfigs.config
    }
}
```

Add the signing configuration for the **debug** and **release** builds inside the **buildTypes** block. This is used to automatically sign your debug APK and release APK.

Once you have completed the configuration, click the ▶ icon to install the app onto your phone or emulator and launch the app. Figure 3.17 shows what the app looks like once it is launched.

That's it. Now that we've created our project, let's develop some basic app functions such as home screen and account sign-in.

3.4 BUILDING THE PET STORE APP

Before we delve into integrating HMS Core capabilities, let's get the app ready with the following functions: home screen, video playback, sign-in, registration, personal center, and settings.

The first thing to do is to make our code readable and scalable. To do so, create the **bean, common, constant, network, ui, util,** and **view** packages, as shown in Figure 3.18.

Table 3.1 lists the functions of the newly created packages.

3.4.1 Adding the Home Screen

Create a package named **main** in the **ui** package. Move **MainActivity** to the **main** package, and rename it **MainAct** and its corresponding layout file **main_act.xml**.

FIGURE 3.17   **App successfully launched.**

FIGURE 3.18   App project structure.

TABLE 3.1   Package Functions

Package	Function
bean	Data structure classes.
common	Common classes.
constant	Constant classes.
network	Network request classes.
ui	App screens, such as the home screen and sign-in screen.
util	Utilities classes.
view	Custom views.

The home screen comprises:

1. Top: an ImageView to show the app's background image.

2. Middle: a LinearLayout with two horizontal TextViews inside it, to show pet stores and pet videos.

3. Bottom: an ImageView on the right side, to access the personal center.

For the layout code, please refer to the **main_act.xml** file. Figure 3.19 shows what the app's home screen looks like in practice.

3.4.2 Adding the Video Playback Function

Touching **Videos** on the home screen brings up a list of pet videos for users to stream. To support this function, create a package named **petvideo** in the **ui** package, where all video-related code will be stored. Create an activity named **PetVideoAct.java** for the pet video screen. The layout file is **petvideo_act.xml**.

The pet video screen consists of the following:

1. Top: an ImageView to show the back icon and a TextView to show the title of the pet video screen.

2. Bottom: a RecyclerView to show pet videos.

For the layout code, please refer to the **petvideo_act.xml** file. Figure 3.20 shows the pet video screen.

3.4.3 Adding the Sign-in Function

After adding the home and pet video screens, we'll want to add an account system for the app, to ensure that playback information and user profiles can be saved for future use.

To do so, first create a package named **login** in the **ui** package, and then create an activity named **LoginAct**. The corresponding layout file is **login_act.xml**.

The sign-in screen consists of the following:

1. Top: two ImageViews to show the back icon and app logo respectively, and a TextView to show the title of the sign-in screen.

2. Middle: two EditTexts under the app logo, for entering the user name and password respectively.

3. Bottom right under the password text box: a TextView for account registration.

4. Bottom: a Button for sign-in.

For the layout code, please refer to the **login_act.xml** file. Figure 3.21 shows what this sign-in screen looks like.

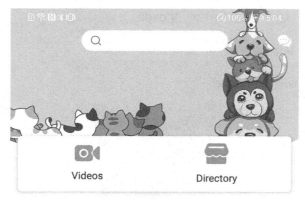

Videos

Directory

 Mr Smith's Pet Store
1000 m

FIGURE 3.19   App home screen.

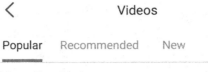

Popular   Recommended   New

What a fun time!

Let's play together!

We're friends!

FIGURE 3.20   Pet video screen.

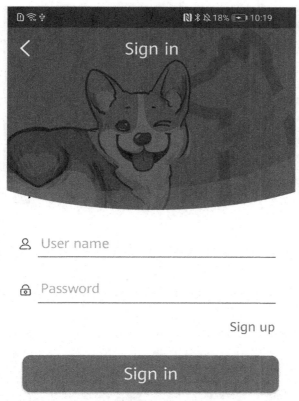

FIGURE 3.21   Sign-in screen.

3.4.4 Adding the Registration Function

Create an activity named **RegisterAct** in the **login** package. The corresponding layout file is **register_act.xml**. The registration screen is similar to the sign-in screen and consists of the following:

1. Top: two ImageViews to show the back icon and app logo respectively, and a TextView to show the title of the registration screen.

2. Middle: three EditTexts under the app logo, for entering the user name, password, and confirm password respectively.

3. Bottom: a Button for account registration.

FIGURE 3.22   Registration screen.

For the layout code, please refer to the **register_act.xml** file. Figure 3.22 shows this registration screen.

To make things simpler for this demo app, we'll save the user name and password in **SharedPreferences**. The sign-in screen will be displayed after registration. Here's the code:

```
/**
* Save the user name and password in
SharedPreferences.
```

```
*/
private void onRegister() {
  String name = mEtUserName.getText().toString().
trim();
  if (TextUtils.isEmpty(name)) {
    ToastUtil.getInstance().showShort(this, R.string.
toast_input_username);
    return;
  }

  String password = mEtPassword.getText().toString().
trim();
  if (TextUtils.isEmpty(password)) {
    ToastUtil.getInstance().showShort(this, R.string.
toast_input_password);
    return;
  }
  String passwordDouble = mEtPasswordDouble.getText().
toString().trim();
  if (TextUtils.isEmpty(passwordDouble)) {
    ToastUtil.getInstance().showShort(this, R.string.
toast_input_password_double);
    return;
  }

  if (!password.equals(passwordDouble)) {
    ToastUtil.getInstance().showShort(this, R.string.
toast_passwords_different);
    return;
  }

  SPUtil.put(this, SPConstants.KEY_LOGIN, true);
  SPUtil.put(this, SPConstants.KEY_USER_NAME, name);
  SPUtil.put(this, SPConstants.KEY_PASSWORD,
password);
  finish();
}
```

Now that we've prepared the sign-in and registration screens, let's take a look at how to direct a user from the home screen to the sign-in screen. To do so, we'll want to create a **LoginUtil** class in the **util** package. The code for this is shown below:

```
/**
* Function description: sign-in tool class.
*/
public abstract class LoginUtil {
  private static final String TAG = "LoginUtil";

  /**
  * Sign-in detection. A user who has not signed in
will be redirected to the sign-in screen.
  */
  public static boolean loginCheck(Context context) {
    boolean isLogin = isLogin(context);
    if (!isLogin) {
      context.startActivity(new Intent(context,
LoginAct.class));
    }
    return isLogin;
  }

  /**
  * Check whether a user has signed in and return true
if the user has signed in or false if not.
  */
  public static boolean isLogin(Context context) {
    if (null == context) {
      return false;
    }
    return (boolean) SPUtil.get(context, SPConstants.
KEY_LOGIN, Boolean.
      FALSE);
  }
}
```

Use the following code to check whether a user has signed in when they attempt to access the pet store list, pet video list, or personal center. If the user has not signed in, they will be redirected to the sign-in screen.

```
/**
 * Sign-in check.
 */
public static boolean loginCheck(Context context) {
  boolean isLogin = isLogin(context);
  if (!isLogin) {
    context.startActivity(new Intent(context,
LoginAct.class));
  }
  return isLogin;
}

/**
 * Check whether the user has signed in.
 */
public static boolean isLogin(Context context) {
  if (null == context) {
    return false;
  }
  return (boolean) SPUtil.get(context, SPConstants.
KEY_LOGIN, Boolean.FALSE);
}
```

3.4.5 Adding the Personal Center

With the home, sign-in, and registration screens in place, now let's add a screen to show a signed-in user their personal information. Create a package named **mine** in the **ui** package, and create an activity named **MineCenterAct** in it. The corresponding layout file is **mine_act.xml**.

The personal center screen is simple and consists of the following:

1. Top: a RelativeLayout with two ImageViews and a TextView inside it, to show the back icon, settings icon, and title of the personal center screen respectively.

2. Bottom: a LinearLayout with a horizontal ImageView and TextView, to show a user's profile picture and user name respectively. For the layout code, please refer to the **mine_act.xml** file.

Add the following snippet to the **onClick** method for the ⊘ icon on the home screen. When a user touches this icon, the app will display either the sign-in screen (if the user has not signed in) or the personal center screen (if the user has signed in).

```
findViewById(R.id.main_user).setOnClickListener(new
View.OnClickListener() {
    @Override
    public void onClick(View v) {
      // Display the personal center screen.
      if (LoginUtil.loginCheck(MainAct.this)) {
        startActivity(new Intent(MainAct.this,
MineCenterAct.class));
      }
    }
});
```

3.4.6 Adding the Settings Function

Here, we'll add a settings screen that is displayed when the user touches the settings icon, for the user to configure their personal information. We'll need to create a package named **setting** in the **ui** package and create an activity named **SettingAct** in it. The corresponding layout file is **setting_act.xml**.

The settings screen consists of the following:

1. Top: a RelativeLayout with an ImageView and a TextView inside it, to show the back icon and title of the settings screen respectively.

2. Bottom: a ScrollView that contains a vertical LinearLayout with two horizontal LinearLayouts and a Button inside it, to show the profile picture, user name, and sign-out button respectively.

For the layout code, please refer to the **setting_act.xml** file. Figure 3.23 shows what this settings screen looks like.

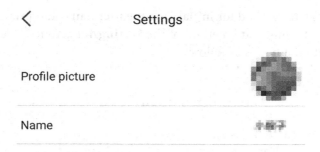

FIGURE 3.23   Settings screen for the app.

The **initData** method for initializing the user name and profile picture is called in the **onCreate** method of the **SettingAct** activity. The code for the **initData** method is as follows:

```
/**
 * Initialize user information.
 */
private void initData() {
  String userName = (String) SPUtil.get(this,
SPConstants.KEY_USER_NAME, "");
  if (TextUtils.isEmpty(userName)) {
    return;
  }
  mTvUserName.setText(userName);
}
```

After touching the sign-out button, the user will be signed out and returned to the app's home screen. The sample code for this is as follows:

```
/**
 * Sign out.
 */
private void onExitLogin() {
  SPUtil.put(this, SPConstants.KEY_LOGIN, false);
  SPUtil.put(this, SPConstants.KEY_USER_NAME, "");
  SPUtil.put(this, SPConstants.KEY_PASSWORD, "");
  finish();
}
```

Next, add the following code in the **onClick** method of the settings icon on the personal center screen. When the user touches this icon, the settings screen is displayed.

```
findViewById(R.id.title_right).setOnClickListener(new
View.OnClickListener() {
    @Override
    public void onClick(View v) {
      // Launch the settings screen.
```

```
    startActivity(new Intent(MineCenterAct.this,
SettingAct.class));
    }
});
```

We've now developed all of the app's basic functions.

3.5 SUMMARY

In this chapter, we've learned the process for becoming a Huawei developer and created a project, through a demo app, to walk you through how to develop certain basic functions. Now that the app's functions are in place, we'll address how you can integrate HMS Core capabilities in subsequent chapters to further enrich the app's features and provide for an optimal user experience.

CHAPTER 4

Account Kit

4.1 ABOUT THE SERVICE

Account Kit complies with OAuth 2.0[1] and OpenID Connect[2] to offer 2FA. To secure digital assets and personal information, 2FA verifies users with password, SMS, email, image (such as dragging a puzzle slider), and identity information (such as ID number). Once your app has Account Kit integrated, users can sign in to it via HUAWEI ID from their phones, tablets, TVs, or head units.

Account Kit consists of three parts:

1. **Account Kit (APK)**, part of HMS Core (APK): provides HUAWEI ID sign-in and authorization capabilities.

2. **Account SDK**: encapsulates capabilities provided by Account Kit for developers to use through open APIs.

3. **Huawei OAuth server**: authorizes developer access and manages authorization data.

Figure 4.1 shows how an app works with Account Kit.
The interactions are detailed as follows:

1. The app calls the Account SDK to request the authorization information from HMS Core (APK). Such information includes the authorization code, profile picture, and nickname.

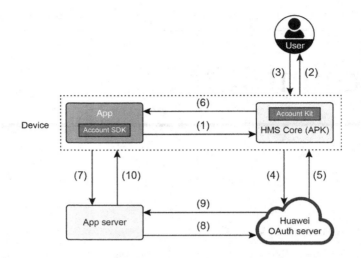

FIGURE 4.1   Interactions between an app and Account Kit.

2. HMS Core (APK) brings up the HUAWEI ID authorization screen for the user to grant authorization.

3. The user grants authorization.

4.–6. HMS Core (APK) obtains the authorization code from the Huawei OAuth server, and returns it to the app.

7. The app sends the code to its server.

8.–9. The app server sends the code and client secret to the Huawei OAuth server to request an access token and a refresh token.

10. The app server verifies the access token. If it's valid, the app server uses it to generate a new service token and returns this token to the app.

4.2 PREPARATIONS

Before integrating HMS Core kits, you'll need to first register as a Huawei developer and complete identity verification on the HUAWEI Developers website.[3] Once you are verified, proceed to the next step as shown in Figure 4.2.

4.2.1 Becoming a Verified Huawei Developer

See 3.1 to register as a Huawei developer and complete identity verification.

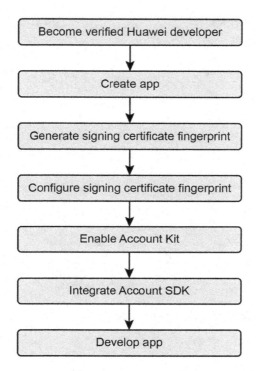

FIGURE 4.2   Account Kit integration process.

4.2.2 Creating an App

To develop a new app with Account Kit integrated, create it in AppGallery Connect.

1. Sign in to the HUAWEI Developers console. On the page shown in Figure 4.3, click **AppGallery Connect**.

2. On the AppGallery Connect home page, click **My projects** (Figure 4.4).

3. On the **My projects** page, click **Add project**, as shown in Figure 4.5.
   Your project makes all your resources and apps accessible in one place. Simply manage your apps without worrying about the details. If an app has different platform versions for Android, iOS, web, and quick app, add them to the same project.

4. On the **New project** page, give your project a name, and click **OK** (Figure 4.6).

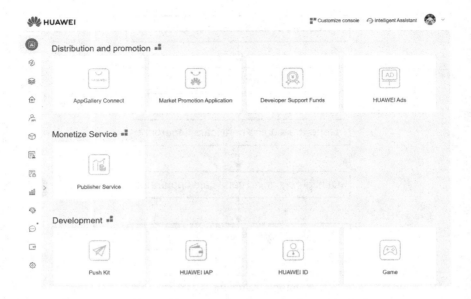

FIGURE 4.3   HUAWEI Developers console.

FIGURE 4.4   AppGallery Connect home page.

FIGURE 4.5   My projects page.

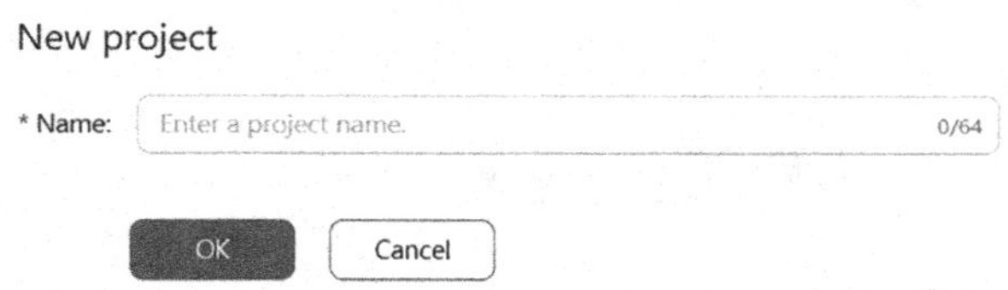

New project

* Name: Enter a project name.   0/64

OK   Cancel

FIGURE 4.6   New project page.

5. On the **Project settings** page, click **Add app** (Figure 4.7).

FIGURE 4.7   Project settings page.

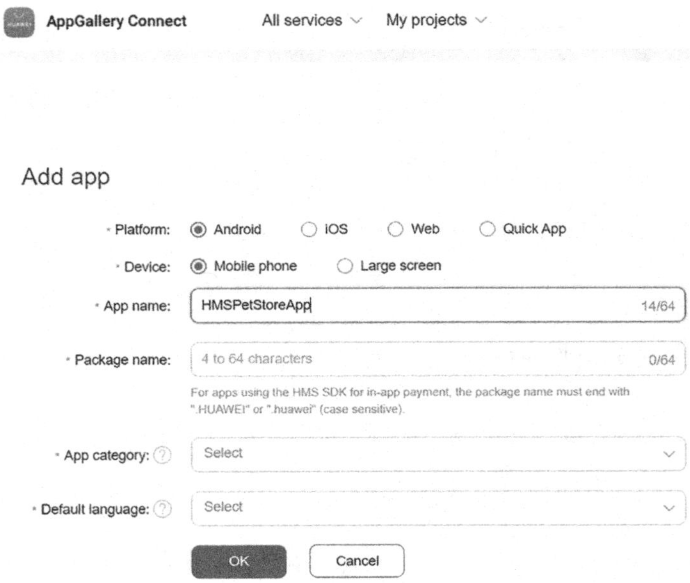

AppGallery Connect   All services ∨   My projects ∨

Add app

· Platform:	⦿ Android ○ iOS ○ Web ○ Quick App
· Device:	⦿ Mobile phone ○ Large screen
· App name:	HMSPetStoreApp 14/64
· Package name:	4 to 64 characters 0/64

For apps using the HMS SDK for in-app payment, the package name must end with ".HUAWEI" or ".huawei" (case sensitive).

· App category: ⑦	Select ∨
· Default language: ⑦	Select ∨

[OK]   [Cancel]

FIGURE 4.8   Creating an app.

6. On the **Add app** page, set required parameters, and click **OK** (Figure 4.8).

4.2.3 Generating a Signing Certificate Fingerprint

When your app calls HMS Core (APK) using the HMS Core SDK to access HMS Core services, HMS Core (APK) will authenticate your app with a valid certificate fingerprint. To make this fingerprint, use the signing certificate created in Section 3.3.3.

1. Open the command-line interface (CLI) using the **cmd** command, and run the **cd** command to go to the directory where **keytool.exe** is located, as shown in Figure 4.9.

2. Run **keytool -list -v -keystore** *<keystore-file>* and respond as prompted. In the command, *<keystore-file>* indicates the absolute path to the app's signing certificate.

C:\Users\█████.CHINA>cd C:\Program Files\Java\jdk-13.0.1\bin

FIGURE 4.9   Accessing the keytool installation directory.

```
C:\Program Files\Java\jdk-13.0.1\bin>keytool -list -v -keystore D:\HMSPetStoreApp.jks
Enter keystore password:

Keystore type: JKS
Keystore provider: SUN

Your keystore contains 1 entry

Alias name: key0
Creation date: Feb 27, 2020
Entry type: PrivateKeyEntry
Certificate chain length: 1
Certificate[1]:
Owner: CN=HMS, OU=HMS, O=HUAWEI, L=NanJing, ST=JiangSu
Issuer: CN=HMS, OU=HMS, O=HUAWEI, L=NanJing, ST=JiangSu
Serial number: 60293a2f
Valid from: Thu Feb 27 11:07:01 CST 2020 until: Mon Feb 20 11:07:01 CST 2045
Certificate fingerprints:
         SHA1: A3:C8:DE:23:                                    :81:4D
         SHA256: 8A:26:D9:7E:04:CB:B2:8B:C3:B3:                          :7C:E4:79:50:5E
Signature algorithm name: SHA256withRSA
Subject Public Key Algorithm: 2048-bit RSA key
Version: 3
```

FIGURE 4.10   Obtaining the SHA-256 certificate fingerprint.

Example:

```
keytool -list -v -keystore D: \HMSPetStoreApp.jks
```

3. Obtain the SHA-256 certificate fingerprint, as shown in Figure 4.10.

4.2.4 Configuring the Signing Certificate Fingerprint

Now, let's start configuring the signing certificate fingerprint.

1. Sign in to AppGallery Connect and click **My projects**. Find the project that has the Pet Store app, and click the app to go to the page shown in Figure 4.11.

FIGURE 4.11   Project settings page.

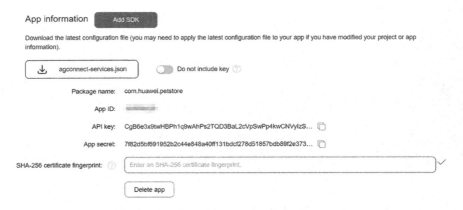

FIGURE 4.12   Entering the SHA-256 certificate fingerprint.

2. On the **General information** tab, find the **SHA-256 certificate fin-gerprint** parameter, click the plus icon (+) next to it, and enter the certificate fingerprint generated earlier, as shown in Figure 4.12.

4.2.5 Enabling Account Kit

An HMS Core kit works for your app only after you enable it. To do so, on the **Project settings** page, go to **Manage APIs** and toggle on the **Account Kit** switch, as shown in Figure 4.13.

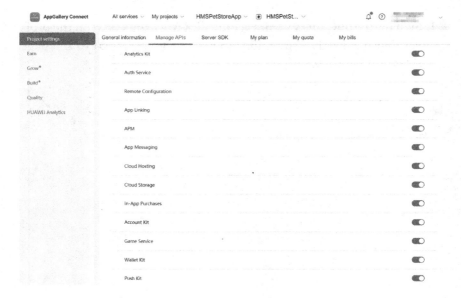

FIGURE 4.13   Account Kit enabled.

4.2.6 Integrating the Account SDK

You can integrate the Account SDK into your app regardless of whether you are developing it in Android Studio or Eclipse. Here, we'll complete the integration in Android Studio. You can find the integration instructions for Eclipse apps in the *Account Kit Development Guide*[4] on the HUAWEI Developers website.

1. On the **Project settings** page, go to the **General information** tab, and scroll down to **App information**. Click the **agconnect-services. json** button to download this file (Figure 4.14).

2. Copy the **agconnect-services.json** file to the **app** directory of the **HMSPetStoreApp** project, as shown in Figure 4.15.

3. Open the project-level **build.gradle** file and add the Maven repository of the HMS Core SDK under **allprojects > repositories** and under **buildscript > repositories**.

```
repositories {
  // Add the Maven repository of the HMS Core SDK.
  maven { url 'https://developer.huawei.
    com/repo/' }
}
```

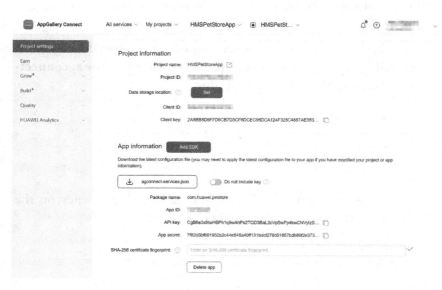

FIGURE 4.14   Downloading the AppGallery Connect configuration file.

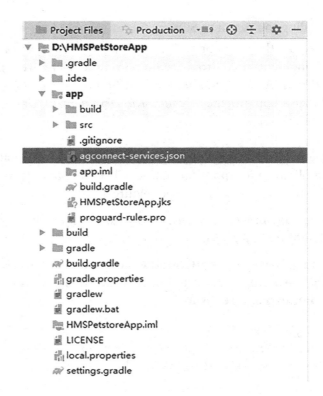

FIGURE 4.15 Copying the AppGallery Connect configuration file to the app directory.

Add the AppGallery Connect plug-in to the **dependencies** block of **buildscript**. This plug-in will parse the content of the **agconnect-services.json** file during app running.

```
dependencies {
    // Add the AppGallery Connect plug-in.
    classpath 'com.huawei.agconnect:agcp:
        1.2.1.301'
}
```

4. Open the app's **build.gradle** file and add the dependency on the Account SDK to the **dependencies** block.

```
dependencies {
    // Add the dependency on the Account SDK.
    implementation 'com.huawei.hms:hwid:4.0.1.300'
}
```

Add the configuration for referencing the AppGallery Connect plug-in at the end of the **build.gradle** file.

```
apply plugin: 'com.huawei.agconnect'
```

5. (Optional) Specify supported languages. Open the app's **build.gradle** file. Then go to **android > defaultConfig**, add **resConfigs**, and specify supported languages. English (**en**) and Simplified Chinese (**zh-rCN**) are mandatory.

```
android {
  defaultConfig {
    resConfigs "en","zh-rCN","Other languages supported
by your app"
  }
}
```

6. Configure obfuscation scripts.

Open the obfuscation configuration file **proguard-rules.pro** and add necessary configurations to exclude the HMS Core SDK from obfuscation.

Find the latest obfuscation configurations in the *Account Kit Development Guide* on the HUAWEI Developers website.

```
-ignorewarnings
-keepattributes *Annotation*
-keepattributes Exceptions
-keepattributes InnerClasses
-keepattributes Signature
-keepattributes SourceFile,LineNumberTable
-keep class com.hianalytics.android.**{*;}
-keep class com.huawei.updatesdk.**{*;}
-keep class com.huawei.hms.**{*;}
```

If you are using AndResGuard or similar tools, add the following configurations in the obfuscation configuration file:

```
"R.string.hms*",
"R.string.connect _ server _ fail _ prompt _ toast",
"R.string.getting _ message _ fail _ prompt _ toast",
"R.string.no _ available _ network _ prompt _ toast",
"R.string.third _ app _ *",
"R.string.upsdk _ *",
"R.layout.hms*",
"R.layout.upsdk _ *",
```

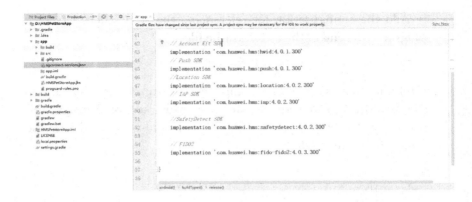

FIGURE 4.16   Performing synchronization.

FIGURE 4.17   Successful synchronization.

```
"R.drawable.upsdk*",
"R.color.upsdk*",
"R.dimen.upsdk*",
"R.style.upsdk*",
"R.string.agc*"
```

7. Click **Sync Now** in the upper right corner of Android Studio and wait for the synchronization to complete (Figure 4.16).

Now, we've made all of the necessary preparations for integrating Account Kit into the Pet Store app (Figure 4.17).

4.3 SIGNING IN WITH A HUAWEI ID

In this section, we'll guide you through how to design a HUAWEI ID sign-in button and how to sign in to your app with a HUAWEI ID in ID token or authorization code mode, or silently.

4.3.1 Designing a HUAWEI ID Sign-In Button

If you want your app to let users sign in with their HUAWEI ID, follow the HUAWEI ID sign-in button usage rules[5] and make a button.

Customize how it looks with Account Kit's UI service class named **HuaweiIdAuthButton,** then make it work by using **setOnClickListener (OnClickListener)** to register a listener.

Now, let's use **HuaweiIdAuthButton** to develop a HUAWEI sign-in button for the Pet Store app.

1. Open the layout file **login_act.xml** of the sign-in screen and add **HuaweiIdAuthButton.**

```
<com.huawei.hms.support.hwid.ui.HuaweiIdAuthButton
  android:id="@+id/hwid _ signin"
  android:layout _ width="wrap _ content"
  android:layout _ height="wrap _ content"
  android:layout _ gravity="center _
    horizontal"
  android:layout _ marginTop="@dimen/
    petstore _ 10 _ dp" />
```

2. Open **LoginAct.java**, register a listener for the HUAWEI ID sign-in button in the **initView** method, and set the theme, radius of the rounded corner, and color scheme for the button.

```
mHuaweiIdAuthButton = findViewById(R.id.hwid _ signin);
// Register a listener to listen for touch events.
mHuaweiIdAuthButton.setOnClickListener(this);
// Set the theme.
mHuaweiIdAuthButton.setTheme(HuaweiIdAuthButton.
THEME _ NO _ TITLE);
// Set the radius of the rounded corner, in px.
mHuaweiIdAuthButton.setCornerRadius(HuaweiIdAuthButton.
CORNER _ RADIUS _ LARGE);
// Set the color scheme.
mHuaweiIdAuthButton.setColorPolicy(HuaweiIdAuthButton.
COLOR _ POLICY _ WHITE);
```

To learn more about the methods in the **HuaweiIdAuthButton** class, please refer to the Account Kit documentation[6] on the HUAWEI Developers website.

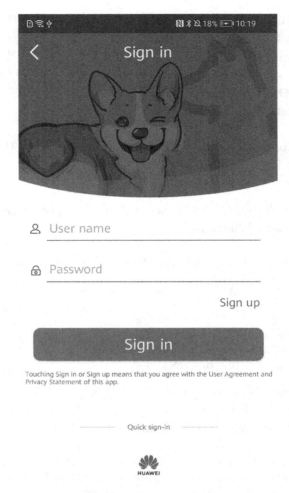

FIGURE 4.18   Checking the HUAWEI ID sign-in icon.

Now, let's run the app. The sign-in screen shown in Figure 4.18 will appear, with the HUAWEI ID sign-in icon at the bottom, which enables users to sign in to your app just by touching it.

4.3.2 Signing In with a HUAWEI ID in ID Token Mode

We've added the HUAWEI ID sign-in button in the previous section. Now, let's start adding code to make the sign-in functional. Since apps can be deployed on servers or standalone, Account Kit provides two sign-in modes: authorization code for server apps and ID token for both.

If your app is deployed on a server, choose between authorization code and ID token modes:

- If you save HUAWEI ID information on your server and periodically synchronize it with the Huawei OAuth server, or generate your own service tokens for your users based on their HUAWEI IDs, use the authorization code mode.

- If you only want to obtain HUAWEI ID information, but neither update it afterward nor generate your own service tokens, then use the ID token mode.

We'll first walk you through the ID token mode on our Pet Store app.

4.3.2.1 Service Process

Figure 4.19 shows the process of signing in with a HUAWEI ID in ID token mode.

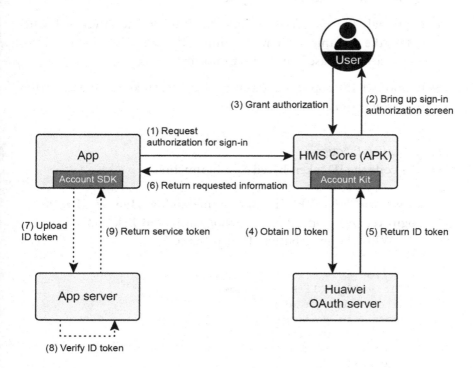

FIGURE 4.19   Sign-in (ID token mode).

The process is described as follows:

1. Your app sends a sign-in authorization request to HMS Core (APK).

2. HMS Core (APK) brings up the sign-in authorization screen, explicitly notifying the user of what they are about to authorize.

3. The user grants authorization.

4. HMS Core (APK) requests an ID token from the Huawei OAuth server.

5. The Huawei OAuth server returns an ID token to HMS Core (APK). The APK parses the token to obtain the information, such as the profile picture and nickname, as requested in the authorization scope.

6. HMS Core (APK) returns the ID token and the information parsed from it to the app.

7. (Optional) To save the user information on the app server, the app uploads the ID token to the app server.

8. (Optional) The app server verifies the ID token and, if verified, will obtain the user information. If required, the app server will generate a service token based on the user information.

9. (Optional) The app server returns the service token to the app. The user is now signed in.

4.3.2.2 Coding Practice
Now, let's code the ID token-based sign-in function.

1. Define the HUAWEI ID sign-in method **onHuaweiIdLogin** in **LoginAct.java**, and call this method in the **onClick** method of the HUAWEI ID sign-in button. Here is the code:

```
@Override
public void onClick(View view) {
  switch (view.getId()) {
    case R.id.hwid_ signin:
      // Sign in with a HUAWEI ID.
      onHuaweiIdLogin();
      break;
    default:
```

```
   break;
  }
 }
// Sign in with a HUAWEI ID.
private void onHuaweiIdLogin() {
}
```

2. Implement the **onHuaweiIdLogin** method with the following code:

```
// Define a HUAWEI ID sign-in button.
private HuaweiIdAuthButton mHuaweiIdAuthButton;
public static final int REQUEST_SIGN_IN_LOGIN = 1002;
private HuaweiIdAuthService mAuthService;
/**
 * Sign in with a HUAWEI ID.
 */
private void onHuaweiIdLogin() {
  // Specify authorization settings for ID token-based
sign-in.
  HuaweiIdAuthParams authParam = new
   HuaweiIdAuthParamsHelper(HuaweiIdAuthParams.
DEFAULT_AUTH_REQUEST_PARAM)
     .createParams();
  mAuthService    =    HuaweiIdAuthManager.getService(
LoginAct.this, authParam);
  // Obtain the intent of the authorization screen and
bring up the screen through startActivityForResult.
  startActivityForResult(mAuthService.getSignInIntent(),
REQUEST_SIGN_IN_LOGIN);
 }
```

So far, we have:

a. Defined authorization settings. Here, the default settings are used. For more details, please refer to the **HuaweiIdAuthParamsHelper** class in the *Account Kit API Reference*.

b. Obtained the **HuaweiIdAuthService** instance that is used to initiate a HUAWEI ID sign-in authorization request.

c. Obtained the intent of the authorization screen and brought up the screen.

3. Override the **onActivityResult** method to obtain the sign-in result, and return **DisplayName** and **AvatarUriString** if the sign-in is successful.

```
@Override
protected void onActivityResult(int requestCode, int
resultCode, @Nullable Intent data) {
  super.onActivityResult(requestCode, resultCode, data);
  if (requestCode == REQUEST _ SIGN _ IN _ LOGIN) {
    Task<AuthHuaweiId>         authHuaweiIdTask       =
HuaweiIdAuthManager.parseAuthRe
      sultFromIntent(data);
    if (authHuaweiIdTask.isSuccessful()) {
    // The sign-in is successful.
    AuthHuaweiId  huaweiAccount  =  authHuaweiIdTask.
getResult();
      Log.i(TAG, "signIn success");
      Log.i(TAG,  "DisplayName:  "  +  huaweiAccount.
getDisplayName());
      Log.i(TAG, "AvatarUriString: " + huaweiAccount.
        getAvatarUriString());
      } else {
      // The sign-in failed.
      String message = "signIn failed: "
      + ((ApiException)
      authHuaweiIdTask.
      getException()).
      getStatusCode();
    ToastUtil.getInstance().
      showShort(this, message);
    }
  }
}
```

Relaunch the Pet Store app, and touch the HUAWEI ID sign-in icon. Figure 4.20 shows the next screen, which requests user authorization and also clearly lists the information that the app will obtain. If the app icon does not appear on this screen, configure required settings in AppGallery Connect by following the instructions in Section 12.2.2.

Touch **Authorize and log in**. As shown in Logcat in Figure 4.21, we've successfully obtained the nickname (**DisplayName**) and profile picture (**AvatarUriString**).

4. Verify the ID token.

For an app deployed on a server, ID token verification is best performed server-side. Once a user has successfully signed in, the app uses HTTPS to send the ID token to the server for secure verification. If the ID token is valid, the app will set up a session with your own

🔋 📶 📵 ✻ 📶   📷100% 🔋 4:55

✕ **HUAWEI ID login**

Pet Store

This app will be authorized to:

- Link your HUAWEI ID

- Access your profile pic, name, and nickname (or anonymized phone number/email if none is set).

Data shared with HMSPetStoreApp is managed by a third party and subject to their privacy policy. You can revoke this authorization at any time in the HUAWEI ID Privacy center.

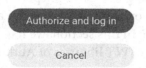

Authorize and log in

Cancel

FIGURE 4.20   HUAWEI ID sign-in authorization screen.

2021-01-30 17:02:14.904 17087-17087/? I/LoginAct: signIn success
2021-01-30 17:02:14.904 17087-17087/? I/LoginAct: DisplayName:
2021-01-30 17:02:14.904 17087-17087/? I/LoginAct: AvatarUriString: https://unfile1.hicloud.com/FileServer/image/b_02600860002475399E0_20200331110910_QACS8byOvxAveDdr;

FIGURE 4.21   Sign-in result in Logcat.

account system to associate the user information contained in the ID token with an already existing or newly created account in the system. For a stand-

---

NOTE

Calling the ID token verification API takes some time, depending on network conditions. Therefore, this verification method is only suitable for debugging. In the production environment, please verify the token locally on the app server.

---

alone app, ID token verification is not mandatory. The app obtains user information directly from HMS Core (APK).

Next, let's move on to verifying an ID token by either:

— Verifying it locally on the app server, or

— Calling the ID token verification API provided by Account Kit. The Huawei OAuth server will directly return the verification result. Get the API at https://oauth-login.cloud.huawei.com/oauth2/ v3/tokeninfo. For more details on this API, please refer to the *Account Kit API Reference*[7] on the HUAWEI Developers website.

Since local verification is more practical, let's learn how to do it here with key snippets. Get the full code from **IDTokenValidateUtil. java** in the sample code of the Pet Store app.

The ID token is actually a JWT, so we recommend that you verify the ID token by using a general-purpose JWT library, rather than your own code. If you want to learn more about JWT, visit https:// jwt.io/introduction/. In this section, we'll use **java-jwt** and **jwks-rsa**, two general-purpose JWT libraries of Auth0.

a. Obtain a public key URI from the **jwks_uri** field at https://oauth-login.cloud.huawei.com/.well-known/openid-configuration. Then use the public key URI to obtain a public key, which is used to verify the ID token. The public key is updated once a day and cached on the app server. The code for requesting the public key is as follows:

```
/**
 * Obtain the public key from the Account Kit server to
verify the ID token.
 */
```

```
private JSONArray getJwkPublicKeys() throws IOException
{
    // Obtain the public key URI.
    String certUrl = "https://oauth-login.cloud.huawei.
com/oauth2/v3/certs";
    InputStream in = null;
    HttpURLConnection urlConnection = null;
    BufferedReader bufferedReader = null;
    InputStreamReader inputStreamReader = null;
    JSONArray keysJsonArray = null;
    try {
      URL url = new URL(certUrl);
      urlConnection        =        (HttpURLConnection)url.
openConnection();
      urlConnection.setRequestMethod("GET");
      urlConnection.setDoOutput(true);
      urlConnection.setDoInput(true);
      urlConnection.connect();
      if (urlConnection.getResponseCode() == 200) {
        in = urlConnection.getInputStream();
        inputStreamReader = new InputStreamReader(in,
StandardCharsets.UTF _ 8);
        bufferedReader = new BufferedReader(inputStream
Reader);
        StringBuilder strBuf = new StringBuilder();
        String line;
        while ((line = bufferedReader.readLine()) != null)
{
          strBuf.append(line);
        }
      JSONObject jsonObject = JSONObject.parseObject(-
strBuf.toString());
      keysJsonArray = jsonObject.getJSONArray("keys");
      }
    } finally {
      if (bufferedReader != null) {
        bufferedReader.close();
      }
      if (inputStreamReader != null) {
        inputStreamReader.close();
      }
      if (in != null) {
        in.close();
      }
        if (urlConnection != null) {
          urlConnection.disconnect();
```

```
    }
  }
  return keysJsonArray;
```

b. Verify the signature. The key code snippet is as follows:

```
// Parse the ID token.
DecodedJWT decoder = JWT.decode(idToken);
RSAPublicKey   rsaPublicKey   =   getRSAPublicKeyByKid(-
decoder.getKeyId());
Algorithm   algorithm   =   Algorithm.RSA256(rsaPublicKey,
null);
JWTVerifier verifier = JWT.require(algorithm).build();
// Verify the signature.
verifier.verify(decoder);
```

c. Check whether the value of the **iss** field in the ID token is **https://accounts.huawei.com**.

```
if (!decoder.getIssuer().equals("https://accounts.huawei.
com")) {
  System.err.println("The iss field does not match.");
  return;
}
```

(d) Check whether the value of the **aud** field in the ID token is the same as that of **client_id** of the app.

```
if (!decoder.getAudience().get(0).equals(CLIENT _ ID)) {
  System.err.println("The aud field does not match.");
  return;
}
```

(e) Check whether the ID token has expired based on the value of **exp**.

```
// If the ID token has expired, an exception
TokenExpiredException is thrown.
verifier.verify(decoder);
```

This checklist proves that the ID token is valid. Your app can associate the HUAWEI ID with an already existing or newly created account in your own account system.

In reality, you can decide whether to verify the ID token. In this book, we will simplify things by not letting the Pet Store app upload user information to the app server or associate an account with your account system. The ID token will not be verified, either.

5. Define the **onHuaweiId-LoginSuccess** method in **LoginAct.java** and call the method to save the user information in **SharedPreferences**. A successful save will trigger the Pet Store app to show its home screen. Here's the code:

NOTICE

Apps are not allowed to directly send user information, such as **GivenName** obtained using the **AuthHuaweiId.getGivenName()** method, to the app server. This avoids sending information from attackers that use fake user accounts to sign in to your app. Instead, the app server uses the ID token to obtain user information securely.

```
/**
 * Save user information in SharedPreferences.
 */
private void onHuaweiIdLoginSuccess(AuthHuaweiId hua-
weiAccount) {
    // Save the OpenID of the HUAWEI ID.
    String openId = huaweiAccount.getOpenId();
    SPUtil.put(this, SPConstants.KEY _ HW _ OEPNID, openId);
    try {
        JSONObject jsonObject = new JSONObject();
        // Save the profile picture of the HUAWEI ID.
        jsonObject.put(SPConstants.KEY _ HEAD _ PHOTO, huawe-
iAccount.getAvatarUri().
            toString());
        SPUtil.put(this, openId, jsonObject.toString());
    } catch (JSONException e) {
        e.printStackTrace();
    }
    // Add a sign-in status flag.
    SPUtil.put(this, SPConstants.KEY _ LOGIN, true);
    // Add a HUAWEI ID sign-in status flag.
    SPUtil.put(this, SPConstants.KEY _ HW _ LOGIN, true);
    // Save the nickname of the HUAWEI ID.
    SPUtil.put(this, SPConstants.KEY _ NICK _ NAME, huawei
Account.getDisplayName());
    finish();
}
```

Relaunch the Pet Store app, touch the HUAWEI ID sign-in icon, and touch the **Authorize and log in** button. You'll see the home screen of the app, as shown in Figure 4.22, meaning that you're now signed in to the app with a HUAWEI ID.

6. To display the HUAWEI ID's profile picture and nickname on the **Settings** screen of the app, open the **SettingAct.java** file and use the **initData** method to obtain the HUAWEI ID information that you've previously saved.

Videos

Directory

 Mr Smith's Pet Store
1000 m

FIGURE 4.22   Home screen.

```java
/**
 * Initialize user information.
 */
private void initData() {
  String nickName = (String) SPUtil.get(this, SPConstants.
KEY _ NICK _ NAME, "");
  if (TextUtils.isEmpty(nickName)) {
    return;
  }
  // Set a nickname.
  mTvNickName.setText(nickName);
  boolean isHuaweiLogin = (boolean) SPUtil.get(this,
SPConstants.KEY _ HW _ LOGIN,
    false);
  if (!isHuaweiLogin) {
    return;
  }
  String openId = (String) SPUtil.get(this, SPConstants.
KEY _ HW _ OEPNID, "");
  if (TextUtils.isEmpty(openId)) {
    // No user information found in the app.
    return;
  }
  String userInfo = (String) SPUtil.get(this, openId,
"");
  if (TextUtils.isEmpty(userInfo)) {
    // No user information found in the app.
    return;
  }
  String headPhoto = "";
  try {
    JSONObject jsonObject = new JSONObject(userInfo);
    headPhoto = jsonObject.optString(SPConstants.
KEY _ HEAD _ PHOTO,"");
  } catch (Exception e) {
    e.printStackTrace();
  }
  // Set a profile picture.
  if (!TextUtils.isEmpty(headPhoto)) {
    Glide.with(this)
      .load(headPhoto)
      .into(mIvHeadImg);
  }
}
```

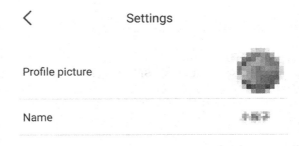

FIGURE 4.23   Settings screen.

Now, let's relaunch the app and access the **Settings** screen shown in Figure 4.23. On this screen, we'll find the profile picture and nick-name of our HUAWEI ID.

4.3.3 Signing In with a HUAWEI ID in Authorization Code Mode

In the previous section, we introduced sign-in with a HUAWEI ID in ID token mode. Now, let's learn the authorization code mode.

4.3.3.1 Service Process

Figure 4.24 shows the process of signing in to an app with a HUAWEI ID in authorization code mode.

The process is described as follows:

1. The app sends a sign-in authorization request to HMS Core (APK) to obtain an authorization code.

2. HMS Core (APK) brings up the sign-in authorization screen, explicitly notifying the user of what they are about to authorize. The user grants authorization.

3. HMS Core (APK) requests an authorization code from the Huawei OAuth server.

4. The Huawei OAuth server returns an authorization code to HMS Core (APK).

5. HMS Core (APK) sends the authorization code to the app.

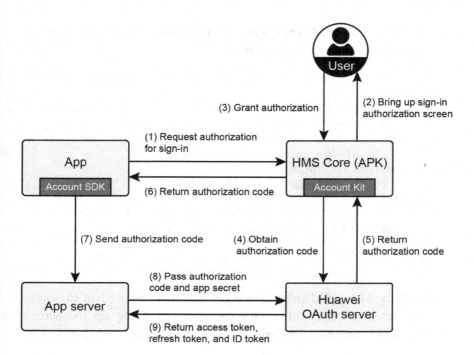

FIGURE 4.24   Sign-in (authorization code mode).

6. The app sends the authorization code to the app server for verification.

7. The app server calls the token obtaining API and passes the authorization code and app secret to obtain an access token, a refresh token, and an ID token.

   This ID token is returned only when the authorization scope in the sign-in authorization request contains the OpenID.

8. The Huawei OAuth server returns the three tokens to the app server.

   The app server can then use the access token to obtain the OpenID and UnionID via the **getTokenInfo** API. When the access token expires, the app server uses the refresh token to obtain a new access token. The app server can also parse the ID token to get user information such as the nickname and profile picture.

4.3.3.2 Coding Practice

Now, let's write the code that enables the authorization code-based sign-in function.

1. Call the **HuaweiIdAuthParamsHelper.setAuthorizationCode** method to request authorization as follows:

```
// Specify authorization settings for authorization
code-based sign-in.
HuaweiIdAuthParams authParam = new HuaweiIdAuthParams
Helper(HuaweiIdAuthParams.DEFAULT _ AUTH _ REQUEST _
PARAM)
    // Obtain an authorization code.
    .setAuthorizationCode()
    .createParams();
```

2. Call the **getService** method of **HuaweiIdAuthManager** to initialize the **HuaweiIdAuthService** object. Here's the code:

```
HuaweiIdAuthService authService = HuaweiIdAuthManager.
getService(HuaweiIdActivity.this, mAuthParam);
```

3. Call the **HuaweiIdAuthService.getSignInIntent** method to obtain the intent of the authorization screen and bring up the screen through **startActivityForResult** to request user authorization. Here's the code:

```
startActivityForResult(authService.getSignInIntent(),
Constant.REQUEST _ SIGN _ IN _ LOGIN _ CODE);
```

4. Process the sign-in result after the authorization is complete. Here is the code:

```
@Override
protected void onActivityResult(int requestCode, int
resultCode, @Nullable
    Intent data) {
  super.onActivityResult(requestCode, resultCode, data);
  if (requestCode == Constant.REQUEST _ SIGN _ IN _
LOGIN _ CODE) {
    Task<AuthHuaweiId> authHuaweiIdTask = HuaweiIdAuth
Manager.parseAuthResultF
      romIntent(data);
    if (authHuaweiIdTask.isSuccessful()) {
    // The sign-in is successful, and the user's HUAWEI
ID information and authorization code are obtained.
      AuthHuaweiId huaweiAccount = authHuaweiIdTask.
getResult();
      Log.i(TAG, "Authorization code:" + huaweiAccount.
getAuthorizationCode());
    } else {
    // The sign-in failed.
      Log.e(TAG, "sign in failed : " + ((ApiException)auth
HuaweiIdTask.
      getException()).getStatusCode());
    }
  }
}
```

5. After a successful sign-in, call the token obtaining API to send a request to the Huawei OAuth server to obtain an ID token, an access token, and a refresh token. This request is a POST request, and its body should contain the parameters listed in Table 4.1.

The body of the response upon a successful API call would contain the parameters listed in Table 4.2.

TABLE 4.1   Parameters in the Request Body

Parameter	Value
grant_type	Always **authorization_code**.
code	Authorization code obtained in the previous step.
client_id	App ID that you obtained when creating your app in AppGallery Connect.
client_secret	App secret that you obtained when creating your app in AppGallery Connect.
redirect_uri	Redirection URI that you specified in AppGallery Connect.

TABLE 4.2 Parameters in the Response Body

Parameter	Mandatory	Type	Description
token_type	Yes	String	Always **Bearer**.
access_token	Yes	String	Access token.
scope	Yes	String	Scope of an access token.
expires_in	No	String	Validity period of an access token, in seconds. The default value is **3600**.
refresh_token	No	String	Refresh token. It will be returned if the **access_type** parameter is set to **offline** in the request for calling the token obtaining API. The refresh token is required when you want to obtain a new access token.
id_token	No	String	ID token, which is a JWT. It will be returned if the input parameter **scope** contains **openId** in the request for calling the token obtaining API.

The code to obtain the three tokens from the Huawei OAuth server is here:

```
/**
 * Obtain an access token and a refresh token.
 */
public static void getAccessToken(String code) throws
Exception {
  // Specify the app ID.
  String clientId = ""; // your app ID
  // Specify the app secret.
  String clientSecret = "";
  // Call the token obtaining API.
  String tokenUrl = "https://oauth-login.cloud.huawei.
com/oauth2/v3/token";
  // To use the authorization code to obtain the access
token, refresh token, and ID token,
  // set grant _ type to authorization _ code.
  String grant _ type = "authorization _ code";
  String contentType = "application/x-www-form-
urlencoded; charset=UTF-8";
  // Format the request body.
  String msgBody = MessageFormat.
format("grant _ type={0}&code={1}&client _
    id={2}&client _ secret={3}&redirect _ uri={4}", grant _
type, URLEncoder.
```

```
      encode(code,    "utf-8"),    clientId,    clientSecret,
"https://com.huawei.apps.101742901/oauth2redirect");
    String response = httpPost(tokenUrl, contentType, msg-
Body, 5000, 5000, null);
    JSONObject obj = JSONObject.parseObject(response);
    String accessToken = obj.getString("access _ token");
    String refreshToken = obj.getString("refresh _ token");
    System.out.println("Access Token : " + accessToken);
    System.out.println("Refresh Token : " + refreshToken);
}
```

httpPost is a public method for sending an HTTP POST request. Here is the code:

```
/**
 * Send an HTTP POST request.
 */
public static String httpPost(String httpUrl, String
contentType, String data,
    int  connectTimeout,  int  readTimeout,  Map<String,
String> headers) throws
    IOException {
    OutputStream output;
    InputStream in = null;
    HttpURLConnection urlConnection = null;
    BufferedReader bufferedReader = null;
    InputStreamReader inputStreamReader = null;
    try {
      URL url = new URL(httpUrl);
      urlConnection      =         (HttpURLConnection)url.
openConnection();
      urlConnection.setRequestMethod("POST");
      urlConnection.setDoOutput(true);
      urlConnection.setDoInput(true);
      urlConnection.setRequestProperty("Content-Type",
contentType);
      if (headers != null) {
        for (String key : headers.keySet()) {
          urlConnection.setRequestProperty(key,    headers.
get(key));
        }
      }
      urlConnection.setConnectTimeout(connectTimeout);
      urlConnection.setReadTimeout(readTimeout);
```

```
    urlConnection.connect();

    output = urlConnection.getOutputStream();
    output.write(data.getBytes(StandardCharsets.UTF_8));
    output.flush();
    if (urlConnection.getResponseCode() < 400) {
      in = urlConnection.getInputStream();
    } else {
      in = urlConnection.getErrorStream();
    }
    inputStreamReader   =   new   InputStreamReader(in,
StandardCharsets.UTF_8);
    bufferedReader = new BufferedReader(inputStreamReader);
    StringBuilder strBuf = new StringBuilder();
    String str;
    while ((str = bufferedReader.readLine()) != null) {
      strBuf.append(str);
    }
    return strBuf.toString();
  } finally {
    if (bufferedReader != null) {
      bufferedReader.close();
    }
    if (inputStreamReader != null) {
      inputStreamReader.close();
    }
    if (in != null) {
      in.close();
    }
    if (urlConnection != null) {
      urlConnection.disconnect();
    }
  }
}
```

6. The access token has a short validity period (currently 60 minutes). When the access token has expired or is about to expire, use the refresh token (valid by default for 180 days) to request a new access token from the Huawei OAuth server through the token obtaining API. Here's the code:

```
/**
 * When an access token has expired, use the refresh
token to obtain a new access token.
 */
```

```
public static void refreshAccessToken(String code,
String refreshToken) throws
  Exception {
  // Specify the app ID.
  String clientId = "";
  // Specify the app secret.
  String clientSecret = "";
  // Call the token obtaining API.
  String tokenUrl = "https://oauth-login.cloud.huawei.
com/oauth2/v3/token";
  // To use the refresh token to obtain a new access
token, set grant.type to refresh_token.
  String grant_type = "refresh_token";
  String contentType = "application/x-www-form-
urlencoded; charset=UTF-8";
  // Format the request body.
  String msgBody = MessageFormat.
format("grant_type={0}&client_id={1}&client_
  secret={2}&refresh_token={3}", grant_type,
clientId,clientSecret, URLEncoder.
  encode(refreshToken, "utf-8"));
  String response = httpPost(tokenUrl, contentType, msg-
Body, 5000, 5000, null);
  JSONObject obj = JSONObject.parseObject(response);
  System.out.println(obj.toJSONString());
  String accessToken = obj.getString("access_token");
  System.out.println("Access Token : " + accessToken);
}
```

(7) After obtaining a new access token, call the **getTokenInfo** API to verify the token. If it is valid, you will obtain the information including **union_id**, **open_id**, **expire_in**, and **scope**. Here is the code:

```
/**
 * Obtain the OpenID and UnionID.
 */
public static void getTokenInfo(String accessToken)
throws IOException {
  // Call the getTokenInfo API.
  String tokenInfoUrl = "https://api.cloud.huawei.com/
rest.php?nsp_fmt=JSON&nsp_
    svc=huawei.oauth2.user.getTokenInfo";
```

```
String   contentType   =   "application/x-www-form-
urlencoded; charset=UTF-8";
    String       msgBody       =       MessageFormat.
format("access _ token={0}&open _ id=OPENID",
        URLEncoder.encode(accessToken, "UTF-8"));
    String response = httpPost(tokenInfoUrl, contentType,
msgBody, 5000, 5000,
        null);
    JSONObject obj = JSONObject.parseObject(response);
    String openId = obj.getString("open _ id");
    String unionId = obj.getString("union _ id");
    System.out.println("openId : " + openId);
    System.out.println("unionId : " + unionId);
}
```

Now, we've successfully developed the function of HUAWEI ID sign-in via an authorization code. Since you've obtained the OpenID and UnionID, you can then use them to associate a user's HUAWEI ID information with your own account system.

4.3.4 Silently Signing In with a HUAWEI ID

When a user signs in to an app with their HUAWEI ID, the app will show an authorization screen, asking them to allow it to obtain their ID information. Even if already authorized at the first sign-in, the app will still show the authorization screen briefly before displaying the sign-in screen shown in Figure 4.25. To completely skip this authorization screen, Account Kit provides the silent sign-in function.

4.3.4.1 Service Process

Once your app has silent sign-in enabled, user authorization is only required for the first sign-in to your app with a HUAWEI ID. Subsequent sign-ins using the same HUAWEI ID do not require any authorization, and thus the authorization screen won't appear. Figure 4.26 shows how silent sign-in works.

The process is described as follows:

1. Your app calls the **HuaweiIdAuthService.silentSignIn** method to send a silent sign-in request to HMS Core (APK).

2. HMS Core (APK) checks whether the access token in the cache has expired. If it is still valid, HMS Core (APK) returns the authorization

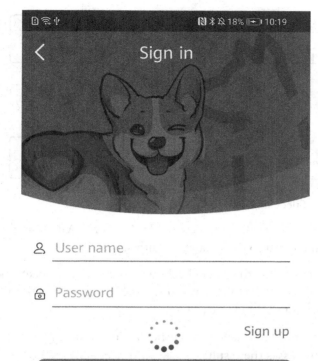

FIGURE 4.25 Signing in after user authorization.

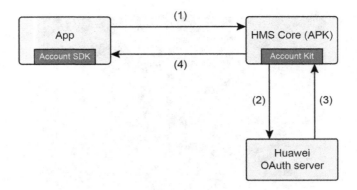

FIGURE 4.26   Silent sign-in.

result in the cache. Otherwise, HMS Core (APK) sends a silent sign-in request to the Huawei OAuth server.

3. The Huawei OAuth server checks whether your app meets the authorization condition for silent sign-in and, if so, returns the authorization result to HMS Core (APK).

4. HMS Core (APK) sends the authorization result to your app, which then processes the result.

4.3.4.2 Coding Practice
To build a better user experience, implement silent sign-in for your app.

1. Open the **LoginAct.java** file and create the **silentSignIn** method as follows:

```java
/**
 * Silent sign-in
 */
private void silentSignIn() {
    // Specify authorization settings for silent sign-in.
    HuaweiIdAuthParams        authParams        =        new
HuaweiIdAuthParamsHelper(HuaweiIdAuthParams.DEFAULT _
AUTH _ REQUEST _ PARAM).createParams();
    // Initialize the HuaweiIdAuthService object.
    mAuthService     =     HuaweiIdAuthManager.getService(-
LoginAct.this, authParams);
    // Send a silent sign-in request.
    Task<AuthHuaweiId> task = mAuthService.silentSignIn();
```

```
// Processing after a successful authorization
task.addOnSuccessListener(new OnSuccessListener<AuthH
uaweiId>() {
  @Override
  public void onSuccess(AuthHuaweiId authHuaweiId) {
    // Already authorized.
    onHuaweiIdLoginSuccess(authHuaweiId, false);
    Log.d(TAG, authHuaweiId.getDisplayName() + " silent
signIn success ");
  }
});
// Processing after an authorization failure
task.addOnFailureListener(new OnFailureListener() {
  @Override
  public void onFailure(Exception e) {
    if (e instanceof ApiException) {
      ApiException apiException = (ApiException) e;
      if (apiException.getStatusCode() == 2002) {
        // Unauthorized. Call the onHuaweiIdLogin
method to show the authorization screen to request user
authorization.
        onHuaweiIdLogin();
      }
    }
  }
});
}
```

So far, the code has enabled us to:

a. Specify authorization settings for silent sign-in.

b. Obtain the **HuaweiIdAuthService** instance to make a silent sign-in request.

c. Process the authorization result.

   If the authorization is successful, your app will obtain and save the user's HUAWEI ID information. If the authorization fails, your app may have not obtained authorization from the user. In this case, your app will call the **getSignInIntent** method of **HuaweiIdAuthService** to display the authorization screen, an optional step. Here, the **onHuaweiIdLogin** method created in Section 4.3.2 is called to bring up the authorization screen. Once granting authorization, the user will be signed in.

2. Call the **silentSignIn** method in the **onClick** method of the HUAWEI ID sign-in button. The code looks like the following:

```
@Override
  public void onClick(View view) {
    switch (view.getId()) {
      case R.id.hwid _ signin:
        // Sign in with a HUAWEI ID.
        silentSignIn();
        break;
      default:
        break;
    }
  }
```

Relaunch the Pet Store app to test the silent sign-in function. You'll find that the app shows the authorization screen only at the first sign-in.

Now, we've finished HUAWEI ID sign-in. It's time for us to move on to signing out from a HUAWEI ID.

4.4 SIGNING OUT FROM A HUAWEI ID

Your app will need to provide a portal for a signed-in user to sign out. When the user signs out, the app should notify HMS Core (APK) to remove the user's HUAWEI ID information, for privacy purposes.

4.4.1 Service Process

First, let's take a look at the sign-out process, as shown in Figure 4.27.

The process is described as follows:

1. The app calls the **HuaweiIdAuthService.signOut** method to send a request to HMS Core (APK) for signing out from a HUAWEI ID.

2. HMS Core (APK) removes the user's HUAWEI ID information and returns the sign-out result to the app.

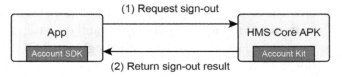

FIGURE 4.27   Sign-out.

4.4.2 Coding Practice

Signing out from a HUAWEI ID is quite easy – all you need to do is to call the **signOut** method. Open the **SettingAct.java** file and add the **huaweiSignOut** method. Here is the code:

```
/**
 * Sign out from a HUAWEI ID.
 */
private void huaweiSignOut() {
  HuaweiIdAuthParams authParams = new
HuaweiIdAuthParamsHelper(HuaweiIdAuthParams.DEFAULT_
AUTH_REQUEST_PARAM).createParams();
  HuaweiIdAuthService authService =
HuaweiIdAuthManager.getService
    (SettingAct.this, authParams);
  Task<Void> signOutTask = authService.signOut();
  signOutTask.addOnSuccessListener(new
OnSuccessListener<Void>() {
  @Override
  public void onSuccess(Void aVoid) {
     Log.d(TAG, "signOut Success");
     // Remove the sign-in status flag.
     SPUtil.put(SettingAct.this, SPConstants.KEY_HW_
LOGIN, false);
     SPUtil.put(SettingAct.this, SPConstants.KEY_
LOGIN, false);
     finish(); }
  }).addOnFailureListener(new OnFailureListener() {
    @Override
    public void onFailure(Exception e) {
     Log.d(TAG, "signOut fail");
     ToastUtil.getInstance().showShort(SettingAct.
this, "signOut fail");
    }
  });
}
```

In the **onClick** method of the sign-out button, call the **huaweiSignOut** method to sign out. The code is as follows:

```
findViewById(R.id.setting_exit).setOnClickListener(new
View.OnClickListener() {
```

```
@Override
public void onClick(View v) {
  // Sign out from a HUAWEI ID.
  huaweiSignOut();
}
});
```

Relaunch the Pet Store app and go to the **Settings** screen. Touch the **Sign out** button. You'll be signed out and redirected to the home screen, as shown in Figure 4.28.

In addition to signing out, your users may want to revoke authorization for privacy purposes. Next, let's take a look at the function of revoking authorization.

4.5 REVOKING AUTHORIZATION

Now, let's learn the authorization revoking process and the code for implementing it.

4.5.1 Service Process

Figure 4.29 shows the process of revoking authorization.

The process is described as follows:

1. The app calls the **HuaweiIdAuth-Service.cancelAuthorization** method to send a request to HMS Core (APK) for revoking authorization.

2. HMS Core (APK) forwards the authorization revoking request to the Huawei OAuth server.

3. The Huawei OAuth server removes the HUAWEI ID authorization information and returns the authorization revoking result to HMS Core (APK).

4. HMS Core (APK) deletes the HUAWEI ID authorization information from the local cache and returns the authorization revoking result to the app.

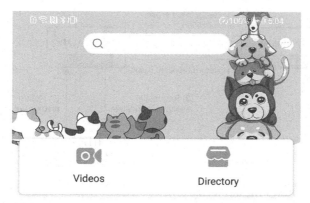

Videos

Directory

 Mr Smith's Pet Store

1000 m

FIGURE 4.28 Home screen of the Pet Store app.

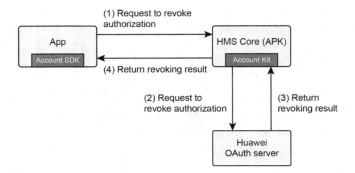

FIGURE 4.29   Revoking authorization.

4.5.2 Coding Practice

Revoking authorization involves only two steps: calling the **cancelAuthorization** method and processing the revoking result. Take a look at the following code:

```
/**
 * Revoke authorization.
 */
private void cancelAuthorization() {
  HuaweiIdAuthParams authParams = new
HuaweiIdAuthParamsHelper(HuaweiIdAuthP
    arams.DEFAULT_AUTH_REQUEST_PARAM).createParams();
  mAuthService = HuaweiIdAuthManager.getService(-
LoginAct.this, authParams);
  // Register a listener to listen for the
authorization revoking result.
  mAuthService.cancelAuthorization().
addOnCompleteListener(new
    OnCompleteListener<Void>() {
    @Override
    public void onComplete(Task<Void> task) {
      if (task.isSuccessful()) {
        // Authorization is revoked successfully, and
the HUAWEI ID information is also deleted.
        Log.d(TAG, "Cancel Authorization Success");
      } else {
        // Authorization revoking failed.
      }
```

```
      }
    });
}
```

Now, we've completed the development of HUAWEI ID sign-in, sign-out, and authorization revoking functions.

4.6 AUTOMATICALLY READING AN SMS VERIFICATION CODE

If your app requires users to bind their mobile number for further verification, Account Kit's automatic SMS verification code reader can come in handy. This function enables quick identity verification by saving users the trouble of manually inputting verification codes. This additional verification also safeguards their privacy and assets. Now, let's learn how to integrate this function.

4.6.1 Service Process

Figure 4.30 shows the process of automatically reading an SMS verification code for a user who has already signed in to your app with a HUAWEI ID. The process is described as follows:

1. The user enters a mobile number to request a verification code. The app calls the **ReadSmsManager.start()** method to request HMS Core (APK) to enable the SMS reading service.

2. HMS Core (APK) returns the result.

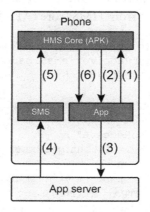

FIGURE 4.30 Automatically reading an SMS verification code.

3. The app sends the mobile number to the app server.

4. The app server uses the template[8] to generate an SMS containing a verification code and sends the SMS to the user.

5. HMS Core (APK) listens for the SMS that contains the matching verification code.

6. HMS Core (APK) sends the found message to the app through a directed broadcast.

NOTE

ReadSmsManager allows for fully automated verification. However, you still need to define a hash value in the SMS message body. If you are not the message sender, such as because you are using a third-party app server, **ReadSmsManager** is not recommended.

4.6.2 Coding Practice

For a user already signed in with a HUAWEI ID, your app can further verify their identity by asking the user for their mobile number and verification code.

1. Create an activity named **VerifyAct** in the **login** package to add a mobile number binding screen. The screen's layout file is **verify_act.xml**. This screen (as shown in Figure 4.31) has a simple layout, so we won't discuss it in detail here. Please find how to code the screen in the layout file.

2. Open the **VerifyAct.java** file and create **smsBroadcast-Receiver** to receive the broadcast from HMS Core (APK). Here's the code:

```
// Receive the broadcast from HMS Core (APK).
  private BroadcastReceiver smsBroadcastReceiver =
    new BroadcastReceiver() {
    @Override
    public void onReceive(Context context,
      Intent intent) {
      Log.d(TAG, "onReceive");
      Bundle bundle = intent.getExtras();
      if (bundle != null) {
        Status     status    =     bundle.getParcelable(-
ReadSmsConstant.EXTRA _ STATUS);
        if (status != null && status.getStatusCode() ==
CommonStatusCodes.
```

FIGURE 4.31 Mobile number binding screen of the Pet Store app.

```
            SUCCESS) {
            if        (bundle.containsKey(ReadSmsConstant.
    EXTRA _ SMS _ MESSAGE)) {
                // An SMS that meets the requirement is read.
                final String smsMessage = bundle.getString
                  (ReadSmsConstant.EXTRA _ SMS _ MESSAGE);
                runOnUiThread(new Runnable() {
                  @Override
                  public void run() {
                      // Extract the SMS verification code
    from the obtained SMS.
                      onGetVerifyCode(smsMessage);
                  }
                });
            } else {
                // Failed to obtain the verification code.
```

```
                    onVerifyGainError();
                  }
              } else {
                  // No SMS that meets the requirements is
read before the service times out.
                  Log.d(TAG, "receive sms failed");
                  // Failed to obtain the verification code.
                  onVerifyGainError();
              }
          } else {
              // Failed to obtain the verification code.
              onVerifyGainError();
          }
        }
    };
```

The code for the **onGetVerifyCode** method is as follows:

```
/**
 * Extract the verification code from an SMS.
 */
private void onGetVerifyCode(String smsMessage) {
  Log.e(TAG, "read sms success, sms content is " +
smsMessage);
    if (TextUtils.isEmpty(smsMessage)) {
      onVerifyGainError();
      return;
    }
    // Extract the verification code from an SMS. The mes-
sage content is "[#]Welcome to the Pet Store app. The
    // verification code is 200002. yKaTWEGHzyV"
    int indexOf = smsMessage.lastIndexOf(". ");
    mVerifyCode  =  smsMessage.substring(indexOf  -  6,
indexOf);
    Log.e(TAG, "verifyCode : " + mVerifyCode);
    mEtVerifyCode.setText(mVerifyCode);
}
```

The code for the **onVerifyGainError** method is as follows:

```
/**
 * Show a message upon a failure to obtain the verifi-
cation code.
 */
private void onVerifyGainError() {
```

```
mTvVerifyGain.setText(getString(R.string.verify _ code));
ToastUtil.getInstance().showShort(VerifyAct.this,
getString(R.string.
    toast _ verifycode _ error));
}
```

3. Open the **VerifyAct.java** file, create the **onGainVerifyCode** method, and enable the SMS reading service. Once enabled, register **sms-BroadcastReceiver** for receiving the SMS, and call the **onGainVerifyCode** method in the **onClick** method of the button for obtaining the SMS verification code. The code is as follows:

```
/**
 * Obtain the verification code.
 */
private void onGainVerifyCode() {
  mTvVerifyGain.setText(getString(R.string.
verify _ gain));
  // Enable the SMS reading service.
  Task<Void> task = ReadSmsManager.start(this);
  task.addOnSuccessListener(new OnSuccessListener<Void>()
{
    @Override
    public void onSuccess(Void aVoid) {
      Log.d(TAG, "open read sms permission success");
      // Dynamically register a broadcast receiver for
automatic SMS reading.
      if (!isRegisterBroadcast) {
        IntentFilter       intentFilter      =      new
IntentFilter(ReadSmsConstant.
          READ _ SMS _ BROADCAST _ ACTION);
          registerReceiver(smsBroadcastReceiver,
intentFilter);
      }
    }
  }).addOnFailureListener(new OnFailureListener() {
    @Override
    public void onFailure(Exception e) {
      Log.d(TAG, "open read sms permission fail");
      // Failed to obtain the verification code.
      onVerifyGainError();
    }
  });
}
```

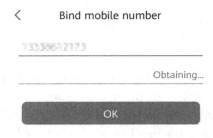

FIGURE 4.32   Verification code to be auto-filled.

4. Now, the Pet Store app has enabled the reader function. Relaunch the app, and simulate the verification process by using another phone to send a verification SMS. Figure 4.32 shows the mobile number binding screen on which the verification code will be auto-filled.

Account Kit has now been fully integrated, equipping our Pet Store app with a range of highly functional features.

4.7 SUMMARY

In this chapter, you got an introduction to the Account Kit's main functions and use cases, and you also learned how to integrate it into an app for better user experience. In the next chapter, you'll learn about how to integrate IAP into the app so users can make purchases, such as a membership, to watch pet videos.

NOTES

1 To learn more about OAuth 2.0, please visit https://oauth.net/2/.
2 To learn more about OpenID Connect, please visit https://openid.net/connect/.
3 Visit the HUAWEI Developers website at https://developer.huawei.com/consumer/en/.
4 You can find this guide at https://developer.huawei.com/consumer/en/doc/development.
5 You can find the rules at https://developer.huawei.com/consumer/en/doc/development/HMSCore-Guides-V5/dev-specifications-0000001050048916-V5.
6 Youcanfinditathttps://developer.huawei.com/consumer/en/doc/development.
7 You can find it at https://developer.huawei.com/consumer/en/doc/development/HMSCore-References-V5/account-verify-id-token_hms_reference-0000001050050577-V5.
8 You can find the template at https://developer.huawei.com/consumer/en/doc/development/HMSCore-References-V5/account-support-sms-readsmsmanager-0000001050050553-V5.

CHAPTER 5

In-App Purchases

5.1 ABOUT THE SERVICE

Thanks to an assortment of supported payment channels, your app will be equipped to deliver payment services on a truly global scale, without having to integrate third-party payment systems. Furthermore, IAP offers a product management system (PMS) for managing product price and language settings, giving your app an edge when establishing a presence in global markets. With PMS, all you need to do is integrate IAP to avoid the hassles associated with fund transfers between IAP, third-party payment providers, and clearing organizations. First, we'll outline some of the key working principles behind IAP. Figure 5.1 shows the IAP architecture, which consists of the following:

- IAP SDK: provides APIs for integrating IAP into apps.

- IAP Kit: runs on the device to process payment logic.

- IAP server: runs on the cloud to store order and payment data.

- PMS: runs on the cloud to manage products.

PMS helps you manage a product after you have entered the relevant product information in AppGallery Connect. Once your app has integrated the IAP SDK, it will be able to call APIs from IAP to carry out a wide range

DOI: 10.1201/9781003206699-5

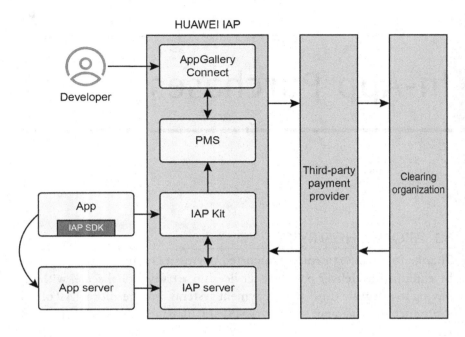

FIGURE 5.1   IAP architecture.

of services, such as obtaining product information, initiating payments, and querying payment records. If you have an app server, it will be able to obtain the data from your app to perform digital signature verification. Alternatively, you can call the IAP server's APIs for product management to better serve your users.

IAP lets users of your app complete transactions via payment cards, third-party payment channels, DCB, and HUAWEI Points. Supported payment cards include almost all of those supported by major providers such as Visa and Mastercard. DCB is now supported by many major carriers around the globe. Users can bind payment cards and phone numbers to their HUAWEI IDs and complete payments simply by entering previously set HUAWEI ID payment passwords, rather than having to complete all of the steps associated with traditional payment methods. IAP is currently available in 184 countries and regions. To check which they are, please go to the HUAWEI Developers website and find them in the *IAP Development Guide*.

5.2 PREPARATIONS

This section details the preparations and steps required for integrating IAP. First, let us take a look at the functional requirements for IAP in the Pet Store app as mentioned earlier in Section 3.3. These include:

- Membership purchase: enables the user to view and purchase products, and review purchase orders.

- Pet videos: enables the user to browse video material and play content of interest.

The Pet Store app offers a wide range of pet videos that are viewable by purchasing a membership package. The following details the process for integrating IAP by defining a membership package, purchasing the package, and viewing a video after the purchase.

5.2.1 Enabling IAP

Enable IAP in AppGallery Connect, to ensure that the Pet Store app will be able to integrate it.

1. Sign in to AppGallery Connect, click **My projects**, find the project for the Pet Store app, and go to **Project settings**, as shown in Figure 5.2.

2. On the **Manage APIs** tab, enable **In-App Purchases**, as shown in Figure 5.3.

3. Go to **Earn > In-App Purchases** and click **Settings**, as shown in Figure 5.4.

   If this is your first time performing the configuration, you will be prompted to sign an agreement. After the configuration is successful, the public key used for digital signature verification will be displayed, as shown in Figure 5.5.

FIGURE 5.2   Project settings.

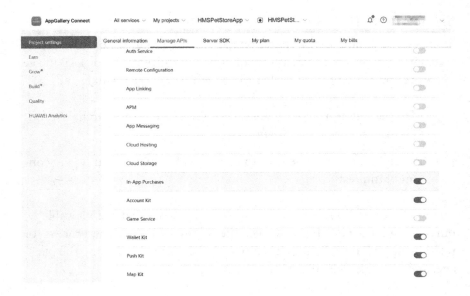

FIGURE 5.3   Enabling IAP.

FIGURE 5.4   IAP status before configuration.

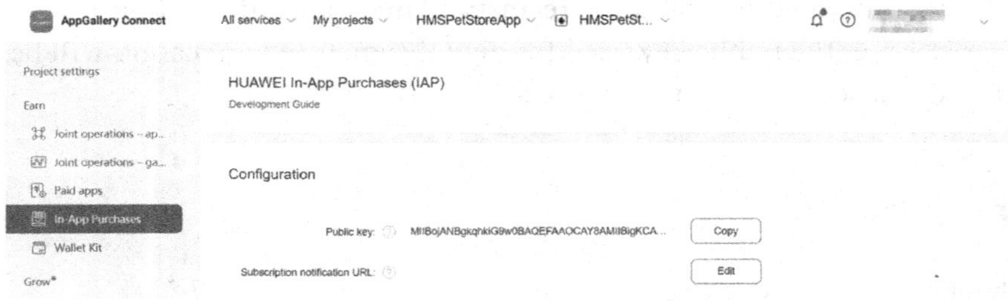

FIGURE 5.5   Public key displayed after configuration.

5.2.2 Integrating the IAP SDK

Next, we'll outline the process for integrating the IAP SDK. It's similar to integrating the Account SDK.

1. Open the **build.gradle** file in the **app** directory of your project, and add the following dependency to the **dependencies** block:

```
dependencies {
...
implementation 'com.huawei.hms:iap:4.0.2.300'
}
```

Here, **4.0.2.300** is an example SDK version number. You can obtain the latest SDK version number from the HUAWEI Developers website.

2. Click **Sync Now** in the upper right corner of Android Studio and wait for the synchronization to complete.

   After completing the steps above, you'll need to configure the information related to the membership package for the Pet Store app in AppGallery Connect. But before doing so, let's learn a bit more about how to use PMS.

5.3 PRODUCT CREATION IN PMS

This section describes how to create and configure a product in PMS.

5.3.1 Principles Behind PMS

As mentioned earlier, PMS is the part of IAP that enables the display of in-app products in local languages and currencies. In PMS, a default currency and a default language are specified for each country or region. Once you have entered the product description in multiple languages via AppGallery Connect, you'll only need to enter the price in a familiar currency, after which PMS will automatically calculate the prices in other currencies, using the real-time exchange rate. When the user queries a product, IAP detects the user's location and determines their local language and currency in PMS, and returns the product information in the corresponding language and currency to facilitate convenient in-app payments.

Figure 5.6 outlines the product management in PMS.

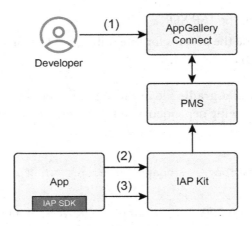

FIGURE 5.6   Product management in PMS.

1. Configure the product information in AppGallery Connect. PMS supports the following types of products.

TABLE 5.1   Product Types

Type	Description	Example
Consumables	Consumables are used a single time and can be re-purchased once depleted.	Extra lives and gems in a game
Non-consumables	Non-consumables are purchased a single time and never expire.	Extra levels within a game or permanent membership for an app
Subscriptions	A subscription is a purchase that ensures access to value-added functions or content for a specified period of time. It can be automatically renewed on a recurring basis, until the user decides to cancel.	Non-permanent membership for an app

2. Before displaying the product information, your app will need to call an API of the IAP SDK, in order for the app to determine whether IAP is supported in the user's service location.

3. If IAP is supported, your app will obtain the product information corresponding to the product ID.

TABLE 5.2   Package Types and Rights

Package	Type	Right	Fee
Monthly membership	Consumable	One month of pet video access	US$0.06
Quarterly membership	Consumable	Three months of pet video access	US$0.12
Permanent membership	Non-consumable	Unrestricted pet video access	US$0.2
Subscribed membership	Subscription	One week of pet video access	US$0.01 per week

5.3.2 Configuring Products

5.3.2.1 Planning Products

The packages outlined in Table 5.2 have been planned for the Pet Store app and include tiered fees and rights, to meet varying user requirements.

5.3.2.2 Configuring a Consumable

Consumables will be used up or expire. To use a consumable on a continuous basis, the user will need to purchase it again once it has been depleted. In the preceding plan, the consumables include monthly and quarterly membership options.

1. Sign in to AppGallery Connect, click **My apps**, and select the Pet Store app.

2. Click **Operate**. The **Product Management** page appears. On the **Products** tab, click **Add Product**, as shown in Figure 5.7.

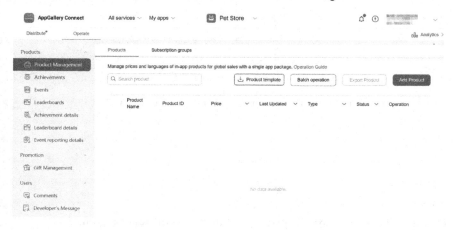

FIGURE 5.7   Products tab.

FIGURE 5.8 Configuring the product information.

3. On the displayed page, configure the product information, such as the product ID and name, and click **Save**, as shown in Figure 5.8.

4. Click **View and edit** next to **Product price (tax included)**. On the displayed page, set the default currency and price, select countries or regions, and then click **Convert prices**. The prices for the countries or regions that you have selected will be updated accordingly, as shown in Figure 5.9.

FIGURE 5.9 Setting product prices for different countries or regions.

FIGURE 5.10   New product on the list.

5. Click **Save**. Then in the displayed dialog box, click **OK** to complete product configuration. You will find the new product on the product list, as shown in Figure 5.10.

6. Since the product status is **Invalid**, click **Activate** in the **Operation** column for the product. In the displayed dialog box, click **OK**, as shown in Figure 5.11. The product status will then be changed to **Valid**, after which the product is open for purchase.

Through the preceding steps, we have configured two consumables, a monthly membership priced at US$0.06 and a quarterly membership priced at US$0.12.

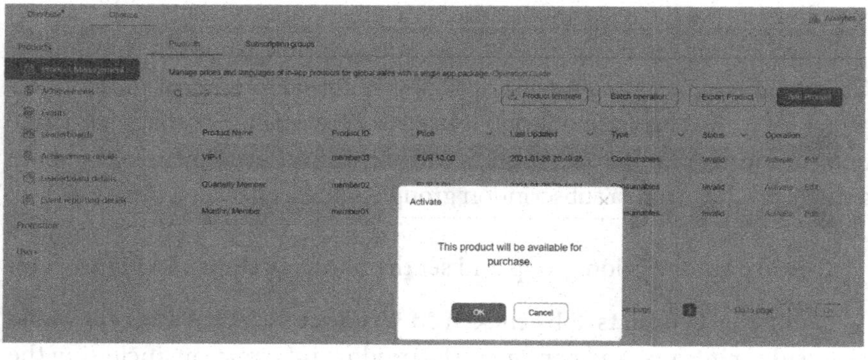

FIGURE 5.11   Activating the product.

FIGURE 5.12   Product configuration.

5.3.2.3 Configuring a Non-consumable

Non-consumables will not expire or exhaust as they are being used, and users only purchase them a single time. The permanent membership is one such example of a non-consumable.

Similar to a consumable, configuring a non-consumable only requires you to select **Non-consumables** on the **Add Product** page. For other configurations, please refer to the earlier procedure of adding a consumable.

Figure 5.12 shows the configuration for the said product.

After the configuration is complete, you'll need to activate the permanent membership to enable users to purchase it.

5.3.2.4 Configuring a Subscription

Subscriptions can be automatically renewed, and the renewal fees are deducted periodically from the user's payment account. The subscribed membership we have planned earlier is a subscription.

Subscriptions can be managed under **Subscription groups** in AppGallery Connect. Before creating a subscription, you'll need to create a subscription group for it. A subscription group is used to conveniently manage subscriptions to a range of different products with similar service functions, but only a single product from a subscription group will take effect at a time.

1. Add a subscription group and set the name, as shown in Figure 5.13.

2. On the **Products** tab, click **Add Product**, select **Auto-renewable subscriptions**, and configure the product information, including the subscription period and group, as shown in Figure 5.14.

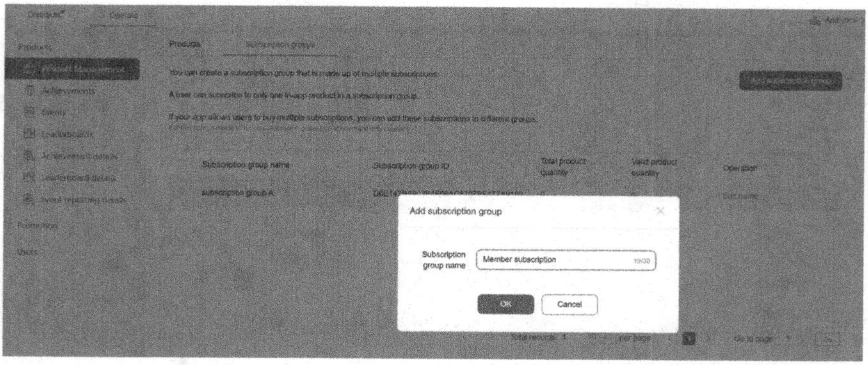

FIGURE 5.13   Adding a subscription group.

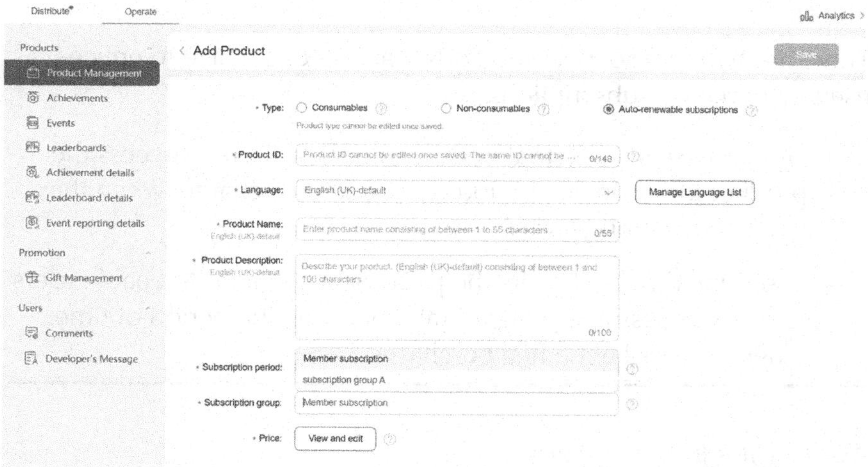

FIGURE 5.14   Adding a subscription.

In this example, set the subscription period to one week, and the price to US$0.01. For details about how to set the price, please refer to the process for configuring consumables.

3. Activate the subscription. Figure 5.15 shows an example of configured products.

Confirm that the status of all relevant products is **Valid**, to ensure that the Pet Store app can query and display the product details via IAP.

FIGURE 5.15   All planned products.

NOTE

There are two promotional methods that you can utilize to entice users to purchase subscriptions:

1. Free trial: sets a free trial period, to enable users to access the product for a specific period of time free-of-charge, when they make the first purchases.

2. Discounted price: lowers the price for a product, to enable users to enjoy access at a reduced rate for a specific period of time, when they make the first purchases.

5.4 PRODUCT PURCHASE

After browsing and selecting a product, a user will need to pay to access it. During this phase, your app will need to provide a payment function, confirm the rights granted to the user after payment, and call the consumption API to notify IAP that the user has received the product. This section also details the process for redelivering products and querying purchased products and order information via IAP. The purchasing process is as follows:

1. Your app checks whether the user's service location supports IAP.

2. If so, your app will obtain the product information.

3. Your app will then call the **IapClient.createPurchaseIntent()** API, based on the product ID, to display the checkout screen.

4. After the user completes payment, IAP will send the payment result to your app via **Activity.setResult()**. Your app will then process the data in **onActivityResult()**, such as the digital signature verification and product consumption.

5. For a consumable, after the right is assigned to the user, your app will call the **IapClient.consume-OwnedPurchase()** API, to notify IAP that the product has been processed by the app.

The following sections outline the steps above using a consumable as an example.

5.4.1 Checking Whether IAP Is Supported

Whether IAP is available will depend on the HUAWEI ID used to sign in to the device. To use IAP, you'll also need to make sure IAP is supported in the user's service location. To do this, your app calls the **isEnvReady()** method in the **IapClient** class, listens for the callback result, and then determines whether the user's service location is included within the list of locations[1] supported by IAP. In the callback result, if **ORDER_STATE_SUCCESS** is returned, IAP is supported in the user's service location; if an error code is thrown, you'll need to take the appropriate measure based on its handling suggestion. Here's the code:

```
@Override
protected void onCreate(@Nullable Bundle
savedInstanceState) {
  super.onCreate(savedInstanceState);
  setContentView(R.layout.membercenter_act);
  // Initialize the view.
  initView();
  // Check whether IAP is supported.
  checkEnv();
}
/**
* Check whether IAP is supported in the service
location of the signed-in user.
*/
private void checkEnv() {
  IapClient mClient = Iap.getIapClient(this);
```

```java
mClient.isEnvReady().addOnSuccessListener(new OnSucc
essListener<IsEnvReadyResult>() {
   @Override
   public void onSuccess(IsEnvReadyResult result) {
      if (result.getReturnCode() == OrderStatusCode.
ORDER_STATE_SUCCESS) {
         // If IAP is supported, load the product
information.
Log.i(TAG, "is support IAP");
         loadProducts();
      }
   }
}).addOnFailureListener(new OnFailureListener() {
   @Override
   public void onFailure(Exception e) {
      if (e instanceof IapApiException) {
         IapApiException exception = (IapApiException) e;
         Status status = exception.getStatus();
         int returnCode = status.getStatusCode();
         // If the user is not signed in, display the
HUAWEI ID sign-in screen.
         if (OrderStatusCode.ORDER_HWID_NOT_LOGIN ==
returnCode) {
            boolean hasResolution = startResolution(
MemberCenterAct.this,
               status, REQ_CODE_LOGIN);
            if (hasResolution) {
               return;
            }
         }
      }

      refreshHandler.
sendEmptyMessage(REFRESH_NOT_SUPPORT_IAP_WHAT);
   }
});
}
```

5.4.2 Obtaining the Product Information

Call the **IapClient.obtainProductInfo()** API each time to obtain the information for a single type of products. IAP will return the product description in the local language and price in the local currency, based on the service location of the user's HUAWEI ID.

The code for obtaining the product information will be stored in **MemberCenterAct.java** of your project. The following sample code describes how to construct a product information query request.

```
private void loadProducts() {
  // Construct a listener for product query results.
  OnUpdateProductListListener
updateProductListListener = new OnUpdateProduct
    ListListener(3, refreshHandler);

  // Construct a consumable query request.
  ProductInfoReq consumeProductInfoReq = new
ProductInfoReq();
  consumeProductInfoReq.setPriceType(IapClient.
PriceType.IN_APP_CONSUMABLE);
  consumeProductInfoReq.
setProductIds(CONSUMABLE_PRODUCT_LIST);

  // Construct a non-consumable query request.
  ProductInfoReq nonCousumableProductInfoReq = new
ProductInfoReq();
  nonCousumableProductInfoReq.setPriceType(IapClient.
PriceType.IN_APP_NONCON
    SUMABLE);
  nonCousumableProductInfoReq.
setProductIds(NON_CONSUMABLE_PRODUCT_LIST);

  // Construct a subscription query request.
  ProductInfoReq subscriptionProductInfoReq = new
ProductInfoReq();
  subscriptionProductInfoReq.setPriceType(IapClient.
PriceType.IN_APP_SUBSCRI
    PTION);
  subscriptionProductInfoReq.
setProductIds(SUBSCRIPTION_PRODUCT_LIST);

  // Query the product information.
  getProducts(consumeProductInfoReq,
updateProductListListener);
```

```
  getProducts(nonCousumableProductInfoReq,
updateProductListListener);
  getProducts(subscriptionProductInfoReq,
updateProductListListener);
}
```

In the preceding code, **ProductIds** indicates the product ID you have entered when configuring the product in AppGallery Connect. The following sample code illustrates how to call the **obtainProductInfo** API:

```
private void getProducts(ProductInfoReq
productInfoReq, OnUpdateProductListListener
  productListListener) {
  IapClient mClient = Iap.getIapClient(this);
  Task<ProductInfoResult> task = mClient.
obtainProductInfo(productInfoReq);
  task.addOnSuccessListener(new OnSuccessListener<Prod
uctInfoResult>() {
    @Override
    public void onSuccess(ProductInfoResult result) {
      // Product information is found.
      productListListener.onUpdate(productInfoReq.
getPriceType(), result);
    }
  }).addOnFailureListener(new OnFailureListener() {
    @Override
    public void onFailure(Exception e) {
      // Product information fails to be queried.
      productListListener.onFail(e);
    }
  });
}
```

A list is provided within the project to display all product information and offer an intuitive view of the data returned by the API. Define a **RecyclerView** class in the **membercenter_act.xml** layout file, and initialize it in the code.

```
private void initView() {
  // Initialize RecyclerView.
  mRecyclerView = findViewById(R.
id.membercenter_recyclerView);
```

```
LinearLayoutManager manager = new
LinearLayoutManager(this);
// Set a layout manager.
mRecyclerView.setLayoutManager(manager);
// Set the vertical layout (default).
manager.setOrientation(RecyclerView.VERTICAL);
// Set the adapter.
MemCenterAdapter mMemCenterAdapter = new
MemCenterAdapter(mItemData);
mRecyclerView.setAdapter(mMemCenterAdapter);
mMemCenterAdapter.setListener(new
IRecyclerItemListener() {
  @Override
  public void onItemClick(View view, int position) {
    onAdapterItemClick(position);
  }
});
mRecyclerView.setItemAnimator(new Default
  ItemAnimator());
ImageView mIvBack = findViewById(R.id.
  title_back);
mIvBack.setOnClickListener(new View.On
  ClickListener() {
  @Override
  public void onClick(View v) {
    finish();
  }
});
}
```

The found product information is then displayed on the **Member center** screen of the Pet Store app, as shown in Figure 5.16.

5.4.3 Initiating a Payment

This section describes how to use IAP to carry out purchases and payments. The user can initiate the purchase by touching the **Buy now** button, located next to the product. The sample code is as follows:

```
private void buy(final int type, String product
  Id) {
  // Construct a purchase request.
```

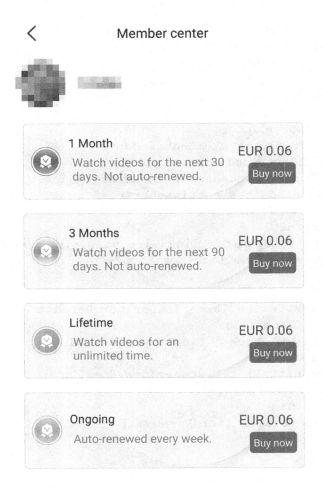

FIGURE 5.16 Member center screen.

```
PurchaseIntentReq req = new PurchaseIntentReq();
req.setProductId(productId);
req.setPriceType(type);
req.setDeveloperPayload(MemberRight.
getCurrentUserId(this));

IapClient mClient = Iap.getIapClient(this);
Task<PurchaseIntentResult> task = mClient.
createPurchaseIntent(req);
task.addOnSuccessListener(new OnSuccessListener<Purc
haseIntentResult>() {
```

```
    @Override
    public void onSuccess(PurchaseIntentResult result)
{
        if (result != null && result.getStatus() != null)
{
            // Display the checkout screen.
            boolean success = startResolution(-
MemberCenterAct.this, result.
                getStatus(), getRequestCode(type));
            if (success) {
                return;
            }
        }
        refreshHandler.
sendEmptyMessage(REQUEST_FAIL_WHAT);
    }
    }).addOnFailureListener(new OnFailureListener() {
    @Override
        public void onFailure(Exception e) {
            Log.e(TAG, "buy fail, exception: " +
e.getMessage());
            refreshHandler.
sendEmptyMessage(REQUEST_FAIL_WHAT);
        }
    });
}
```

After receiving a success response from the **createPurchaseIntent** API, your app will call the **startResolution** method to display the checkout screen. Here is what your code should look like:

```
private static boolean startResolution(Activity
activity, Status status, int reqCode) {
  if (status.hasResolution()) {
    try {
      status.startResolutionForResult
        (activity, reqCode);
      return true;
    } catch (IntentSender.SendIntentException exp) {
      Log.i(TAG, "startResolution fail, "
        + exp.getMessage());
```

```
  }
} else {
  Log.i(TAG, "startResolution, intent
    is null");
}
  return false;
}
```

When the user launches the Pet Store app and touches **Buy now**, the checkout screen will be displayed, as shown in Figure 5.17.

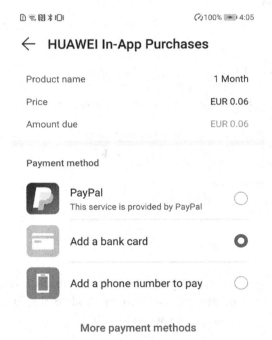

FIGURE 5.17 Checkout screen.

After the user selects a payment method and completes the payment, the payment result will be returned to the Pet Store app via **Activity.setResult()** for further processing.

5.4.4 Confirming the Transaction

After the user completes the payment, your app will need to process the payment data returned by

NOTICE

The payment in this example will incur fees, so exercise caution when performing this operation. Section 5.6 will detail a sandbox testing approach. After the signed-in HUAWEI ID is added to the sandbox testing environment, no fees will be deducted when you test out payments.

IAP, and then perform further processing based on the result.

Here, we've used processing the payment result for a consumable as an example. Open **MemberCenterAct.java** of your project, obtain the payment data returned by IAP from **onActivityResult**, and parse the Intent data through **parsePurchaseResultInfoFromIntent** to obtain the payment result object **PurchaseResultInfo**. Call the **getReturnCode** method of the object to obtain the payment status code, and then call the **getInAppPurchaseData** method to obtain the payment data and perform further processing based on your predefined service logic.

```
@Override
protected void onActivityResult(int requestCode, int
resultCode, @Nullable Intent
  data) {
  super.onActivityResult(requestCode, resultCode,
data);
  PurchaseResultInfo buyResultInfo = Iap.
getIapClient(this).parsePurchaseRes
    ultInfoFromIntent(data);
  Log.i(TAG, "confirmOrder, returnCode: " +
buyResultInfo.getReturnCode() +
    "errMsg: " + buyResultInfo.getErrMsg());

  // The user cancels payment.
  if (buyResultInfo.getReturnCode() ==
OrderStatusCode.ORDER_STATE_CANCEL) {
    Log.i(TAG, "cancel buy product");
```

```
    return;
  }
  switch (requestCode) {
    case REQ_CODE_LOGIN:
      if (data != null) {
        int returnCode = data.getIntExtra("returnCode",
-1);
        if (returnCode == OrderStatusCode.ORDER_STATE_
SUCCESS) {
          // The sign-in is successful. Check the
payment environment again.
          checkEnv();
          return;
        }
      }
      refreshHandler.
sendEmptyMessage(LOGIN_ACCOUNT_FIRST_WHAT);
      break;
    case REQ_CODE_PAY_CONSUMABLE:
    case REQ_CODE_PAY_NON_CONSUMABLE:
    case REQ_CODE_PAY_SUBSCRIPTION:
      int priceType = getPriceType(requestCode);
      if (resultCode == RESULT_OK) {
        // The purchase is successful.
        if (buyResultInfo.getReturnCode() ==
OrderStatusCode.ORDER_STATE_
          SUCCESS) {
          // Verify the digital signature.
          boolean success = CipherUtil.doCheck(
buyResultInfo.getInApp
          PurchaseData(), buyResultInfo.
getInAppDataSignature());
          if (success) {
          PurchasesOperation.deliverProduct(this,
buyResultInfo.
            getInAppPurchaseData(), priceType);
        } else {
          // The signature verification failed.
          Log.e(TAG, "check sign fail");
          return;
        }
```

```
    } else if (buyResultInfo.getReturnCode() ==
OrderStatusCode.ORDER_
      PRODUCT_OWNED) {
      // The product needs to be consumed before it
is purchased again.
      PurchasesOperation.replenish(this, "",
priceType);
      refreshHandler.sendEmptyMessageDelayed(BUY_
ALREADY_WHAT, 500);
    } else {
      Log.e(TAG, "buy fail, returnCode: " +
buyResultInfo.getReturn
        Code() + " errMsg: " + buyResultInfo.
getErrMsg());
      refreshHandler.sendEmptyMessage(BUY_FAIL_WHAT);
    }
  } else {
    Log.i(TAG, "cancel pay");
  }
    break;
  default:
    break;
  }
}
```

Your app will identify the type of the purchased product through **onActivityResult** and use the processing logic that corresponds to the product type for the payment result. It will then get the payment status based on the status code returned in the payment result. If the payment is successful, your app will be able to obtain the payment data. After the digital signature verification, your app will assign the right to use the purchased product (using a method in the **PurchasesOperation.java** file) and call the consumption API.

```
public static void deliverProduct(Context context,
String data, int priceType) {
  InAppPurchaseData inAppPurchaseData;
  try {
    inAppPurchaseData = new InAppPurchaseData(data);
  } catch (JSONException e) {
```

```java
        Log.e(TAG, "parse inAppPurchaseData error");
        return;
    }
    updateMemberRightData(context, inAppPurchaseData);
    if (priceType == IapClient.PriceType.IN_APP_
CONSUMABLE) {
        PurchasesOperation.consumePurchase(context,
inAppPurchaseData.getPurchase
        Token());
    }
}

/**
 * Assign rights based on product types.
 * @param context Context.
 * @param inAppPurchaseData Order data.
 */
private static void updateMemberRightData(Context
context, InAppPurchaseData
    inAppPurchaseData) {
    String productId = inAppPurchaseData.getProductId();
    switch (productId) {
      case "member01":
        MemberRight.updateNormalVideoValidDate(context,
30 * ONE_DAY);
        break;
      case "member02":
        MemberRight.updateNormalVideoValidDate(context,
60 * ONE_DAY);
        break;
      case "member03":
        MemberRight.setVideoAvailableForever(context);
        break;
      case "subscribeMember01":
        MemberRight.updateVideoSubscriptionExpireDate(
context, inAppPurchaseData);
        break;
      default:
        break;
    }
}
```

After the right assignment, your app will need to call the consumption API to notify IAP that the product has been processed.

```
public static void consumePurchase(Context context,
String purchaseToken) {
  // Construct a request for consuming the product.
  ConsumeOwnedPurchaseReq req = new
ConsumeOwnedPurchaseReq();
  req.setPurchaseToken(purchaseToken);

  IapClient mClient = Iap.getIapClient(context);

  Task<ConsumeOwnedPurchaseResult> task = mClient.
consumeOwnedPurchase(req);
  task.addOnSuccessListener(new OnSuccessListener<Cons
umeOwnedPurchaseResult>() {
    @Override
    public void onSuccess(ConsumeOwnedPurchaseResult
result) {
      if (result != null && result.getStatus() != null)
{
        if (result.getStatus().getStatusCode() ==
OrderStatusCode.ORDER_
          STATE_SUCCESS) {
          // The consumption is successful.
          Log.i(TAG, "consumePurchase success");
        }
      }
    }
  }).addOnFailureListener(new OnFailureListener() {
    @Override
    public void onFailure(Exception e) {
      // The consumption failed.
      Log.e(TAG, "consumePurchase fail, exception: " +
e.getMessage());
    }
  });
}
```

Thus far, the user has purchased the consumable and has the right to view pet videos.

5.4.5 Redelivering a Product

Your app is now able to provide IAP services for its users. However, a number of complications can occur during the actual purchasing process. For example, your app may be stopped in the background after the user has paid for the product due to system restrictions or a user misoperation, and as a result be unable to receive the payment result returned by IAP. In this case, the user may not receive the product that they paid for. To address this issue, IAP offers a product redelivery mechanism, which ensures that user rights and interests are rigorously protected.

5.4.5.1 Service Process

Figure 5.18 shows the redelivery process for a consumable.

1. The user restarts your app.

2. Your app obtains the information related to the product that has been purchased but not consumed from IAP.

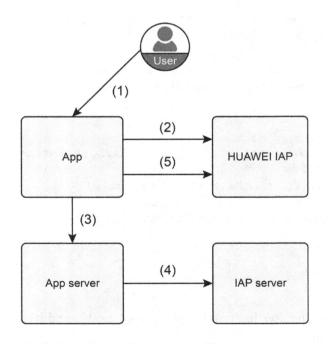

FIGURE 5.18 Redelivery process for a consumable.

3–4. Your app or server verifies the purchase information for the product.

5. Your app assigns the corresponding right to the user and calls the consumption API to notify IAP that the product has been received.

5.4.5.2 Coding Practice

In the **PurchasesOperation.java** file of your project, define the **replenish** method for redelivery. The sample code is as follows:

```
/**
 * Implement redelivery.
 *
 * @param context Context.
 * @param continuationToken Token of querying the next
page for purchased products. This parameter is left
empty in the first query.
 */
public static void replenish(final Context context,
String continuationToken,
  final int priceType) {
  OwnedPurchasesReq req = new OwnedPurchasesReq();
  req.setPriceType(priceType);
  req.setContinuationToken(continuationToken);
  IapClient mClient = Iap.getIapClient(context);

  Task<OwnedPurchasesResult> task = mClient.
obtainOwnedPurchases(req);
  task.addOnSuccessListener(new OnSuccessListener<Owne
dPurchasesResult>() {
    @Override
    public void onSuccess(OwnedPurchasesResult result)
{
      if (result != null && result.getStatus() != null)
{
        if (result.getStatus().getStatusCode() ==
OrderStatusCode.ORDER_
          STATE_SUCCESS) {
          if (result.getInAppPurchaseDataList() != null)
{
            int index = 0;
```

```
            for (String data : result.
getInAppPurchaseDataList()) {
            boolean success = CipherUtil.doCheck(data,
result.
              getInAppSignature().get(index));
            if (success) {
              // Redeliver the product.
              deliverProduct(context, data, priceType);
            } else {
              // Signature verification failed.
              Log.e(TAG, "check sign fail");
            }
            index++;
            }
          }
          if (!TextUtils.isEmpty(result.
getContinuationToken())) {
            replenish(context, result.
getContinuationToken(),
              priceType);
          }
        }
      }
    }
  }).addOnFailureListener(new OnFailureListener() {
    @Override
    public void onFailure(Exception e) {
      // Request error.
      Log.e(TAG, "getPurchase exception: " +
e.getMessage());
    }
  });
}
```

The redelivery is executed when your app's home screen has loaded.

```
/**
* Execute the redelivery when your app has started.
* @param context Context.
*/
public static void replenishForLaunch(final Context
context) {
```

```
IapClient mClient = Iap.getIapClient(context);
mClient.isEnvReady().addOnSuccessListener(new OnSucc
essListener<IsEnvReadyResult>() {
  @Override
  public void onSuccess(IsEnvReadyResult result) {
    if (result.getReturnCode() == OrderStatusCode.
ORDER_STATE_SUCCESS) {
      // IAP is supported.
      Log.i(TAG, "is support IAP");
      // Execute the redelivery.
      replenish(context, "", IapClient.PriceType.
IN_APP_CONSUMABLE);
      replenish(context, "", IapClient.PriceType.
IN_APP_NONCONSUMABLE);
      replenish(context, "", IapClient.PriceType.
IN_APP_SUBSCRIPTION);
    }
  }
});
}
```

By contrast, the redelivery for non-consumables does not require the consumption API to be called. Therefore, it's important to note that a non-consumable that has been delivered to the user will not be redelivered.

For a subscription, the user can modify the subscription relationship at any time within the validity period. This means that, in addition to offering the subscription upon successful payment, you'll need to query the current subscription status of the user before providing the service. If the user has not received the offer, the redelivery process will be triggered.

5.4.6 Querying Purchased Products and Orders

This section details the process for querying the records of purchased products and orders. For consumables, you'll need to call the **obtainOwnedPurchaseRecord** API to obtain the corresponding information for all products that have been delivered and consumed. For non-consumables and subscriptions, you'll need to call the **obtainOwnedPurchase** API to pass a specific product type to query the information about the products purchased by the user.

Open **PurchasesOperation.java** in your project, and define the **getRecords** method for querying purchase records. When **priceType** is set to consumable, all purchase records can be queried.

```java
public static void getRecords(Context context, int
priceType, String continuationToken,
  RecordListener listener) {
  OwnedPurchasesReq req = new OwnedPurchasesReq();
  req.setPriceType(priceType);
  req.setContinuationToken(continuationToken);
  IapClient mClient = Iap.getIapClient(context);

  Task<OwnedPurchasesResult> task = mClient.
obtainOwnedPurchaseRecord(req);
  task.addOnSuccessListener(new OnSuccessListener<Owne
dPurchasesResult>() {
    @Override
    public void onSuccess(OwnedPurchasesResult result)
{
      if (result != null && result.getStatus() !=
null) {
      if (result.getStatus().getStatusCode() ==
OrderStatusCode.ORDER_
        STATE_SUCCESS) {

        listener.onReceive(result.
getInAppPurchaseDataList());
        // If the next page exists, continue the
query.
        if (!TextUtils.isEmpty(result.
getContinuationToken())) {
          getRecords(context, priceType, result.
getContinuationToken(),
          listener);
        } else {
        // The query is complete.
        listener.onFinish();
        }
      }
    }
  }
}
```

```
}).addOnFailureListener(new OnFailureListener() {
  @Override
  public void onFailure(Exception e) {
    // Request error.
    Log.e(TAG, "getPurchase exception: " +
e.getMessage());
    listener.onFail();
  }
});
}
```

You'll then need to add a screen to display the order records through **OrderAct.java**. You can then call the **getRecords** method to display all of the order records on this screen. You can add an entry to **initView** in **MineCenterAct.java** to redirect to the order record screen.

```
findViewById(R.id.mine_orders).setOnClickListener(new
View.OnClickListener() {
  @Override
  public void onClick(View v) {
    startActivity(new Intent(MineCenterAct.this,
OrderAct.class));
  }
});
```

Then call the implemented **getRecords** method in **OrderAct.java** to obtain order records.

```
/**
 * Display the list data.
 */
private void initRecyclerData() {
  mItemData.clear();
  if (MemberRight.isVideoAvailableForever(this)) {
    PurchasesOperation.getRecords(this, IapClient.
PriceType.IN_APP_NONCONSUMABLE,
      "", new RecordListener() {
      @Override
      public void onReceive(List<String>
inAppPurchaseDataList) {
        Message message = refreshHandler.
obtainMessage(REFRESH_NONCONSU
```

```
        MABLE_DATA, inAppPurchaseDataList);
      refreshHandler.sendMessage(message);
    }

    @Override
    public void onFinish() {
      Log.i(TAG, "load finish");
    }

    @Override
    public void onFail() {
      Log.i(TAG, "load fail");
    }
  });
}
PurchasesOperation.getRecords(this, IapClient.
PriceType.IN_APP_CONSUMABLE, "",
  new RecordListener() {
  @Override
  public void onReceive(List<String>
inAppPurchaseDataList) {
    Message message = refreshHandler.
obtainMessage(REFRESH_CONSUMABLE_DATA,
      inAppPurchaseDataList);
    refreshHandler.sendMessage(message);
  }

  @Override
  public void onFinish() {
    Log.i(TAG, "load finish");
  }

  @Override
  public void onFail() {
    Log.i(TAG, "load fail");
    }
  });
}
```

Start the Pet Store app. The purchase records will be displayed, as shown in Figure 5.19.

< My purchases

02/01/2021   Completed

1 Month   €0.06
€0.06   1

1 item, total: €0.06

Details

FIGURE 5.19   Purchase record screen.

Open the **MineCenterAct.java** file in your project, and define the **initMemberInfo** method to display member information.

```
/**
 * Configure a loyalty card.
 */
private void initMemberInfo() {
  initData();

  // Display the member status.
  if (MemberRight.isVideoAvailableForever(this)) {
    mTvMembersTime.setText(R.string.iap_buy_forever);
    mTvMembers.setVisibility(View.GONE);
  } else if (MemberRight.isVideoSubscriptionValid(
this)) {
    mTvMembersTime.setText(getString(R.string.iap_
member_valid, new Simple
      DateFormat("YYYY-MM-dd", Locale.US).format(
MemberRight.getVideoSubscriptionExpireDate(this))));
    mTvMembers.setVisibility(View.GONE);
  } else if (MemberRight.isVideoAvailable(this)) {
    mTvMembers.setVisibility(View.GONE);
    mTvMembersTime.setText(getString(R.string.iap_
member_valid, new Simple
      DateFormat("YYYY-MM-dd", Locale.US).format(
MemberRight.getNorm
      alVideoExpireDate(this))));
  } else {
```

```
        mTvMembers.setVisibility(View.VISIBLE);
}

    // Display the member details.
    if (MemberRight.isVideoAvailableForever(this)) {
      mLlMemberLayout.setVisibility(View.VISIBLE);
      mTvMemberName.setText(R.string.
iap_buy_member_forever);
      mTvMemberDesc.setText(R.string.member_desc);
      mTvMemberPay.setVisibility(View.GONE);
    } else if (System.currentTimeMillis() <
MemberRight.getVideoSubscriptionExpireDate(this)) {
      mLlMemberLayout.setVisibility(View.VISIBLE);
      mTvMemberName.setText(R.string.
iap_buy_member_subscription);
      mTvMemberDesc.setText(R.string.member_desc);
      mTvMemberPay.setText(R.string.
iap_buy_subscription);
    } else if (MemberRight.isVideoAvailable(this)) {
      mLlMemberLayout.setVisibility(View.VISIBLE);
      mTvMemberName.setText(R.string.iap_buy_member);
      mTvMemberDesc.setText(R.string.member_desc);
      mTvMemberPay.setOnClickListener(new View.
OnClickListener() {
        @Override
        public void onClick(View view) {
          startActivity(new Intent(MineCenterAct.this,
MemberCenterAct.
          class));
        }
      });
    } else {
      mLlMemberLayout.setVisibility(View.GONE);
    }
  }
```

Start the Pet Store app. The member information will be displayed in the personal center, as shown in Figure 5.20.

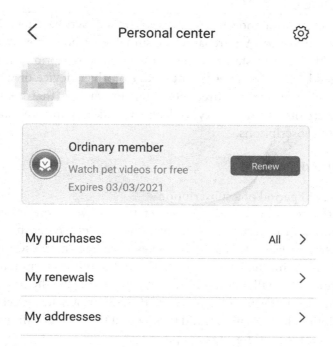

FIGURE 5.20   Personal center screen.

5.5 PRODUCT USAGE

This section describes how to provide services for users based on the products they purchased. A purchased consumable or non-consumable will remain with the same status, while a purchased subscription's status may be changed by the user in **Account center** on their device or within the app, and this status has a direct effect on the services that the user can access. Therefore, it's necessary to delve more deeply into the status and lifecycle of subscriptions.

5.5.1 Subscriptions

1. Renewal period of a subscription

   The renewal period can be set to one week, one month, two months, three months, six months, or one year. After the user purchases a subscription and completes payment, the subscription will take effect immediately. Prior to the end of the subscription validity period, IAP will automatically deduct the fees for the next renewal from the user's payment account. If the user opts to cancel the subscription, it will remain valid throughout the current validity period, but not renewed for the next period.

2. Status change of a subscription

   The user can change the status of a subscription using the following methods:

   Method 1: Automatic renewal

   If the user does not modify the subscription and the account balance is sufficient, the subscription will be automatically renewed, as shown in Figure 5.21.

   IAP automatically deducts fees for renewal 24 hours prior to expiration of the subscription.

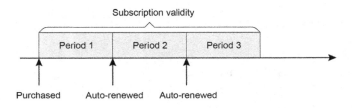

FIGURE 5.21   Automatic renewal process.

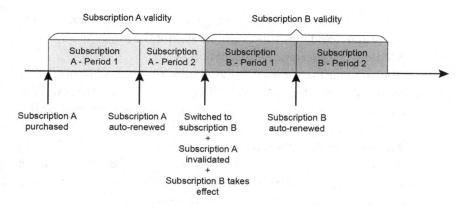

FIGURE 5.22 Taking effect immediately.

Method 2: Subscription switching

The user can switch between different subscriptions within the same subscription group. The new subscription then:

(1) Takes effect immediately. Figure 5.22 shows the process of switching from subscription A to subscription B.

After the switch, the original subscription's amount will be refunded to the initial payment channel in the correct proportion, and the user will be charged the complete price for the new subscription, which takes effect immediately. Currently, the switch is triggered when the renewal period of the original subscription matches the new subscription.

(2) Takes effect in the next period. Figure 5.23 shows the process of switching from subscription A to subscription C.

After the switch, the original subscription's status is set to expiring while the new subscription is set to pending. The new subscription will be charged and take effect when the original subscription

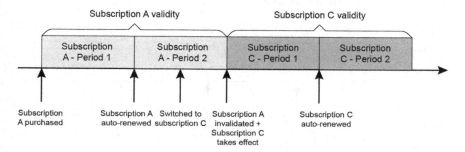

FIGURE 5.23 Taking effect in the next period.

expires. Currently, the switch is triggered when the renewal periods of the original and new subscriptions are not the same.

Method 3: Subscription cancellation

The user opts to cancel a purchased subscription, and if successful, the subscription will not be renewed in the next period. However, the use of the subscription in the current period is not affected by the cancellation, as shown in Figure 5.24.

Method 4: Subscription renewal suspension

The user can also suspend the renewal of a subscription that is under renewal, for a certain period of time. Figure 5.25 shows the process of suspending a subscription renewal.

After the user suspends the renewal of the subscription, the subscription is not automatically renewed when its current validity period has ended. During the suspension period, the subscription is invalid, and thereafter will be automatically restored as valid and renewed as before.

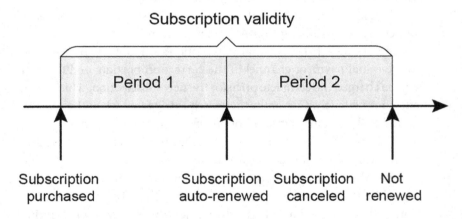

FIGURE 5.24   Subscription cancellation.

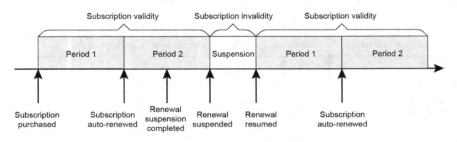

FIGURE 5.25   Subscription renewal suspension.

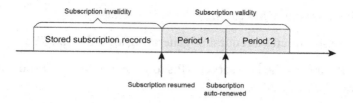

FIGURE 5.26   Subscription resumption.

Method 5: Subscription resumption

The user can choose to resume a subscription that has been canceled or lapsed, to enjoy the services included in the subscription once again, as outlined in Figure 5.26.

The user can resume a subscription on the subscription management screen on their device.

5.5.2 Service Provisioning

This section details the process through which product services, such as pet video viewing, are offered for users. After the user subscribes to a membership package in the Pet Store app, they will enjoy access to view pet videos. Figure 5.27 outlines this service provisioning process.

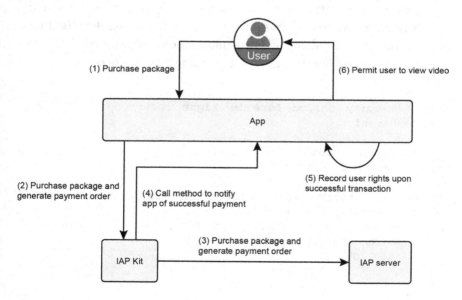

FIGURE 5.27   Service provisioning.

1. The user subscribes to a membership package.

2. The app initiates a request of generating an order to IAP Kit.

3. IAP Kit calls the IAP server APIs to generate the order and complete payment.

4. IAP Kit returns the successful payment result to the app.

5. The app records the right granted to the user. In this example, the right enables the user to access and view pet videos.

6. The user then views pet videos in the app at their leisure.

The following are in-depth descriptions of the service process for each product type.

1. Consumables

   After the user purchases a consumable, you'll need to complete the service processing that is not directly related to IAP. You can define the right of the consumable as permitted viewing duration, based on the corresponding rights of membership packages. After the user purchases a monthly or quarterly membership, the Pet Store app will update the permitted viewing duration accordingly. Here, we have used Android's **SharedPreferences** to record the user data. Open **MemberRight.java** in your project and define the methods for obtaining and updating the validity period, for the right corresponding to a membership.

```
/**
 * Validity period for the right corresponding to a
 membership.
 *
 * @param context Context.
 * @return Timestamp.
 */
public   static   long   getNormalVideoExpireDate(Context
context) {
    return   (long)   SPUtil.get(context,   getCurrentUserId(
context), VIDEO _ NORMAL _
    KEY, 0L);
}

/**
 * Update the validity period.
```

```
*
* @param context Context.
* @param extension Validity period.
*/
public static void updateNormalVideoValidDate(Context
context, long extension) {
  long videoExpireDate = getNormalVideoExpireDate(
context);
  long currentTime = System.currentTimeMillis();
  if (currentTime < videoExpireDate) {
    videoExpireDate += extension;
  } else {
    videoExpireDate = currentTime + extension;
  }
  SPUtil.put(context, getCurrentUserId(context), VIDEO _
NORMAL _ KEY, videoExpire
    Date);
}
```

The validity periods are recorded in **SharedPreferences**, a framework that makes user rights management easier than ever. Simply define a method in **MemberRight.java** to determine whether the user has the right to view pet videos after they purchase a membership.

```
/**
* Check whether the user has the right to view pet
videos.
* @param context Context.
* @return boolean
*/
public static boolean isVideoAvailable(Context context)
{
  return isVideoAvailableForever(context) || isVideo
SubscriptionValid(context)
        || System.currentTimeMillis() < getNormalVideo
ExpireDate(context);
}
```

Before a video is played, use the following method to check whether the user has the right to view the video. If the user does not have this right, prompt them to purchase a membership. The implementation logic in **VideoPlayAct.java** is as follows:

```
@Override
protected void onCreate(@Nullable Bundle savedInstance
State) {
```

```
super.onCreate(savedInstanceState);
setContentView(R.layout.videoplay_act);
if (MemberRight.isVideoAvailable(this)) {
  play();
} else {
  startActivityForResult(new                Intent(this,
MemberCenterAct.class), REQ_CODE_
    MEMBER_CENTER);
}
}

/**
* Play a video.
*/
private void play() {
  // Initialize the view.
  initView();
  // Initialize the playback.
  initVideoPlay();
}

@Override
protected void onActivityResult(int requestCode, int
resultCode, @Nullable
  Intent data) {
  super.onActivityResult(requestCode, resultCode, data);
  if (requestCode == REQ_CODE_MEMBER_CENTER) {
    if (MemberRight.isVideoAvailable(this)) {
      play();
    } else {
      finish();
    }
  }
}
}
```

2. Non-consumables

   After a user purchases a non-consumable, the app calls the
   IapClient.obtainOwnedPurchases() API to obtain the corresponding product information. As mentioned earlier, permanent membership in the Pet Store app is a non-consumable, and the permitted
   viewing duration may not apply. Instead, you can use the purchasing
   records for this product to indicate that the user is entitled to view
   videos on a permanent basis. In **MemberRight.java**, you'll need to
   define the methods for determining whether the user is a permanent
   member and updating the status of a permanent member.

```
/**
 * Determine whether the user is a permanent member.
 *
 * @param context Context.
 * @return boolean
 */
public static boolean isVideoAvailableForever(Context
context) {
  return (boolean) SPUtil.get(context, getCurrentUserId(
context), VIDEO _ FOREVER _
    KEY, false);
}

/**
 * Update the status of a permanent member.
 *
 * @param context Context.
 */
public   static   void   setVideoAvailableForever(Context
context) {
  SPUtil.put(context, getCurrentUserId(context), VIDEO _
FOREVER _ KEY, true);
}
```

Based on the sample code above, you can use a flag to record a permanent membership purchase. For details about how to determine the user's right to view videos, please refer to the description in the consumable section.

3. Subscriptions

Similar to the preceding product types, you'll need to check for the validity of a subscription. After a subscription is purchased, the app will obtain the purchase details through **InApppurchaseData** and query the purchased subscription through **IapClient.obtain OwnedPurchases()**. For services (such as membership services) that depend on the renewal status, a value of **true** in **inApppurchaseData. isSubValid** indicates that the subscription relationship is valid and that the user is free to access the service.

The Pet Store app offers membership services, and therefore, you can use **inAppPurchaseData.isSubValid** to quickly determine whether the subscription is valid. To do so, you'll need to open **PurchasesOperation.java** in your project and grant rights to the user.

```java
/**
 * Update the expiration time of the membership.
 *
 * @param inAppPurchaseData Purchase information.
 */
public static void updateVideoSubscriptionExpireDate(
Context context, InAppPurchaseData inAppPurchaseData)
{
  if (inAppPurchaseData == null) {
    return;
  }
  // The subscription relationship is valid.
  if (inAppPurchaseData.isSubValid()) {
    long       expireDate    =       inAppPurchaseData.
getExpirationDate();
    String uuid = inAppPurchaseData.getDeveloperPayload();
    if (TextUtils.isEmpty(uuid)) {
      uuid = getCurrentUserId(context);
    }
    long videoExpireDate = getVideoSubscriptionExpireDate
(context);
    if (videoExpireDate < expireDate) {
      SPUtil.put(context,    uuid,    VIDEO _ SUBSCRIPTION _
KEY, expireDate);
    }
  }
}

/**
 * Obtain the expiration time of the membership.
 *
 * @param context Context.
 * @return Timestamp.
 */
public    static    long    getVideoSubscriptionExpireDate(
Context context) {
  return    (long)    SPUtil.get(context,    getCurrentUserId(
context), VIDEO _ SUBSCRIPTION _
    KEY, 0L);
}
```

Obtain the subscription through **obtainOwnedPurchases** and verify the validity of the subscription data. After the verification is successful, convert the JSON data into **InAppPurchaseData** and pass it to the **updateVideoSubscriptionExpireDate** method to update the member right. For details about how to determine the user's right to view videos, please refer to the description in the consumable section.

5.5.3 Subscription Management

In addition to displaying purchase records for non-subscription products, IAP also enables users to access the subscription management screen from **Account center** on devices that run EMUI, to make it easy for users to manage their subscriptions. This screen displays all of the user's subscriptions and related settings. When the user has purchased a subscription, the app will provide a portal for the user to directly access the subscription details screen provided by IAP.

By setting the intent scheme URL, you enable the user to proceed to the subscription management or subscription details screen from the app. On the subscription details screen, you'll see key details, as well as all other subscriptions in the same group. The intent scheme URL can be set to **pay://com.huawei.hwid.external/subscriptions**. Table 5.3 describes the URL parameters.

The values of **package** and **appid** can be found in the **agconnect-services.json** file, as shown in Figure 5.28.

After the user purchases a subscription, the Pet Store app will display a portal for the user to directly access the subscription details screen. You'll need to add an entry to **initView** in **MineCenterAct.java** for subscription management.

```
findViewById(R.id.sub_manage).setOnClick
  Listener(new View.OnClickListener() {
  @Override
  public void onClick(View view) {
    Intent intent = new Intent(Intent.
    ACTION_VIEW);
```

TABLE 5.3 URL Parameters

Parameter	Mandatory	Description
package	No	App package name.
appid	No	App ID allocated when you create an app in AppGallery Connect.
sku	No	Subscription ID. If this parameter is specified, the subscription details screen will be displayed. Otherwise, the subscription management screen will be displayed.

```
{
    "agcgw":{
        "backurl":"connect-drcn.dbankcloud.cn",
        "url":"connect-drcn.hispace.hicloud.com"
    },
    "client":{
        "cp_id":"10086000000000293",
        "product_id":"9105385871708501335",
        "client_id":"306274895182955520",
        "client_secret":"21612FAF565A22A3A48DB11A92377D9E8911C413C736D55C95E88FC181F63388",
        "app_id":"101778417",
        "package_name":"com.huawei.hmspetstore",
        "api_key":"CV5+5mO4bX1LRRShmnN09Z5Ks8h/rxNYxDmI+0gZtBR04idqbNtwRdoOCnrLc87FaxNSz9dUFvZaU4JBrxARceYEDMqX"
    },
    "service":{
        "analytics":{
            "collector_url":"datacollector-drcn.dt.hicloud.com,datacollector-drcn.dt.dbankcloud.cn",
            "resource_id":"p1",
            "channel_id":""
        },
        "ml":{
            "mlservice_url":"ml-api-drcn.ai.dbankcloud.com,ml-api-drcn.ai.dbankcloud.cn"
        }
    },
    "region":"CN",
    "configuration_version":"1.0"
}
```

FIGURE 5.28   agconnect-services.json configuration file.

```
intent.setData(Uri.parse("pay:// com.huawei.hwid.
external/subscriptions?
    package=com.huawei.hmspetstore&appid=101778417&sk
u=subscribeMember01"));
    startActivity(intent);
    }
});
```

After a successful purchase, the user can touch **My renewals** in the personal center of the Pet Store app to directly access the subscription details screen, as illustrated in Figure 5.29.

If the user has not purchased a subscription, IAP will display a message telling the user that no subscription is available. Alternatively, you can enable the user to directly access the subscription management screen, without the need to pass the **sku** parameter in the URL. It is up to you whether to display a message or display the subscription management screen.

5.6 SANDBOX TESTING

Sandbox testing simulates the product purchasing process during IAP integration, without having to process real payments. This section details how you can use sandbox testing for several different product types.

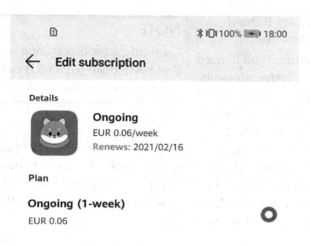

FIGURE 5.29   Subscription details screen.

5.6.1 Principles Behind Sandbox Testing

Prior to testing, you'll need to configure tester accounts, which must be real HUAWEI IDs in AppGallery Connect, before configuring an app version for sandbox testing. If the app you wish to test has not been released

---

NOTE

Currently, sandbox testing requires that HMS Core (APK) 3.0 or later be installed on the testing device.

---

in AppGallery Connect, you'll need to ensure that the **versionCode** value for the app is greater than **0**. If the app has been released in AppGallery Connect, the **versionCode** value for the app to be tested will need to be greater than that for the released app.

1. Testing non-subscription payments

   When a request is initiated to purchase a non-subscription product, IAP will detect the sandbox testing account and then skip the payment-related steps by directly returning a payment success message. The **purchaseType** field in the message refers to the purchase type. If the value of this field is **0**, it means that the purchase has been logged as a sandbox test. The purchase process in the sandbox testing environment uses real-world conditions.

2. Testing subscription renewals

   The time machine concept lets you test out subscription renewals in the most efficient way. For example, the renewal period of one week in the real world is equivalent to 3 minutes in the time machine. Table 5.4 lists the time conversions in sandbox testing.

TABLE 5.4   Time Conversions

Real Time	Test Time
1 week	3 minutes
1 month	5 minutes
2 months	10 minutes
3 months	15 minutes
6 months	30 minutes
1 year	1 hour

To purchase a subscription, you'll need to sign a contract or add a payment card, but will not be charged for the purchase. In the sandbox testing environment, the renewal interval is a fraction of the actual time, as described in the table above. To prevent a large amount of useless data from being accumulated, a single subscription can be automatically renewed for a maximum of six times. After these six times have elapsed, you can go to the subscription management screen to renew the subscription once again or call the API to resume the subscription. Once the subscription is resumed, it will be automatically renewed for an additional period.

5.6.2 Coding Practice

Now, we'll detail the process for configuring a tester account.

1. Sign in to AppGallery Connect and click **Users and permissions**, as shown in Figure 5.30.

2. In the navigation tree on the left, go to **Sandbox > Test accounts**, and click **Add**, as shown in Figure 5.31.

3. Enter the tester account information and click **OK**, as shown in Figure 5.32. Please note that the account must be a real HUAWEI ID that has been previously registered.

   After account configuration, you'll need to confirm that the APK version meets the requirements for the sandbox testing environment.

FIGURE 5.30 Clicking Users and permissions.

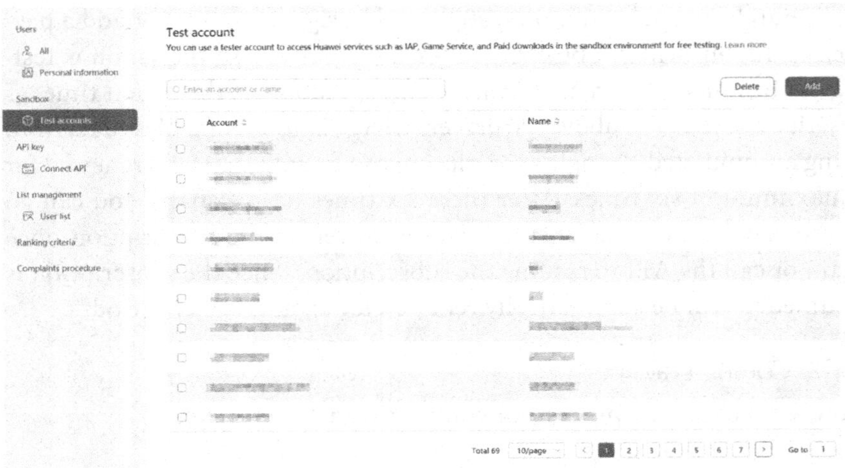

FIGURE 5.31   Adding a tester account.

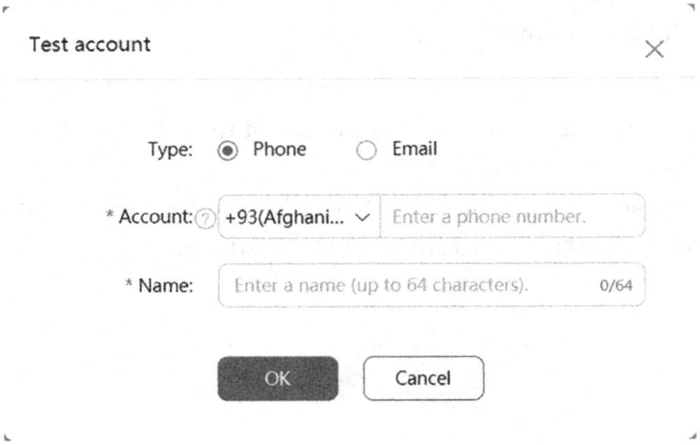

FIGURE 5.32   Entering the tester account information.

This helps ensure that you'll be able to sign in to the mobile phone via the tester account and proceed to the sandbox testing environment to purchase a product. IAP offers the **isSandboxActivated** API, which checks whether the sandbox testing environment is available, to facilitate a more seamless sandbox testing process. If the environment is not available, you'll be able to find the reason from the result returned by the API. To do this, add a method that performs the check to the **PurchaseOperation.java** file of the project.

```
/**
 * Check whether the sandbox testing environment is
available.
 */
public static void checkSandbox(Context context) {
  IapClient mClient = Iap.getIapClient(context);
  Task<IsSandboxActivatedResult> task = mClient.
isSandboxActivated(new IsSandbox
    ActivatedReq());
  task.addOnSuccessListener(new OnSuccessListener<IsSa
ndboxActivatedResult>() {
    @Override
    public void onSuccess(IsSandboxActivatedResult
result) {
      Log.i(TAG, "isSandboxActivated success");
      StringBuilder stringBuilder = new
StringBuilder();

      stringBuilder.append("errMsg: ").append(result.
getErrMsg()).append
        ('\n');
      stringBuilder.append("match version limit :
").append(result.getIs
        SandboxApk()).append('\n');
      stringBuilder.append("match user limit :
").append(result.getIs
        SandboxUser());
      Log.i(TAG, stringBuilder.toString());
    }
  }).addOnFailureListener(new OnFailureListener() {
    @Override
    public void onFailure(Exception e) {
      Log.e(TAG, "isSandboxActivated fail");
      if (e instanceof IapApiException) {
      IapApiException apiException =
(IapApiException) e;
        int returnCode = apiException.getStatusCode();
        String errMsg = apiException.getMessage();
        Log.e(TAG, "returnCode: " + returnCode + ",
errMsg: " + errMsg);
      } else {
        Log.e(TAG, "isSandboxActivated fail, unknown
error");
```

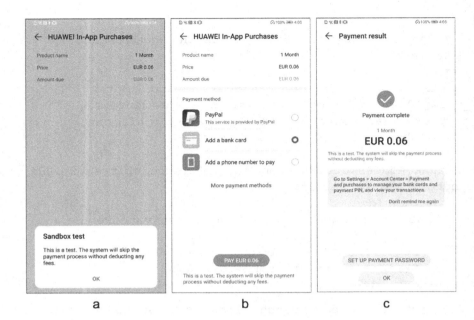

FIGURE 5.33 Sandbox testing message.

```
        }
      }
    });
}
```

From **IsSandboxActivatedResult** returned by the API, you'll be able to determine whether the sandbox testing environment is available. Then sign in using a HUAWEI ID that has not been already configured as a tester account, call **IsSandboxActivatedResult** in **onCreate** of the **Member center** screen, and start the app. You'll be able to see if the HUAWEI ID is not a tester account, by referring to the response from the API.

Use the configured tester account to initiate a payment, and a sandbox testing message will appear when the checkout screen is displayed, as shown in Figure 5.33. You can then use the sandbox testing environment to perform debugging.

5.7 IAP SERVER CAPABILITY OPENNESS

You can connect your app server to the IAP server through APIs, to assist with product management and ensure a high degree of data security, by verifying orders on the app server. By enabling the user to manage subscriptions through the app server, this framework provides for a more flexible and convenient purchasing experience.

NOTE

Although these APIs were not used in the Pet Store app, they may be useful for your own app.

5.7.1 Service Process

IAP provides a range of different functions through its server APIs, including subscription management and token verification for purchasing common products. App operations personnel can use these APIs to process subscription-related transactions, such as to cancel subscriptions, refund fees, revoke subscriptions, and receive notifications for key subscription events. Figure 5.34 shows this service process.

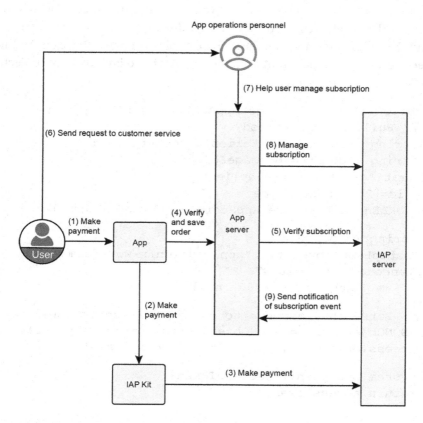

FIGURE 5.34   Service process.

Steps 1–5 are for verifying user payment orders (including consumable, non-consumable, and subscription orders). Steps 6–8 address subscription management, including canceling renewals, postponing settlement dates, refunding fees, revoking subscriptions, and querying refund records. Step 9 involves notifying the app server of any subscription status changes.

5.7.2 Coding Practice

Before using the APIs on the IAP server, you'll need a thorough understanding of the API call specifications. For more details, please refer to the *API Reference*.[2]

To call an API, use the service authentication API provided by the open platform to obtain an access token, and carry it in a request header. For more details, please refer to Section 2.3.2. Here, we've used the Client Credentials mode. Each access token has a specific validity period of repeated use. It is recommended that you apply for a new access token only when HTTP status code 401 is returned during the access to the server API. Now, let's take a look at how you can obtain an access token. You'll need to define the **getAppAT** method in **AtDemo.java** of your project, which is on the app server.

```java
public static String getAppAT() throws Exception {
  // Build a request body.
  String grant_type = "client_credentials";
  String msgBody = MessageFormat.
format("grant_type={0}&client_secret={1}&client_
    id={2}", grant_type,
    URLEncoder.encode(appSecret, "UTF-8"), appId);

  String response =
    httpPost(tokenUrl, "application/x-www-form-
urlencoded; charset=UTF-8",
      msgBody, 5000, 5000, null);

  // Parse the response to obtain the access token.
  JSONObject obj = JSONObject.parseObject(response);
  accessToken = obj.getString("access_token");

  System.out.println(accessToken);
  return accessToken;
}
```

FIGURE 5.35   App details page in AppGallery Connect.

The values for **appSecret** and **appId** in the preceding information can be found on the app details page in AppGallery Connect, as shown in Figure 5.35.

Use the obtained access token to build request headers for other services.

```
public static Map<String, String> buildAuthorization(
String appAt) {
  String oriString = MessageFormat.format("APPAT:{0}",
appAt);
  String authorization =
    MessageFormat.format("Basic {0}", Base64.
encodeBase64String(oriString.
      getBytes(StandardCharsets.UTF_8)));
  Map<String, String> headers = new HashMap<>();
  headers.put("Authorization", authorization);
  headers.put("Content-Type", "application/json;
charset=UTF-8");
  return headers;
}
```

During an API call, the requester may receive a response that contains a signature string from the recipient. In this case, the requester can use the payment public key to verify the signature string, in order to determine whether the response has been tampered with. For more details about how to obtain the public key, please refer to Section 5.2.1. The signature verification process is as follows:

1. Obtain the string to be verified from the returned result. For example, if the product information in **inAppPurchaseDataList** returned by the **obtainOwnedPurchases** API needs to be verified, obtain the JSON string corresponding to the first piece of product information for verification.

2. Obtain the signature string. For example, if **inAppSignature** returned by the **obtainOwnedPurchases** API corresponds to the signature string for **inAppPurchaseDataList**, obtain the signature string corresponding to the first piece of product information for verification.

3. Use the payment public key to verify the result string and the corresponding signature string using the SHA256withRSA algorithm.

The sample code for the signature verification is as follows:

```
public static boolean doCheck(String content, String
sign, String publicKey) {
  if (StringUtils.isEmpty(sign)) {
    return false;
  }
  if (StringUtils.isEmpty(publicKey)) {
    return false;
  }
  try {
    // Use a specified signature verification
algorithm.
    KeyFactory keyFactory = KeyFactory.
getInstance("RSA");
    byte[] encodedKey = Base64.
decodeBase64(publicKey);
    PublicKey pubKey = keyFactory.generatePublic(new
X509EncodedKeySpec(en
      codedKey));
    java.security.Signature signature;
    signature = java.security.Signature.
getInstance("SHA256withRSA");
    signature.initVerify(pubKey);
    signature.update(content.getBytes(
StandardCharsets.UTF_8));
    byte[] bsign = Base64.decodeBase64(sign);
    return signature.verify(bsign);
  } catch (RuntimeException e) {
    throw e;
  } catch (Exception e) {
    e.printStackTrace();
```

```
}
    return false;
}
```

The algorithm enables you to verify the signature on the app or app server. Signature verification on the app server improves security. Next, let's take a look at how to use the server APIs to verify orders and manage subscriptions.

1. Verifying orders (consumables/non-consumables)

For consumables and non-consumables, the IAP server provides an API that verifies orders on the app server, to further confirm that the purchase information is correct. After a payment is completed, HMS Core (APK) will return a purchase order details JSON string **InAppPurchaseData**, as well as a signature string **inAppDataSignature**. The **InAppPurchaseData** string will contain **purchaseToken**, which uniquely identifies the mapping between the product and the user.

You can ensure the validity of **InAppPurchaseData** using signature verification. To further confirm the purchase information, your app server can parse **purchaseToken** in **InAppPurchaseData** and call an API provided by the IAP server, which verifies the purchase token. The verification of the purchase token is not mandatory, because signature verification already ensures data correctness. In **OrderService. java** for the project, define the request for calling the order service API.

```
public static String verifyToken(String purchaseToken,
String productId) throws
    Exception {
    // Obtain an app-level access token.
    // In real world scenarios, the access token does not
need to be obtained each time that a request is initi-
ated. Instead, obtain it when a request is initiated
for the first time, or when result code 401 is returned.
    String appAt = AtDemo.getAppAT();
    // Build a request header.
    Map<String,    String>    headers    =    AtDemo.
buildAuthorization(appAt);
    // Build a request body.
    Map<String, String> bodyMap = new HashMap<>();
```

```
bodyMap.put("purchaseToken", purchaseToken);
bodyMap.put("productId", productId);
String msgBody = JSONObject.toJSONString(bodyMap);
String response = AtDemo.httpPost(ROOT _ URL + "/appli
cations/purchases/tokens/
    verify",
    "application/json; charset=UTF-8", msgBody, 5000,
5000, headers);
System.out.println(response);
return response;
}
```

The preceding code can be implemented easily with the *API Reference*. The following lists the information for the API used in this example:

(1) API prototype

Protocol: HTTPS POST

Direction: App server -> IAP server

URL: {rootUrl}/applications/purchases/tokens/verify

The value of **rootUrl** will vary depending on the site. It is recommended that you select the nearest site for access. For more details, please refer to the site description in the *IAP Development Guide*.

Data format: Request: Content-Type: application/json; Response: Content-Type: application/json

(2) Request parameters

(3) Response parameters

2. Verifying orders (subscriptions)

Similar to non-subscription products, subscription orders can be verified through the API provided by the IAP server. After a

TABLE 5.5   Request Parameters

Parameter	Mandatory	Type	Description
purchaseToken	Yes	String	Purchase token for the product to be delivered. It is returned when the app initiates a purchase request, or queries information about the product to be consumed.
productId	Yes	String	ID for the product to be delivered. The product ID is identical to that you set when configuring product information in AppGallery Connect.

TABLE 5.6   Response Parameters

Parameter	Mandatory	Type	Description
responseCode	Yes	String	Response code. 0: successful Other values: failed For more details, please refer to the API result codes.
responseMessage	No	String	Response description.
purchaseTokenData	No	String	JSON string that contains purchase details. For more details, please refer to the description for **InappPurchaseDetails**. This parameter should be used for signature verification without any changes.
dataSignature	No	String	Signature information for **purchaseTokenData** based on the app's private RSA payment key. The signature algorithm is SHA256withRSA. The app can perform signature verification on the JSON string for **purchaseTokenData**, by using the payment public key. For more details, please refer to the description for verifying the signature in the returned result.

payment is completed, the **InAppPurchaseData** string contains **purchaseToken**, which uniquely identifies the mapping between the product and the user. Before providing the service corresponding to the subscription that the user has purchased, call the API for verifying the subscription service's purchase token to verify the order and obtain the purchase details. In **SubscriptionService.java** for the project, define the request for calling the subscription service API.

The sample code is as follows:

```
public static String getSubscription(String subscrip
tionId, String purchaseToken)
  throws Exception {
  // Obtain an app-level access token.
  String appAt = AtDemo.getAppAT();

  // Build a request header.
  Map<String, String> headers = AtDemo.buildAuthoriza
tion(appAt);
```

```
// Build a request body.
Map<String, String> bodyMap = new HashMap<>();
bodyMap.put("subscriptionId", subscriptionId);
bodyMap.put("purchaseToken", purchaseToken);

String msgBody = JSONObject.toJSONString(bodyMap);

String response = AtDemo.httpPost(ROOT _ URL + "/sub/a
pplications/v2/purchases/
    get",
    "application/json; charset=UTF-8", msgBody, 5000,
5000, headers);

System.out.println(response);
return response;
}
```

The following lists the information for the API used in this example:

(1) API prototype

Protocol: HTTPS POST

Direction: App server -> IAP server

URL: {rootUrl}/sub/applications/{apiVersion}/purchases/get

The value of **rootUrl** will vary depending on the site. It is recommended that you select the subscription service URL at the nearest site for access.

Data format: Request: Content-Type: application/json; Response: Content-Type: application/json

(2) Request parameters

(3) Response parameters

3. Canceling the renewal of a subscription

If a user does not wish to renew a subscription, they can cancel the renewal of the subscription on their own, or the app server can cancel the renewal via the subscription cancellation API provided by the IAP server. In this case, the subscription will remain valid within

TABLE 5.7   Request Parameters

Parameter	Mandatory	Type	Description
subscriptionId	Yes	String	Subscription ID.
purchaseToken	Yes	String	Purchase token for a product, which is returned when the app initiates a purchase request or queries subscription information.

TABLE 5.8   Response Parameters

Parameter	Mandatory	Type	Description
responseCode	Yes	String	Response code. **0**: successful Other values: failed For more details, please refer to the API result codes.
responseMessage	No	String	Response description.
InappPurchaseDetails	No	String	JSON string that contains purchase details. For more details about the format, please refer to the description for **InappPurchaseDetails** in the *API Reference*.

the validity period, for example, 30 days, but the subsequent renewal is stopped. The code to do this is here:

```
public static String stopSubscription(String subscrip
tionId, String purchaseToken)
  throws Exception {
  String appAt = AtDemo.getAppAT();
  Map<String, String> headers = AtDemo.
buildAuthorization(appAt);

  Map<String, String> bodyMap = new HashMap<>();
  bodyMap.put("subscriptionId", subscriptionId);
  bodyMap.put("purchaseToken", purchaseToken);

  String msgBody = JSONObject.toJSONString(bodyMap);

  String response = AtDemo.httpPost(ROOT _ URL + "/sub/a
pplications/v2/purchases/
    stop",
    "application/json; charset=UTF-8", msgBody, 5000,
5000, headers);

  System.out.println(response);
  return response;
}
```

The following lists the information for the API used in this example:

(1) API prototype
Protocol: HTTPS POST
Direction: App server -> IAP server

URL: {rootUrl}/sub/applications/{apiVersion}/purchases/stop

The value of **rootUrl** will vary depending on the site. It is recommended that you select the subscription service URL at the nearest site for access.

Data format: Request: Content-Type: application/json; Response: Content-Type: application/json

(2) Request parameters

(3) Response parameters

4. Postponing the settlement date

When you launch a promotion for your app, such as rewarding users with an extended period of access to a product, your app can call the API provided by the IAP server to postpone the user's settlement date. The user can continue to use the paid service and content and will not be charged during the extended period. IAP updates the subscription renewal date accordingly. Postponing settlement lets you:

(1) Offer free content or services for users as part of a package or discount promotion (e.g., allow the user who subscribes to annual magazines to access specific content free of charge).

TABLE 5.9   Request Parameters

Parameter	Mandatory	Type	Description
subscriptionId	Yes	String	Subscription ID.
purchaseToken	Yes	String	Purchase token for a product, which is returned when the app initiates a purchase request or queries subscription information.

TABLE 5.10   Response Parameters

Parameter	Mandatory	Type	Description
responseCode	Yes	String	Response code. **0**: successful Other values: failed For more details, please refer to the API result codes.
responseMessage	No	String	Response description.

(2) Reward specified users with access to content or services.

The settlement date can be postponed by a minimum of one day and a maximum of one year (365 days). You can call the API again before the new settlement date has arrived to postpone settlement once again. After the postponement, the next renewal will start after the new settlement date has ended. The app may need to notify users by email or within the app that their settlement date has been postponed.

The sample code is as follows:

```
public static String delaySubscription(String
subscriptionId, String purchaseToken,
  Long currentExpirationTime,
  Long desiredExpirationTime) throws Exception {
  String appAt = AtDemo.getAppAT();
  Map<String,    String>    headers    =    AtDemo.
buildAuthorization(appAt);

  Map<String, Object> bodyMap = new HashMap<>();
  bodyMap.put("subscriptionId", subscriptionId);
  bodyMap.put("purchaseToken", purchaseToken);
  bodyMap.put("currentExpirationTime", currentExpiration
Time);
  bodyMap.put("desiredExpirationTime", desiredExpiration
Time);

  String msgBody = JSONObject.toJSONString(bodyMap);

  String response = AtDemo.httpPost(ROOT _ URL + "/sub/a
pplications/v2/purchases/
    delay",
    "application/json;  charset=UTF-8",  msgBody,  5000,
5000, headers);

System.out.println(response);
return response;
}
```

The following lists the information for the API used in this example:

(1) API prototype

Protocol: HTTPS POST

Direction: App server -> IAP server

URL: {rootUrl}/sub/applications/{apiVersion}/purchases/delay

The value of **rootUrl** will vary depending on the site. It is recommended that you select the subscription service URL at the nearest site for access.

Data format: Request: Content-Type: application/json; Response: Content-Type: application/json

(2) Request parameters

(3) Response parameters

5. Refunding subscription fees

If the user applies for a refund after accidentally purchasing a subscription, your app or the IAP server can call the subscription

TABLE 5.11   Request Parameters

Parameter	Mandatory	Type	Description
subscriptionId	Yes	String	Subscription ID.
purchaseToken	Yes	String	Purchase token for a product, which is returned when the app initiates a purchase request or queries subscription information.
currentExpirationTime	Yes	Long	Current subscription expiration time. The value is a standard timestamp.
desiredExpirationTime	Yes	Long	Subscription expiration time after postponement. The value is a standard timestamp and must be later than the current subscription expiration time. The settlement date can be postponed by a minimum of one day and a maximum of 365 days.

TABLE 5.12   Response Parameters

Parameter	Mandatory	Type	Description
responseCode	Yes	String	Response code. **0**: successful Other values: failed For more details, please refer to the API result codes.
responseMessage	No	String	Response description.
newExpirationTime	No	Long	Subscription expiration time after postponement. The value is a standard timestamp.

cancellation API to halt the renewal, before calling the subscription fee refund API. The fee will then be returned to the user through the original payment channel.

NOTICE

1. The subscription fee refund API only refunds the most recent fee from a specified subscription and does not cancel the subscription outright. The validity of the subscription and subsequent renewals are not affected.
2. If the most recent subscription receipt contains refund information, the refund request will be rejected. To refund the fees of previous receipts or the remaining fees from the latest receipt via your app, it is recommended that you use the refund capability in the order service.
3. If a purchase is performed in the sandbox testing environment, or a product is purchased free of charge, the refund will proceed without refund request sent to the IAP server.

The sample code is as follows:

```
public static String returnFeeSubscription(String
subscriptionId, String purchaseToken)
   throws Exception {
   String appAt = AtDemo.getAppAT();
   Map<String, String> headers = AtDemo.
buildAuthorization(appAt);

   Map<String, String> bodyMap = new HashMap<>();
   bodyMap.put("subscriptionId", subscriptionId);
   bodyMap.put("purchaseToken", purchaseToken);

   String msgBody = JSONObject.toJSONString(bodyMap);

   String response = AtDemo.httpPost(ROOT _ URL + "/sub/a
pplications/v2/purchases/
      returnFee",
      "application/json; charset=UTF-8", msgBody, 5000,
5000, headers);

   System.out.println(response);
   return response;
}
```

The following describes the information about the API used in this example:

(1) API prototype

Protocol: HTTPS POST

Direction: App server -> IAP server

URL: {rootUrl}/sub/applications/{apiVersion}/purchases/returnFee

The value of **rootUrl** will vary depending on the site. It is recommended that you select the subscription service URL at the nearest site for access.

Data format: Request: Content-Type: application/json; Response: Content-Type: application/json

(2) Request parameters

(3) Response parameters

6. Revoking subscriptions

If the user wants to revoke their subscription because it was purchased by accident or is no longer needed, your app server can call the subscription revoking API provided by the IAP server to halt the provisioning of services. The purchased subscription will be revoked immediately, and the latest subscription fee will be directly refunded.

> **NOTICE**
>
> It may take some time for the user to receive the refund after a refund request.

TABLE 5.13   Request Parameters

Parameter	Mandatory	Type	Description
subscriptionId	Yes	String	Subscription ID.
purchaseToken	Yes	String	Purchase token for a product, which is returned when the app initiates a purchase request or queries subscription information.

TABLE 5.14   Response Parameters

Parameter	Mandatory	Type	Description
responseCode	Yes	String	Response code. **0**: successful Other values: failed For more details, please refer to the API result codes.
responseMessage	No	String	Response description.

The sample code is as follows:

```
public static String withdrawSubscription(String
subscriptionId, String purchase
  Token) throws Exception {
  String appAt = AtDemo.getAppAT();
  Map<String, String> headers = AtDemo.
buildAuthorization(appAt);

  Map<String, String> bodyMap = new HashMap<>();
  bodyMap.put("subscriptionId", subscriptionId);
  bodyMap.put("purchaseToken", purchaseToken);

  String msgBody = JSONObject.toJSONString(bodyMap);

  String response = AtDemo.httpPost(ROOT _ URL + "/sub/a
pplications/v2/purchases/
    withdrawal",
    "application/json;  charset=UTF-8",  msgBody,  5000,
5000, headers);

  System.out.println(response);
  return response;
}
```

The following lists the information for the API used in this example:

(1) API prototype

Protocol: HTTPS POST

Direction: App server -> IAP server

URL: {rootUrl}/sub/applications/{apiVersion}/purchases/withdrawal

The value of **rootUrl** will vary depending on the site. It is recommended that you select the subscription service URL at the nearest site for access.

Data format: Request: Content-Type: application/json; Response: Content-Type: application/json

(2) Request parameters

TABLE 5.15   Request Parameters

Parameter	Mandatory	Type	Description
subscriptionId	Yes	String	Subscription ID.
purchaseToken	Yes	String	Purchase token for a product, which is returned when the app initiates a purchase request or queries subscription information.

TABLE 5.16 Response Parameters

Parameter	Mandatory	Type	Description
responseCode	Yes	String	Response code. **0**: successful Other values: failed For more details, please refer to the API result codes.
responseMessage	No	String	Response description.

(3) Response parameters

7. Querying canceled or refunded purchases

To view cancellation or refund information for recent subscriptions via your app, call the API provided by the IAP server to query these records generated within the past month.

The sample code is as follows:

NOTICE

To keep batch querying efficient, the returned purchase information does not contain signatures information, in compliance with HTTPS security requirements.

```
public static void cancelledListPurchase(Long endAt,
Long startAt, Integer maxRows,
    Integer type,
        String continuationToken) throws Exception {
    String appAt = AtDemo.getAppAT();
    Map<String, String> headers = AtDemo.buildAuthorization
(appAt);

    Map<String, Object> bodyMap = new HashMap<>();
    bodyMap.put("endAt", endAt);
    bodyMap.put("startAt", startAt);
    bodyMap.put("maxRows", maxRows);
    bodyMap.put("type", type);
    bodyMap.put("continuationToken", continuationToken);

    String msgBody = JSONObject.toJSONString(bodyMap);

    String response = AtDemo.httpPost(ROOT _ URL + "/appli
cations/v2/purchases/cancelledList",
        "application/json; charset=UTF-8", msgBody, 5000,
5000, headers);
    System.out.println(response);
}
```

The following lists the information for the API used in this example:

(1) API prototype

Protocol: HTTPS POST

Direction: App server -> IAP server

URL: {rootUrl}/applications/{apiVersion}/purchases/cancelledList

The value of **rootUrl** will vary depending on the site. It is recommended that you select the order service URL at the nearest site for access.

Data format: Request: Content-Type: application/json; Response: Content-Type: application/json

(2) Request parameters

TABLE 5.17   Request Parameters

Parameter	Mandatory	Type	Description
endAt	No	Long	End timestamp (in UTC) for the most recent canceled or refunded purchases that you wish to query. If **continuationToken** is passed, ignore **endAt**. The value cannot be later than the current time, and the default value is the current time. The value of **endAt** must be greater than or equal to that of **startAt**.
startAt	No	Long	Start timestamp (in UTC) for the most recent canceled or refunded purchases that you wish to query. If **continuationToken** is passed, ignore **startAt**. The value cannot be later than the current time, and the default value is the current time. The value of **endAt** must be greater than or equal to that of **startAt**.
maxRows	No	Integer	Maximum number of query result records. The value must be greater than 0, and both the default and maximum values are **1000**.
continuationToken	No	String	Token returned during the most recent query for the data on the next page.
type	Yes	Integer	Query type. Ignore this parameter if **continuationToken** is set. The options are as follows: **0** (default): queries purchase information for consumables and non-consumables. **1**: queries purchase information for consumables, non-consumables, and subscriptions.

TABLE 5.18 Response Parameters

Parameter	Mandatory	Type	Description
responseCode	Yes	String	Response code. **0**: successful Other values: failed For more details, please refer to the API result codes.
responseMessage	No	String	Response description.
cancelledPurchaseList	No	String	List of canceled or refunded purchases, in JSON string format, with each string indicating a purchase record. For more details about the purchase format, please refer to the description for **cancelledPurchase** in the *API Reference*.
continuationToken	No	String	Token for querying data on the next page. If a value is returned, pass it in the next query request, to query data on the next page.

(3) Response parameters (Table 5.18)

8. Receiving notifications about key subscription events

You can configure an app server callback URL, that is, **Subscription notification URL** shown in Figure 5.36, in

FIGURE 5.36 Configuring a URL for receiving subscription notifications.

AppGallery Connect to receive notifications about key subscription events from the IAP server. The URL must support the HTTPS protocol and have a valid commercial certificate. For more details about how to receive notifications, please refer to the *API Reference.*[3]

The sample code is as follows:

```
/**
 * Process notification information.
 *
 * @param information Request content.
 */
public static String dealNotification(String informa
tion) throws Exception {
  if (StringUtils.isEmpty(information)) {
    return "";
  }
  // Parse the callback information returned by the IAP
server to obtain the request object.
  StatusUpdateNotificationRequest request = MAPPER.
readValue(information, Status
    UpdateNotificationRequest.class);
  StatusUpdateNotificationResponse response = new
StatusUpdateNotificationResponse();

  if   (StringUtils.isEmpty(request.getNotifycationSigna
ture())
    || StringUtils.isEmpty(request.getStatusUpdateNoti
fication())) {
    response.setErrorCode("1");
    response.setErrorMsg("the notification message is
empty");
    return response.toString();
  }

  // Verify data validity.
  boolean isCheckOk =
    doCheck(request.getStatusUpdateNotification(),
request.getNotifycation
    Signature(), PUBLIC _ KEY);
  if (!isCheckOk) {
  response.setErrorCode("2");
  response.setErrorMsg("verify the sign failure");
```

```
    return response.toString();
}

// Implement custom notifications.
StatusUpdateNotification statusUpdateNotification =
    MAPPER.readValue(request.getStatusUpdateNotifica
tion(), StatusUpdateNotification.class);
    int notificationType = statusUpdateNotification.
getNotificationType();
    switch (notificationType) {
    // The user purchases a subscription for the first
time.
        case NotificationType.INITIAL _ BUY:
          break;
    // Customer service personnel or the app cancels a
subscription.
        case NotificationType.CANCEL:
          break;
    // An expired subscription is automatically renewed.
        case NotificationType.RENEWAL:
          break;
    // The user proactively resumes an expired
subscription.
        case NotificationType.INTERACTIVE _ RENEWAL:
          break;
    // The user selects another subscription in the
group, and it will take effect after the current
subscription has expired. The current validity period
is not affected.
        case NotificationType.NEW _ RENEWAL _ PREF:
          break;
    // The renewal of a subscription is stopped by the
user, you, or Huawei, but the paid service for the
subscription remains valid.
        case NotificationType.RENEWAL _ STOPPED:
          break;
    // The user resumes a subscription, and the renewal
status is normal.
        case NotificationType.RENEWAL _ RESTORED:
            break;
    // A single renewal is successful for a promotional
period, free trial period, or sandbox testing.
        case NotificationType.RENEWAL _ RECURRING:
```

```
      break;
      // An expired subscription enters the purchase
record retention period.
      case NotificationType.ON _ HOLD:
        break;
      // After the user makes a renewal suspension plan,
the subscription is paused when its validity period has
expired.
      case NotificationType.PAUSED:
        break;
      // The user has made a renewal suspension plan.
      case NotificationType.PAUSE _ PLAN _ CHANGED:
        break;
      // The user has agreed to the price increase.
      case NotificationType.PRICE _ CHANGE _ CONFIRMED:
        break;
      // The subscription renewal time has been postponed.
      case NotificationType.DEFERRED:
        break;
      default:
        break;
  }

  response.setErrorCode("0");
  response.setErrorMsg("success");
  return response.toString();
}
```

The following lists the information for the API used in this example:

(1) API prototype

Protocol: HTTPS POST

Direction: IAP server -> App server

URL: Configured when you apply for the IAP service.

Data format: Request: Content-Type: application/json; Response: Content-Type: application/json

(2) Request parameters

Table 5.20 summarizes parameters of **statusUpdateNotification**.

Table 5.21 summarizes parameters of **notificationType**.

(3) Response parameters

TABLE 5.19   Request Parameters

Parameter	Mandatory	Type	Description
statusUpdateNotification	Yes	String	Notification message, in JSON string format. For details, please refer to the description for **statusUpdateNotification**.
notifycationSignature	Yes	String	Signature string for **statusUpdateNotification**. The signature algorithm is SHA256withRSA. After receiving the signature string, your app server will need to use the payment public key to verify the JSON string for **statusUpdateNotification**. For more details about how to obtain the public key, please refer to Section 5.2.1.

TABLE 5.20   statusUpdateNotification Parameters

Parameter	Mandatory	Type	Description
environment	Yes	String	Environment in which the notification is sent. **PROD**: production environment **SandBox**: sandbox testing environment
notificationType	Yes	Integer	Type for the notification event. For more details, please refer to **notificationType** parameters.
subscriptionId	Yes	String	Subscription ID.
cancellationDate	No	Long	Timestamp, passed only when **notificationType** is set to **CANCEL**.
orderId	Yes	String	Order ID used for payment during subscription renewal.
latestReceipt	No	String	Token for the most recent receipt, which is only passed when **notificationType** is set to **INITIAL_BUY, RENEWAL**, or **INTERACTIVE_ RENEWAL,** and the renewal is successful.

(Continued)

TABLE 5.20 CONTINUED   statusUpdateNotification Parameters

Parameter	Mandatory	Type	Description
latestReceiptInfo	No	String	Most recent receipt, in JSON string format. This parameter is left empty when **notificationType** is set to **CANCEL**. For more details about included parameters, please refer to the description for **InappPurchaseDetails**.
latestReceiptInfoSignature	No	String	Signature string for **latestReceiptInfo**. The signature algorithm is SHA256withRSA. After receiving the signature string, your app server will need to use the payment public key to verify the JSON string for **latestReceiptInfo**. For more details about how to obtain the public key, please refer to Section 5.2.1.
latestExpiredReceipt	No	String	Token for the most recent expired receipt. This parameter only has a value when **notificationType** is set to **RENEWAL** or **INTERACTIVE_RENEWAL**.
latestExpiredReceiptInfo	No	String	Most recent expired receipt, in JSON string format. This parameter only has a value when **notificationType** is set to **RENEWAL** or **INTERACTIVE_RENEWAL**.
ltestExipiredReceiptSignature	No	String	Signature string for **latestExpiredReceiptInfo**. The signature algorithm is SHA256withRSA. After receiving the signature string, your app server will need to use the payment public key to verify the JSON string for **latestExpiredReceiptInfo**. For more details about how to obtain the public key, please refer to Section 5.2.1.

(Continued)

TABLE 5.20 CONTINUED   statusUpdateNotification Parameters

Parameter	Mandatory	Type	Description
autoRenewStatus	Yes	Integer	Renewal status. 1: The subscription will automatically renew at the end of the current subscription period. 0: The user has canceled subscription renewal.
refundPayOrderId	No	String	Refund order ID. This parameter only has a value when **notificationType** is set to **CANCEL**.
productId	Yes	String	Product ID.
applicationId	No	Long	App ID.
expirationIntent	No	Integer	Expiration reason. This parameter only has a value when **notificationType** is set to **RENEWAL** or **INTERACTIVE_RENEWAL**, and the renewal is successful.

TABLE 5.21   notificationType Parameters

Value	Description
INITIAL_BUY(0)	Integer. The user purchases a subscription for the first time.
CANCEL(1)	Integer. Customer service personnel or the app cancels a subscription. The cancellation time (when the refund starts) can be obtained by using **cancellationDate**.
RENEWAL(2)	Integer. An expired subscription is automatically renewed. The next renewal time can be obtained according to the expiration time in the receipt.
INTERACTIVE_RENEWAL(3)	Integer. The user resumes an expired subscription or switches from an expired subscription to a new subscription. The service will take effect immediately after the operation is successful.
NEW_RENEWAL_PREF(4)	Integer. The user selects another subscription in the group, and it will take effect after the current subscription has expired. The current validity period is not affected. The notification will carry the most recent valid receipt and the new subscription information, including the product ID and subscription ID.

(Continued)

TABLE 5.21 CONTINUED   notificationType Parameters

Value	Description
RENEWAL_STOPPED(5)	Integer. The renewal of a subscription is stopped by the user, you, or Huawei, but the paid service for the subscription remains valid. The notification will contain the most recent receipt, product ID, app ID, subscription ID, and subscription token.
RENEWAL_RESTORED(6)	Integer. The user resumes a subscription, and the renewal status is normal. The notification will contain the most recent receipt, product ID, app ID, subscription ID, and subscription token.
RENEWAL_RECURRING(7)	Integer. A single renewal is successful for a promotional period, free trial period, or sandbox testing. The notification will contain the most recent receipt, product ID, app ID, subscription ID, and subscription token. Note: If **notificationType** is set to **INITIAL_BUY**, **RENEWAL**, or **INTERACTIVE_RENEWAL**, **RENEWAL_RECURRING** will not be present, because all of them indicate a successful renewal.
IN_GRACE_PERIOD(8)	Integer. A subscription expires but enters the grace period. Note: Grace periods are not currently supported.
ON_HOLD(9)	Integer. An expired subscription enters the purchase record retention period.
PAUSED(10)	Integer. After the user makes a renewal suspension plan, the subscription is paused when its validity period has expired.
PAUSE_PLAN_CHANGED(11)	Integer. The user has made a renewal suspension plan.
PRICE_CHANGE_ CONFIRMED(12)	Integer. The user has agreed to the price increase.
DEFERRED(13)	Integer. The subscription renewal time has been postponed.

TABLE 5.22   Response Parameters

Parameter	Mandatory	Type	Description
errorCode	No	String	Self-defined error code.
errorMsg	No	String	Error description.

5.8 SUMMARY

Thus far, you've learned how to manage products, guide users toward purchasing products, and process product purchases through IAP. After configuring the product information in AppGallery Connect, you'll be able to obtain this information via the payment SDK API and display it in the app for quick and easy product management. Furthermore, we've delved into the process for completing a purchase process for a consumable, non-consumable, or subscription, including the steps for initiating a purchase and confirming the transaction.

We've also learned about the redelivery mechanism in IAP, which helps you prevent users from accidentally losing access to benefits that they've paid for. Once the purchase has been completed, you can try to entice users to purchase other related services.

You have also mastered the order querying procedures for non-subscription products, as well as the various subscription management mechanisms. When developing IAP functions, you can use the sandbox testing to test out the effects of IAP integration. If your app has a server, by calling the APIs provided by the IAP server, you'll be able to further expand your service scope and develop customized functions that directly address user needs.

The next chapter will detail the process for integrating Push Kit, once again using the Pet Store app. You'll learn how to push messages to users with greater efficiency to boost user engagement and retention to new heights.

NOTES

1 For details about the locations supported by IAP, please visit https://developer.huawei.com/consumer/en/doc/development/HMSCore-Guides-V5/huawei-iap-coverage-0000001050438753-V5.

2 For details about the APIs of the IAP server, please visit https://developer.huawei.com/consumer/en/doc/development/HMSCore-References-V5/-obtain-application-level-at-0000001051066052-V5.

3 For details about the API for receiving notifications about key subscription events, please visit https://developer.huawei.com/consumer/en/doc/development/HMSCore-References/api-notifications-about-subscription-events-0000001050706084.

CHAPTER 6

Push Kit

P<small>USH</small> K<small>IT</small> <small>LETS YOU CHOOSE</small> to push messages either:

1. From the console in AppGallery Connect

2. Through APIs provided by the Push Kit server

Message recipients can be accessed through Android, iOS, and web apps alike.

Now let's use the Pet Store app to deliver information related to pet products, to illustrate how the service can help reach users quickly and efficiently. To do this, we'll need to integrate Push Kit into the app and send push messages to users when new pet products or member promotions are made available.

6.1 ABOUT THE SERVICE

Thanks to the built-in Push module at the EMUI's system layer, the Push Kit server maintains a continual connection to devices, which ensures an online delivery rate in excess of 99%.

Implementing Push Kit involves four major parts:

1. AppGallery Connect: provides a Push Kit service page, for easy push message management.

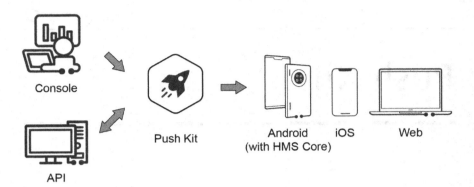

Console

Push Kit

Android
(with HMS Core)

iOS

Web

API

FIGURE 6.1 Push Kit at a glance.

2. Push Kit server: implements service processing for Push Kit on the cloud side.

3. Device-side Push: provides a range of push capabilities, including HMS Push, Notification Center (NC), and Push Core, on the device side. As one of the components built into EMUI, Push Core is crucial to Push Kit functions and will thus be used to refer to the device-side Push.

4. Push SDK: integrates Push Kit into your app.

A seamless channel links the Push Kit server with Push Core. Messages pushed from the cloud are sent to devices through this channel, securely and without delay. Push Kit uses a push token to uniquely identify an app on a device, ensuring that you reach desired users to boost engagement.

Figure 6.2 shows how Push Kit works; the numbers represent the key steps for pushing messages:

Steps 1–4 refer to the process of applying for a push token. When your app is launched, it calls the Push SDK to obtain a push token. The Push Kit server then returns the allocated push token to your app. In step 5, your app uploads the push token to your server for the message sent in step 10.

Steps 6–9 refer to the topic subscription process, in which your app calls the Push SDK to subscribe to a topic. The Push Kit server binds the

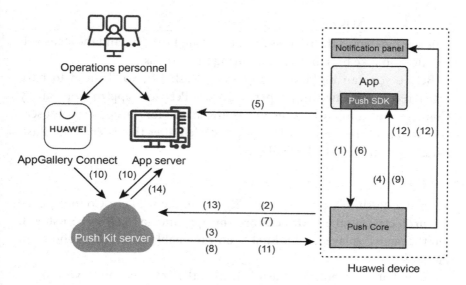

FIGURE 6.2   Message pushing via Push Kit.

topic to the push token, and then returns the subscription result to your app.

Steps 10–12 show the message pushing process. You can push messages through AppGallery Connect or your app server. After a message reaches Push Core through the Push Kit server, Push Core determines the message type. If the message is a notification, the message will appear directly in the notification panel. If instead the message is a data message, the message content is directly passed to the app through the Push SDK. We'll talk more about the two message types in Section 6.5.

Steps 13–14 outline the message receipt process, which involves your app sending the message receiving result to the Push Kit server, followed by the Push Kit server notifying your server of the result by receipt.

Now, let's move on to how to integrate and use Push Kit in the Pet Store app.

NOTE

- HMS Push checks whether your app is eligible to call Push Kit on Huawei devices.
- NC is Push Kit's central message center and displays messages received by devices.

6.2 PREPARATIONS

This section details the process for integrating Push Kit, and the steps you will need to take both before and during the process.

Before you can build your app using Push Kit, you'll need to have registered as a Huawei developer, created a Pet Store app in AppGallery Connect, and configured a certificate fingerprint for the app and obfuscation scripts of the demo project. All that's left after that is enabling Push Kit and integrating the Push SDK.

6.2.1 Enabling Push Kit

To enable Push Kit, do as follows: Sign in to AppGallery Connect, click **My projects**, find the **HMSPetStoreApp** app, and go to **Grow > Push Kit**. On the page displayed, click **Enable now** to enable Push Kit, as shown in Figure 6.3.

Now that we've enabled Push Kit, click the **Settings** tab to view other services, such as **App receipt**, which will be detailed in Section 6.7. For more about **Receive uplink message** and **Configure other Android-based push**, please refer to the development documentation on the HUAWEI Developers website. Figure 6.4 shows the page after Push Kit has been enabled.

FIGURE 6.3   Enabling Push Kit.

FIGURE 6.4   Settings page.

6.2.2 Integrating the Push SDK

To do this, download the **agconnect-services.json** file for your app from AppGallery Connect and save it to the **app** directory of your project in Android Studio. For detailed steps, please refer to previous chapters. Then, continue to configure the dependency on the Push SDK: open the **build. gradle** file in the **app** directory, and add the following to the **dependencies** block, where **{version}** indicates the Push SDK version number:

```
implementation 'com.huawei.hms:push:{version}'
```

You need to obtain the latest version number from the development documentation on the HUAWEI Developers website. Here, we'll use version number 4.0.1.300 in our sample to complete integration.

```
dependencies {
  implementation fileTree(dir: 'libs', include: ['*.
jar'])
  implementation 'androidx.appcompat:appcompat:1.1.0'
  // Configurations partially omitted for brevity.
...
  // Configure the dependency on the Push SDK.
  implementation 'com.huawei.hms:push:4.0.1.300'
}
```

Click **Sync Now** in the upper right corner of Android Studio and wait for the synchronization to complete. So far, we've completed all preparations and can start developing desired functions.

6.3 OBTAINING A PUSH TOKEN

This token is a key for Push Kit to accurately reach users, and it uniquely identifies an app on a device. Push Kit uses the push token to accurately push messages from the cloud to each device. Similar to an express delivery, the push token is like the recipient's address for a delivered package. The following details the process for requesting and receiving a push token.

6.3.1 Requesting a Push Token

Figure 6.5 shows the process of requesting a push token, where the steps for receiving the push token are represented by dotted lines.

The four steps involved are:

1. When a user launches the Pet Store app, the Push SDK sends a token request to Push Core.

2. After the authentication module verifies the certificate fingerprint of the app, Push Core sends a token request to the Push Kit server.

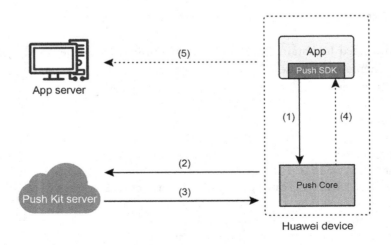

FIGURE 6.5 Process of requesting a push token.

3. The Push Kit server generates a token and sends it to Push Core.

4. Push Core saves the token and app package name to the **SharedPreferences** file (to return results directly when the app requests the token next time) and passes the token to the app.

Next, let's learn how to receive a push token.

6.3.2 Receiving the Push Token

An app that has an app server can report the push token to the app server after receiving it. When a message needs to be pushed, the app server can specify the push token and push the message to users through an API provided by the Push Kit server.

Figure 6.6 shows the process of receiving a push token, where the steps for requesting the push token are represented by dotted lines.

There are two steps associated with this, which are:

1. Push Core sends the token it has received from the Push Kit server to the Push SDK, which then passes it to the app.

2. After receiving the push token, the Pet Store app uploads it to the app server so that messages can be pushed to users through the app server.

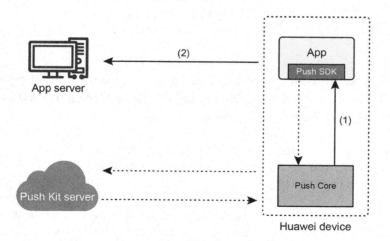

FIGURE 6.6   Process of receiving a push token.

In step 1, the Push SDK receives the push token in either of the following ways:

For EMUI 10.0 or later: Your app directly calls the **getToken** method provided by the Push SDK to obtain the token.

For earlier EMUI versions: Your app inherits the **HmsMessageService** class provided by the Push SDK and overrides the **onNewToken** method to obtain the token. In this method, when Push Core obtains the token, the **onNewToken** method is triggered to report the token to the Push SDK.

During coding, you can use both methods to cater to devices running different EMUI versions. However it's important to note that in some cases, the return value of a **getToken** request is empty. You'll want to take actions to determine how such values are processed to prevent exceptions.

6.3.3 Coding Practice

Your app can only push messages to users after it has obtained a push token. To obtain one, initiate the token request during app building, using the **onCreate** method of **MainAct.java** for the app's home screen. In the sample code, call the initialization method in **MainAct.java** and initiate a token obtaining request.

```
@Override
protected void onCreate(Bundle savedInstanceState) {
  super.onCreate(savedInstanceState);
  setContentView(R.layout.activity_main);
  // Call the initialization method.
  PushService.init(MainActivity.this);
}
```

To make the code simple and clear, add the code for interacting with the Push SDK to **PushService.java**, and call the **getToken** method in the **init** method of **PushService.java**.

```
public static void init(final Context context) {
  // Initiate a token obtaining request.
getToken(context);
  }
private static void getToken(final Context context){
  // Start the sub-thread to execute the task because
this process takes a long time.
```

```
new Thread() {
  @Override
  public void run() {
    // You may fail to obtain a token when calling
getToken. For example, this could happen if you do not
set the certificate fingerprint in AppGallery Connect.
    // Error code 6003 is returned, indicating an
ApiException exception. The error information is
stored in message of the exception.
    try {
      // Read the app_id field from the agconnect-
services.json file in the app directory to verify the
app certificate fingerprint.
      String appId = AGConnectServicesConfig.
fromContext(context).getString("client/app_id");
      String pushToken = HmsInstanceId.getInstance(-
context).getToken(appId, "HCM");
      // pushToken may be empty. In this case, the push
token is passed to the app by the Push SDK through the
Token parameter of the overridden onNewToken method.
      if(!TextUtils.isEmpty(pushToken)) {
        // For devices running EMUI 10.0 or later,
pushToken is not empty.
        // Log the obtained push token.
        Log.i(TAG, "Push Token:" + pushToken);
        // Upload the token to the app server.
        uploadToken(pushToken);
      }
    } catch (Exception e) {
      Log.e(TAG,"getToken failed, Exception: " +
e.toString());
    }
  }
}.start();
}
```

We've now obtained the token. In Section 6.3.2, we learned the two methods for receiving the push token. When developing your app, apply both methods as needed. For devices running EMUI 10.0 or later, use the same code shown earlier to request the token through the **getToken** method above.

For devices running a version of EMUI earlier than 10.0, because Push Core passes the push token to the Push SDK via services, you'll need to create a service that inherits **HmsMessageService** from the Push SDK. Here we've named the service **PushService**.

```
public class PushService extends HmsMessageService {
  private static final String TAG = "HmsPetStore";
  @Override
  public void onNewToken(String pushToken) {
    // For devices running EMUI earlier than 10.0, log
the obtained token if pushToken is not empty.
    Log.i(TAG, "Push Token:" + pushToken);
    // Upload the token to the app server.
    uploadToken(pushToken);
  }
}
```

Declare the **PushService** class in the **AndroidManifest.xml** file.

```
<service
  android:name=".PushService"
  android:exported="false">
  <intent-filter>
    <action android:name="com.huawei.push.action.
MESSAGING_EVENT" />
  </intent-filter>
</service>
```

Thus far, we've learned how to code the key part for obtaining a push token in Push Kit. Next, let's try installing the Pet Store app on a mobile phone and testing the message push function in AppGallery Connect.

6.3.4 Quick Testing

Push Kit supports two types of messages, which differ with regard to what happens once they are pushed to a device: Notification messages are displayed directly in the notification panel by Push Core. The app is not involved in this process, and thus less power is consumed. Data messages are forwarded to the app by Push Core, and the app needs to process the messages. Here, we'll quick-test a notification message:

1. You can build a Pet Store app in Android Studio and debug it. In the preceding code, the push token obtained during app launch is recorded in logs. You'll need to save the push token to test the message push function, as shown in Figure 6.7.

2. Sign in to AppGallery Connect and go to the **Add notification** page for the Pet Store app, as shown in Figure 6.8.

3. On the **Add notification** page, create a test message. Click the **Notification message** option for the message type, set parameters, and click **Test effect**. Then, enter the push token saved in step 1 in the **Token** text box, and click **OK** to push the test message, as shown in Figure 6.9.

The device will receive the push message and display it in the notification panel, as shown in Figure 6.10.

Now that we've successfully sent a notification message, let's learn how to subscribe to a push topic through Push Kit and obtain timely updates.

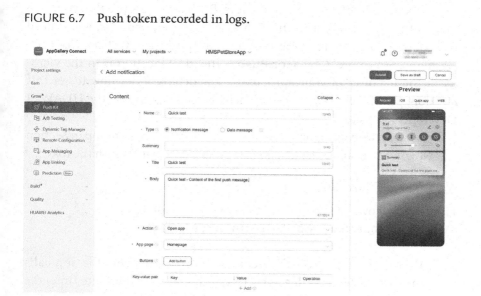

FIGURE 6.7   Push token recorded in logs.

FIGURE 6.8   Add notification page.

FIGURE 6.9   Pushing a test message.

6.4 SUBSCRIBING TO A TOPIC

A push topic is an identifier that you have predefined for the purpose of accurately distinguishing app audiences. Push topics ensure that your app pushes the right content to the right users. To perform this, you'll need to choose a data storage location for your app in AppGallery Connect: Germany, Singapore, China, or Russia. The ideal location is in the vicinity of the majority of your app's users. For details about how to set this location, please refer to the development documentation on the HUAWEI Developers website.

Previously, we had applied for a push token for the Pet Store app in Section 6.2. Now, we will subscribe to a push topic and associate it with the token.

6.4.1 Service Process

Figure 6.11 shows the process of subscribing to a topic.

There are four steps associated with this, which are:

1. When a user browses different contents in your app, the app calls the Push SDK to send a subscription request. At the same time, the app registers the **onComplete** callback for receiving the subscription result. The Push SDK sends a subscription request to Push Core.

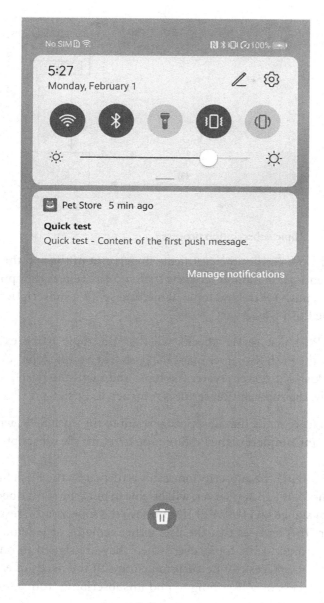

FIGURE 6.10   Test message displayed on a device.

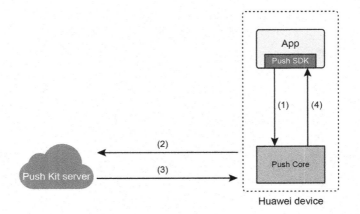

FIGURE 6.11   Topic subscription process.

2. Push Core verifies the certificate fingerprint of the app through the authentication module, collects such information as the app package name, push token, and topic name, and sends a subscription request to the Push Kit server.

3. The Push Kit server checks whether the topic name exists. If it does, the Push Kit server maps the push token to the topic. Otherwise, the Push Kit server creates the topic and maps the push token to it. Lastly, the subscription result is returned to Push Core.

4. Push Core sends the subscription result to the Push SDK, which calls back **onComplete** of the Pet Store app to return the subscription result.

After receiving the subscription result returned by the Push SDK, your app, if armed with an app server, will be able to bind the subscribed topic to the current signed-in HUAWEI ID and save the subscription result on the app server. This ensures that the user either remains or is removed from being subscribed to the topic, even when they are signed in on another device. Other services can be customized to suit the needs of each usage case. The process of subscribing to and unsubscribing from a topic is the same. Now let's practice coding for this process.

6.4.2 Coding Practice

We'll continue to implement the topic subscription function in **Push Service.java**, including initiating topic subscription and then listening to and processing the subscription result.

```
public static void subscribe(final Context context,
final String topic) {
  // Check for repeated subscription. If a topic has
already been subscribed to, the process is terminated.
  if (isSubscribed(context, topic)) {
    return;
  }
  // Create a sub-thread separately to prevent
application not responding (ANR) when the main thread
is called.
  new Thread() {
    @Override
    public void run() {
    // An exception may occur during the subscription.
In this case, capture the exception for fault
locating.
      try {
      // Subscribe to a topic, add a listener, and
implement the OnComplete callback method.
        HmsMessaging.getInstance(context).subscribe(-
topic).addOnCompleteListener
        (new OnCompleteListener<Void>() {
          @Override
          public void onComplete(Task<Void> task) {
            boolean isSuccessful = task.isSuccessful();
            Log.i(TAG, "subscribe " + topic +
(isSuccessful ? "success" :
              "failed, Exception: " + task.getException().
toString())));
            // Persist the subscribed topic.
            if (isSuccessful) {
              PushSharedPreferences.saveTopic(context,
topic);
            }
          }
        });
      } catch (Exception e) {
        Log.e(TAG, "subscribe " +
          topic + " failed, Exception: " + e.toString());
      }
    }
```

```
}.start();
}
```

Here, a topic subscription will be triggered when a user touches **Videos** or **Directory**, or purchases a membership.

Figure 6.12 shows the app screen. When a user touches **Directory**, the PetStore topic subscription is triggered.

```
// Add a listener for the button and implement the
OnClick method.
findViewById(R.id.main_petStore).setOnClick
  Listener(new View.OnClickListener() {
  @Override
  public void onClick(View v) {
  // Trigger a subscription if the user has signed
in and touched the button.
    if (LoginUtil.isLogin(MainAct.this)) {
    // Call the Subscribe method to subscribe to the
Pet Store topic.
      PushService.subscribe(MainAct.
        this, PushConst.TOPIC_STORE);
    }
    // Trigger redirection regardless of whether the
subscription is successful.
    if (LoginUtil.loginCheck(MainAct.this)) {
      startActivity(new Intent(MainAct.this,
PetStoreSearchActivity.class));
    }
  }
});
```

When a user touches **Videos**, the PetVideo topic subscription is triggered.

```
findViewById(R.id.main_petVideo).setOnClickListener(-
new View.OnClickListener() {
  @Override
  public void onClick(View v) {
    // Check whether the user has signed in.
    if (LoginUtil.isLogin(MainAct.this)) {
      // Subscribe to the PetVideo topic.
```

Videos

Directory

 Mr Smith's Pet Store
1000 m

FIGURE 6.12   Pet Store app home screen.

```
    PushService.subscribe(MainAct.this, PushConst.
TOPIC_VEDIO);
    }
    if (LoginUtil.loginCheck(MainAct.this)) {
    startActivity(new Intent(MainAct.this,
PetVideoAct.class));
    }
  }
});
```

When a user successfully purchases a membership, the VIP topic subscription is triggered.

```
// The membership is successfully purchased.
if (buyResultInfo.getReturnCode() == OrderStatusCode.
ORDER_STATE_SUCCESS) {
  // Subscribe to the VIP topic.
  PushService.subscribe(getApplicationContext(),
PushConst.TOPIC_VIP);
  PurchasesOperation.deliverProduct(this,
buyResultInfo.getInAppPurchaseData(),
    buyResultInfo.getInAppDataSignature());
  return;
}
```

You can configure up to 2000 topics for an app, so it's extremely important to exercise judgment when planning them. So far, we have practiced coding for topic subscription and are ready for the subsequent topic-based message pushing.

We previously checked user sign-in status. The topic subscription is only triggered by user sign-in. Therefore, these topics are bound to the signed-in HUAWEI ID. When the user signs out, these topics need to be unsubscribed from.

The following provides the code for unsubscribing from a topic in **PushService.java**:

```
public static void unsubscribe(final Context context,
final String topic) {
  new Thread() {
```

```
    @Override
    public void run() {
      try {
      // Unsubscribe from a topic, add a listener, and
implement the OnComplete callback method.
        HmsMessaging.getInstance(context).unsubscribe(-
topic).addOnComplete
        Listener(new OnCompleteListener<Void>() {
          @Override
          public void onComplete(Task<Void> task) {
          // Log whether the unsubscription is
successful.
            Log.i(TAG, "unsubscribe " + topic + (task.
isSuccessful() ?
              "success" : "failed, Exception: " + task.
              getException().toString()));
            }
          });
      } catch (Exception e) {
        Log.e(TAG, "unsubscribe " + topic + " failed,
Exception: " +
          e.toString());
        }
      }
    }.start();
}
```

When the user signs out, the app reads the user's subscribed topics and initiates a topic unsubscription request.

```
private void onExitLogin() {
  SPUtil.put(this, SPConstants.KEY_LOGIN, false);
  SPUtil.put(this, SPConstants.KEY_PASSWORD, "");
  // Clear the push data after the user signs out.
  pushClear();
  finish();
}

private void pushClear() {
  Context context = getApplicationContext();
```

```
Map<String, String> topics = PushSharedPreferences.
readTopic(context);
  for (String topic : topics.keySet()) {
   // Unsubscribe from all topics.
    PushService.unsubscribe(context, topic);
  }
  // Clear all locally saved topics.
  PushSharedPreferences.clearTopic(context);
  // Clear all locally stored in-app messages.
  PushSharedPreferences.clearMessage(context);
  // Toggle on the push message switch.
  PushSharedPreferences.saveConfig(context, PushConst.
PUSH_MESSAGE_SWITCH, String.
   valueOf(true));
  PushService.turnOnOff(context, true);
}
```

6.5 PUSHING MESSAGES IN APPGALLERY CONNECT

In this section, we'll learn how to use AppGallery Connect to push topic-based messages. As mentioned earlier, Push Kit offers two message types: notification messages and data messages. To help illustrate the differences between them, we'll construct both message types for different topics and push them to the notification panel and the app.

6.5.1 Pushing Notification Messages

When pushing a topic-based notification message in AppGallery Connect, your app is not involved in the process prior to displaying the message. The home screen or an in-app screen will only appear when the user has touched the message or an enclosed button. This process does not require any coding, and thus is less intensive.

The three message display types:

- Open an app: displays the home screen or an in-app screen.

- Open a web page: displays a page specified by a URL in the message.

- Open rich media: displays a static image carried in the message.

Figure 6.13 shows the process of pushing a notification message.

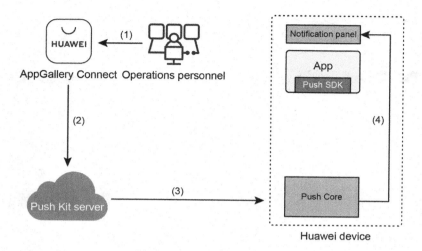

FIGURE 6.13 Process of pushing a notification message.

There are four steps associated with this, which are:

1. Let's suppose that we have added a new product under the PetStore topic. In AppGallery Connect, click **My projects**, click the Pet Store app, go to **Grow > Push Kit** and click **Add notification**, and then create a push message and click **Submit**. Creating the message involves setting **Push scope** to **Subscriber** and **Action** to **Open app**, and selecting **PetStore** from the topic list.

2. AppGallery Connect pushes the message to the Push Kit server.

3. The Push Kit server then searches for all push tokens bound to the topic by topic name and pushes the message to Push Core sequentially by push token.

4. After receiving the message, Push Core determines that it is a notification message and displays it in the notification panel. The user touches the message in the notification panel to trigger the action configured in step 1.

Figures 6.14 and 6.15 show the push notification settings in AppGallery Connect. Figure 6.14 shows how to set the name, title, and content of a notification message, while Figure 6.15 shows how to set the push scope and time.

Figure 6.16 shows the notification message displayed on a device.

FIGURE 6.14 Setting the name, title, and content of a notification message.

FIGURE 6.15 Setting the push scope and time.

FIGURE 6.16   Displaying a notification message on a device.

6.5.2 Pushing Data Messages

We've learned how to push a topic-based notification message in AppGallery Connect. Now, let's move on to how to push topic-based data messages in AppGallery Connect. In this case, Push Kit only serves as the message channel, so we'll need to complete a series of actions, such as parsing, display, and service logic after the message arrives at the app. Doing this provides you with greater flexibility for service implementation and customization, especially for in-depth convergence between the data messages and the app service data and logic.

Figure 6.17 shows the process of pushing a data message.

1. To initiate a promotional activity for users who have subscribed to the VIP topic, sign in to AppGallery Connect, click **My projects**, click the Pet Store app, go to **Grow > Push Kit**, click **Add notification** to go to the message push page, and then select **Data message**.

2. AppGallery Connect pushes the message to the Push Kit server.

3. The Push Kit server searches for all push tokens bound to the topic name **VIP** and pushes the message to Push Core sequentially by push token.

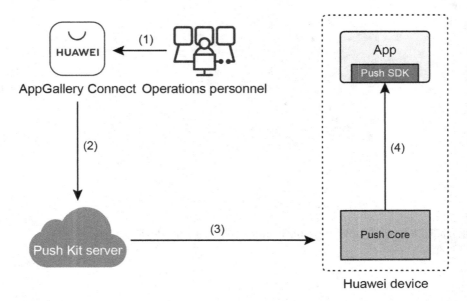

FIGURE 6.17   Process of pushing a data message.

4. After receiving the message, Push Core determines that the message is a data message and sends the message to the app.

The app parses message parameters, determines that the user is a monthly member, and displays the message in its message center.

Let's add a three-month promotional activity for monthly members. This will enable us to push messages to encourage such users to renew their membership.

To configure a monthly member preference activity on the **Operate** page of the Pet Store app in AppGallery Connect:

1. Go to the product management page of the Pet Store app and click **Edit** for the monthly membership product, as shown in Figure 6.18.

2. On the **Edit Product** page, click **View and edit**, as shown in Figure 6.19.

3. On the **Monthly Member - Product price** page, click **Promotional pricing**, as shown in Figure 6.20.

4. On the **Promotional pricing** page, click **Add price promotion**, as shown in Figure 6.21.

5. On the **Promotional pricing** page, set **Promotion name**, **Start time**, and **End time**, and click **Next**, as shown in Figure 6.22.

6. Set the countries/regions that will enjoy access to the promotion, as indicated in Figure 6.23.

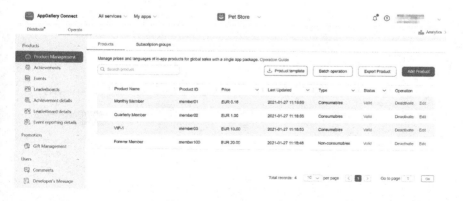

FIGURE 6.18   Product management.

FIGURE 6.19   Editing the monthly membership product.

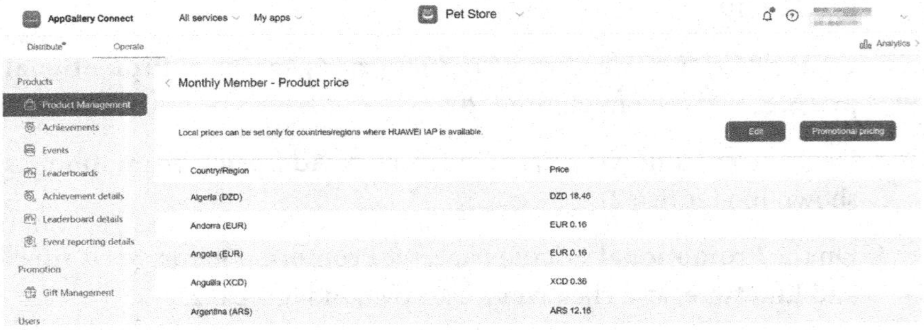

FIGURE 6.20   Price page.

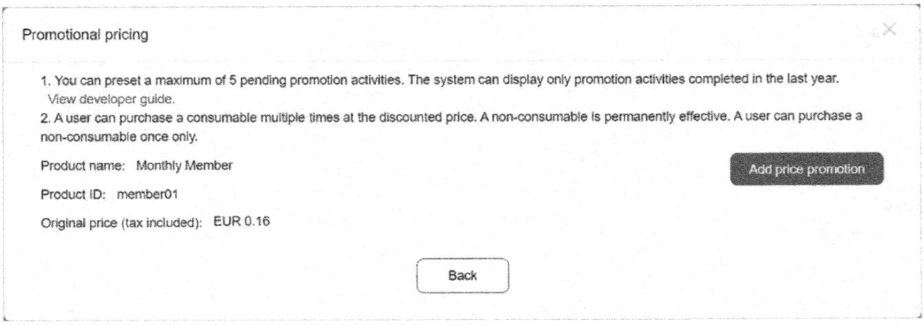

FIGURE 6.21   Setting a promotional price.

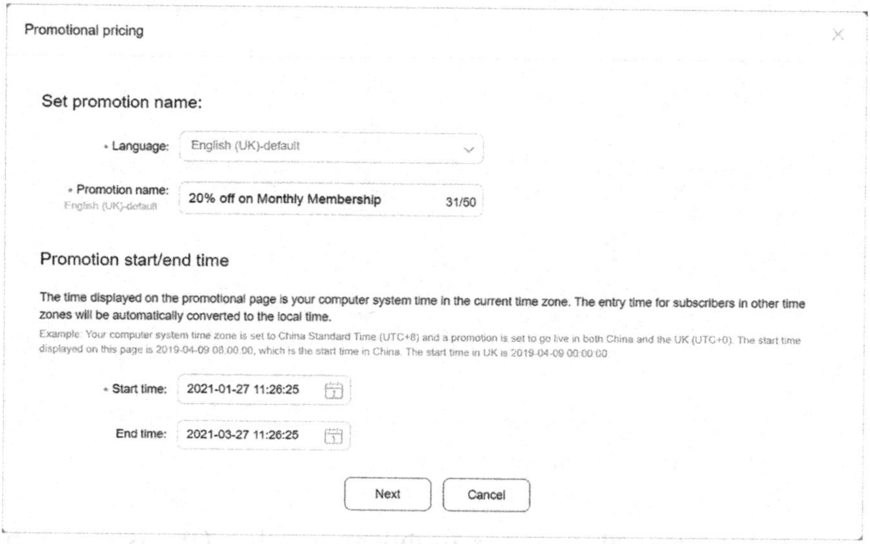

FIGURE 6.22   Configuring promotion information.

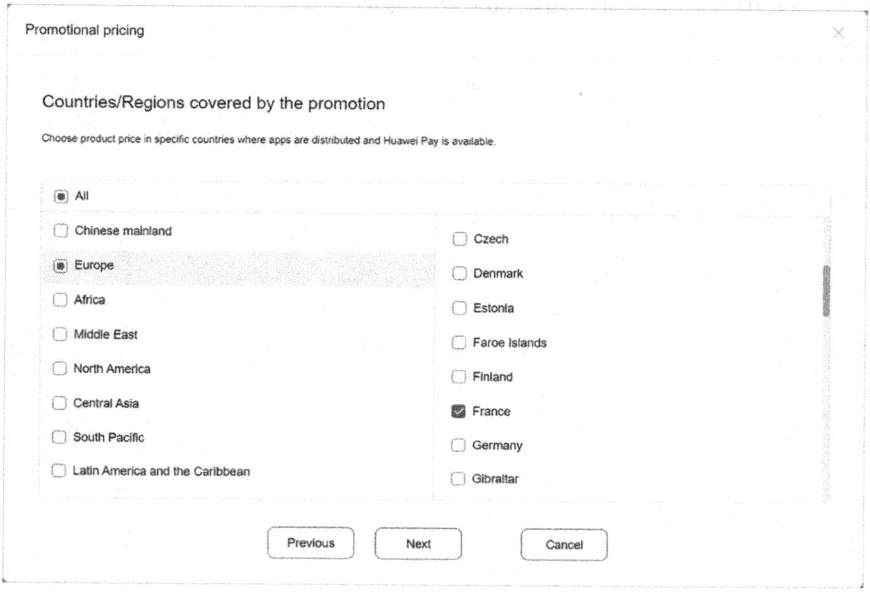

FIGURE 6.23   Setting countries/regions for the promotion.

Promotional pricing   ×

Promotional price for target countries/regions

You can set different promotional prices for different countries/regions. All promotional prices must be lower than the original price.

Default price (tax   EUR 0.13   Convert prices
included):

• Pinned country/region: Europe   ⌄

Local prices can be set only for countries/regions where HUAWEI IAP is available.

You can manually change the promotional price for a country/region, which will be applied in the promotion.

Country/Region	Original price (tax included)	Promotional price (tax included)
France(FR)	EUR 0.16	EUR 0.13

[Previous]   [OK]   [Cancel]

FIGURE 6.24   Setting a promotional price.

7. Set **Promotional price (tax included)** and click **OK**, as shown in Figure 6.24.

So far, we've configured our promotion for monthly members. On the push page of AppGallery Connect, we can push this promotion to them by using a data message, as illustrated in Figure 6.25.

FIGURE 6.25   Setting a data message in AppGallery Connect.

In Figure 6.25, the key in the added key-value pair will need to match the key defined in the code, in order for the app to receive data messages. The code for the app client to parse message parameters is as follows:

```
@Override
public void onMessageReceived(RemoteMessage message) {
  // Override the method for receiving data messages.
  Context context = getApplicationContext();
  Map<String, String> data = message.getDataOfMap();

  // If the user type does not meet the requirement,
discard the message.
  if (data.containsKey(MESSAGE_FILTER_VIP)) {
    if (!getUserType().equals(data.get(MESSAGE_FILTER_
VIP))) {
      return;
    }
  }
  // Write the message to a local file and display all
messages when the user browses the message center in
the app.
  PushSharedPreferences.saveMessage(context, data.
get("title"), data.get("content"));
}
```

When a data message reaches the app, it is displayed in the app's message center, as shown in Figure 6.26.

6.6 PUSHING MESSAGES VIA THE APP SERVER

In this section, we'll learn how to push messages via the app server. The following outlines the process by which the app server pushes messages through APIs on the Push Kit server.

In Section 6.3, we uploaded the push token of our Pet Store app to the app server. Now, we'll use it as an example to illustrate how to push messages via the app server.

6.6.1 Service Process

Calling APIs of the Push Kit server makes message pushing more flexible. Figure 6.27 shows the message push via the app server.

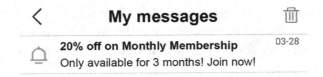

FIGURE 6.26 Displaying a data message in the app's message center.

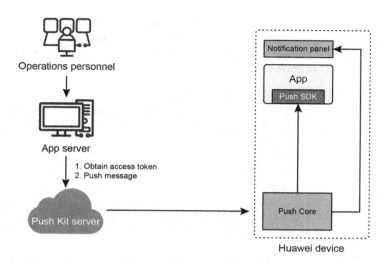

FIGURE 6.27 Pushing a message via the app server.

The app server carries the app ID and app secret to apply for an access token from the Push Kit server, and then uses the token as the authorization credential, in order to use the push token reported by the app (described in Section 6.3.2) to construct a push message. The app server pushes the message to the Push Kit server using the same process as that of pushing a message in AppGallery Connect.

6.6.2 Coding Practice

As mentioned above, we'll need to complete two steps to push messages via the app server.

1. Apply for an access token.

   The app server uses an HTTPS API to apply to the Huawei OAuth server for an access token. The code for constructing the request is as follows:

```
public static String getAccessToken(String appId, String
appSecret) {
  // Construct a message template.
RestTemplate restTemplate = new RestTemplate();
  StringBuilder params = new StringBuilder();
  // Assemble the message. The methods of obtaining
client _ id and client _ secret have been described in
Section 4.3.3.
```

```
params.append("grant _ type=client _ credentials");
params.append("&client _ id=").append(appId);
params.append("&client _ secret=").append(appSecret);
String response = null;
try {
// Send a request to the Huawei OAuth server.
response = restTemplate.postForObject(new URI("https://
oauth-login.cloud.huawei.com/oauth2/v2/token"),   params.
toString(),
    String.class);
} catch (Exception e) {
  Log.catching(e);
}
if (!StringUtils.isEmpty(response)) {
// Obtain the return value and use it to extract the
access token.
JSONObject   jsonObject   =   JSONObject.parseObject
(response);
    return         jsonObject.getString("access _ token").
replace("\\", "");
}
return "";
}
```

Here is a sample constructed request:

```
POST /oauth2/v2/token HTTP/1.1
Host: oauth-login.cloud.huawei.com
Content-Type: application/x-www-form-urlencoded
grant _ type=client _ credentials&client _
id=101778417&client _ secret=79d84ac5ac404a880945430500e2
05a683b5b494fa3df03cf33aefd12e693da9
```

In this example, **client_id** and **client_secret** are the app ID and app secret, respectively. You can obtain their values from the app information in AppGallery Connect, as shown in Figure 6.28.

The response packet of the Huawei OAuth server carries the allocated access token and its validity period (in seconds). The following is an example of a response packet:

```
HTTP/1.1 200 OK
Content-Type: text/html;charset=UTF-8
{"access _ token":"CFyJ7eTl8WIPi9603E7Ro9Icy+K0JYe2qVjS8u
zwCPltlO0fC7mZ0gzZX9p8CCwAaiU17nyP+N8+ORRzjjk1EA==","ex
pires _ in":3600,"token _ type":"Bearer"}
```

FIGURE 6.28   App information.

A backslash (\) in an access token is invalid for authentication. Therefore, we'll want to remove it from the access token, if it's there, to avoid an "Access token expired" error (code: 80200003).

2. Push a message.

After obtaining the access token, the app server constructs a push request packet and sends it to the Push Kit server. These are the types of messages initiated by the app server:

− Push token-based notification messages

− Topic-based notification messages

− Topic-based data messages

For other types of push messages (such as data messages based on the push token), please refer to the development documentation on the HUAWEI Developers website. You can mix and match different message types to suit your needs.

(1) Push token-based notification message

The code for constructing a push token-based notification message is shown below. For details about each field, please refer to the *API Reference* on the HUAWEI Developers website.

```
private JSONObject constructPushMsg(String request) {
    // Construct the message body.
    JSONObject message = new JSONObject();
    // Construct the notification message content.
    message.put("notification", getNotification(request));
    // Android message push control parameters.
    message.put("android", getAndroidPart());
    // Target tokens for message push.
```

```java
    message.put("token", tokens);
    JSONObject pushMsg = new JSONObject();
    // Indicates whether the message is a test message.
The default value is false.
    pushMsg.put("validate _ only", false);
    pushMsg.put("message", message);
    return pushMsg;
}

private JSONObject getNotification(String request) {
    JSONObject notification = new JSONObject();
    // Set request to the message, in which & is used
to separate the title from the content.
    String[] message = request.split("&");
    // Title of the notification message.
    notification.put("title", message[0]);
    // Content of the notification message.
    notification.put("body", message[1]);
    return notification;
}

private JSONObject getAndroidPart() {
    JSONObject android = new JSONObject();
    // Identifier of a message in a batch delivery
task. The identifier is returned to the app server
in a message receipt. The app server can analyze
message delivery statistics by bi _ tag.
    android.put("bi _ tag","pushReceipt");
    android.put("notification", getAnroidNotification());
    return android;
}

private JSONObject getAnroidNotification() {
    JSONObject clickAction = new JSONObject();
    // The Pet Store app details screen is displayed
after a user touches the notification.
    clickAction.put("type",  CLICK _ ACTION _ OPEN _ App _
PAGE);
    // Action of the activity for opening a custom app
screen.
    clickAction.put("action",    "com.huawei.hmspetstore.
OPEN _ PETSTORE");
    JSONObject androidNotification = new JSONObject();
    androidNotification.put("click _ action",
clickAction);
    return androidNotification;
}
```

The code for pushing a message is as follows:

```
public    static    JSONObject    sendPushMessage(String
appId, String appSecret, JSONObject
  messageBody) {
  RestTemplate restTemplate = new RestTemplate();
  HttpHeaders headers = new HttpHeaders();
  JSONObject    accessToken    =    getAccessToken(appId,
appSecret);
  // Replace invalid characters in the access token.
  headers.setBearerAuth(accessToken.getString
("access _ token").replace("\\", ""));
  String response = null;
  HttpEntity<Object>          httpEntity          =          new
HttpEntity<Object>(messageBody, headers);
  try {
    String uri = "https:// push-api.cloud.huawei.
com/v1/[appid]/messages:send".
      replace("[appid]", appId);
    response = restTemplate.postForObject(new URI(-
uri), httpEntity, String.
      class);
  } catch (Exception e) {
    Log.catching(e);
  }
  JSONObject jsonObject = null;
  if (!StringUtils.isEmpty(response)) {
    jsonObject = JSONObject.parseObject(response);
  }
  return jsonObject;
}
```

Now that we've learned the code used to construct the message body and obtain the access token, let's look at the code for the sending process:

```
public JSONObject processSendPush(String request) {
  // Call constructPushMsg -to construct a push mes-
sage, where request is set to the message received
by the app server; & is used to separate the title
from the content.
  JSONObject pushMsg = constructPushMsg(request);
  // Call sendPushMessage to send a message to the
Push Kit server.
  return  HttpsUtil.sendPushMessage(App _ ID,  App _
SECRET, pushMsg);
}
```

The constructed request packet is as follows:

```
POST /v1/101778417/messages:send HTTP/1.1
Host: push-api.cloud.huawei.com
Authorization:  Bearer  CF3X12XV6jMKZgqYSZFws9IPlgDvx
qOfFSmrlmtkTRupbU2VklvhX9kC
  9JCnKVSDX2VrDgAPuzvNm3WccUIaDg==
Content-Type: application/json
{
  "validate _ only":false,
  "message":{
    "notification":{
      "title":"Newest pet products",
      "body":"Come  and  have  a  look!  (Notification
message)"
    },
    "android": {
      "notification": {
        "click _ action": {
        "type": 1,
        "action": "com.huawei.hmspetstore.OPEN _ PETSTORE"
        }
      }
        "bi _ tag":"pushReceipt"
      },
      "token":[

        "ABvGXK23N4PQZa-5vLguUNAuw4C2HzhOftO3iNNm
TX _ ikhWZBH7JV91o5LgYzdX0b0x7ERl
        xjGdLNx5iFUHy74nv4I1zDkQLb4VMZD _ 5yLhrZAz9YjNk
EGxRgTanCS _ pQQ"
      ]
    }
}
```

(2) Topic-based notification message

The code for constructing and sending a topic-based notification message is as follows:

```
public JSONObject processSendTopic(String topic) {
  JSONObject pushMsg = constructTopicMsg(topic);
  return  HttpsUtil.sendPushMessage(App _ ID,  App _
SECRET, pushMsg);
}

private JSONObject constructTopicMsg(String topic) {
  JSONObject message = new JSONObject();
```

```
    // Add a topic-based
message   to   distin-
guish message effects.
   message.
put("notification",
getNotification
("Newest pet prod-
ucts! &Come and
have a look! (Topic
message)"));
```

```
    message.put("android", getAndroidPart());
    // Unlike the token-based push mode, the push mode
is topic here.
    message.put("topic", topic);
    JSONObject pushMsg = new JSONObject();
    pushMsg.put("validate _ only", false);
    pushMsg.put("message", message);
    return pushMsg;
}
```

The constructed request packet is as follows:

```
POST /v1/101778417/messages:send HTTP/1.1
Host: push-api.cloud.huawei.com
Authorization:  Bearer  CF3X12XV6jMKZgqYSZFws9IPlgDvxq
OfFSmrlmtkTRupbU2VklvhX9kC
   9JCnKVSDX2VrDgAPuzvNm3WccUIaDg==
Content-Type: application/json
{
  "validate _ only":false,
  "message":{
  "notification":{
    "title":"Newest pet products",
    "body":"Come and have a look! (Topic message)"
  },
  "android": {
    "notification": {
      "click _ action": {
        "type": 1,
        "action": "com.huawei.hmspetstore.OPEN _ PETSTORE"
      }
    }
      "bi _ tag":"pushReceipt"
    },
    "topic":"PetStore"
  }
}
```

Note that the topic name used on the app client must be the same as that used on the app server.

(3) Topic-based data message

The code for constructing and sending a topic-based data message is as follows:

```
public    JSONObject    processSendDataMessage(String
request) {
    // request: message content received by the app
server, which is a JSON string.
    JSONObject pushMsg = constructDataMsg(request);
    return HttpsUtil.sendPushMessage(App _ ID, App _
SECRET, pushMsg);
}

private JSONObject constructDataMsg(String request)
{
  JSONObject message = new JSONObject();
  // request is directly used as the value of data.
  message.put("data", request);
  message.put("topic", "VIP");
  JSONObject pushMsg = new JSONObject();
  pushMsg.put("validate _ only", false);
  pushMsg.put("message", message);
  return pushMsg;
}
```

The constructed request packet is as follows:

```
POST /v1/101778417/messages:send HTTP/1.1
Host: push-api.cloud.huawei.com
Authorization: Bearer CF3Xl2XV6jMKZgqYSZFws9IPlgDvxq
OfFSmrlmtkTRupbU2VklvhX9kC
    9JCnKVSDX2VrDgAPuzvNm3WccUIaDg==
Content-Type: application/json
{
  "validate _ only":false,
  "message":{
  "data":"{\"title\":\"Membership    benefits    for    Pet
Store! \",\"content\":\"Come    and    have    a    look! (Data
message)\",\
    "vip\":\"normal\"}",
  "topic":"VIP"
  }
}
```

So far, we've coded pushing notification messages and data messages from the app server. For details about the APIs and fields, please refer to the *API Reference* on the HUAWEI Developers website. The following is an example response packet sent by the Push Kit server to the app server:

```
{
    // Success response code.
    "code": "80000000",
    "msg": "Success",
    "requestId": "158571052215233974008001"
}
```

In this example, **requestId** is the tracing index of the message. It is recommended that you record **requestId** in app server logs for subsequent fault locating. In addition, the response by the Push Kit server is only for the push action, and not for the arrival of the push message on devices. For details about the response when the push message reaches a device, please refer to Section 6.7. Figure 6.29 shows how a notification message appears on a screen.

Once a data message is pushed, the app receives and processes the message, and then displays the message in its message center, as shown in Figure 6.30.

We've now gone over the Java code for pushing different message types from the app server. Push Kit also gives you sample code in numerous other languages, including C#, Python, PHP, and Go. For more details, please refer to the development documentation on the HUAWEI Developers website.

6.7 RECEIVING MESSAGE RECEIPTS

The delivery rate and sending status are both crucial, and worthy of attention in message sending. Message receipts are a good way for you to keep track of how your messages are traveling.

A message receipt tells you if the message delivery result was received by the app server. After the Push Kit server pushes a message to a device, Push Core will send back the message delivery result. The Push Kit server then collates this result and sends it to the app server.

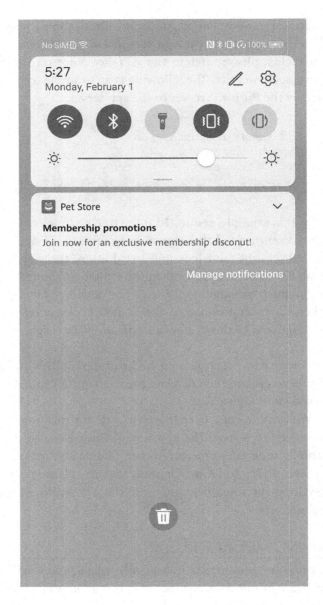

FIGURE 6.29   Notification message effects

FIGURE 6.30 Data message effects.

6.7.1 Service Process

Figure 6.31 outlines the message receipt process.

There are five steps associated with this, which are:

(1)–(3) App operations personnel push a message from the app server to the Push Kit server. The Push Kit server forwards the message to the device, which then processes and displays it.

(4)–(5) The device returns the push result to the Push Kit server, which summarizes the push result and sends the result to the app server as a receipt message.

Currently, message receipts are only available for Android apps. With message receipts, you can determine whether messages have been successfully sent and perform a wide range of operations, including data analysis and message resending, on the app server.

6.7.2 Coding Practice

This section walks you through the coding required to receive a message receipt on the app server. The steps are as follows:

1. Enable **App receipt** under **My projects** in AppGallery Connect, as shown in Figure 6.32.

2. On the receipt parameter settings page, set receipt parameters, as shown in Figure 6.33.

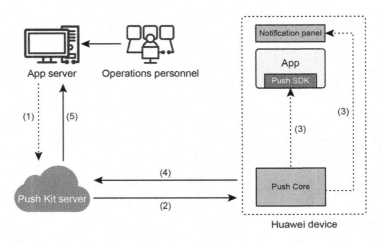

FIGURE 6.31 Message receipt process.

FIGURE 6.32   Enabling the message receipt service.

Note that the HTTPS protocol is used between the Push Kit server and the app server. The Push Kit server checks the validity of your certificate, so you'll need to use a commercial HTTPS certificate.

3. During actual coding, you'll want to make sure that the **bi_tag** field is set in the body of the message pushed by the app server. This field is the message ID of a batch task. The following is an example of the packet that contains this field:

```
{
  "validate _ only":false,
  "message":{
    "notification":{
      "title":"Newest pet products",
      "body":"Come and have a look! (Notification message)"
    },
    "android": {
      "notification": {
        "click _ action": {
          "type": 1,
          "action": "com.huawei.hmspetstore.OPEN _ PETSTORE"
        }
      },
      "bi _ tag":"pushReceipt"
    },
    "token":[
```

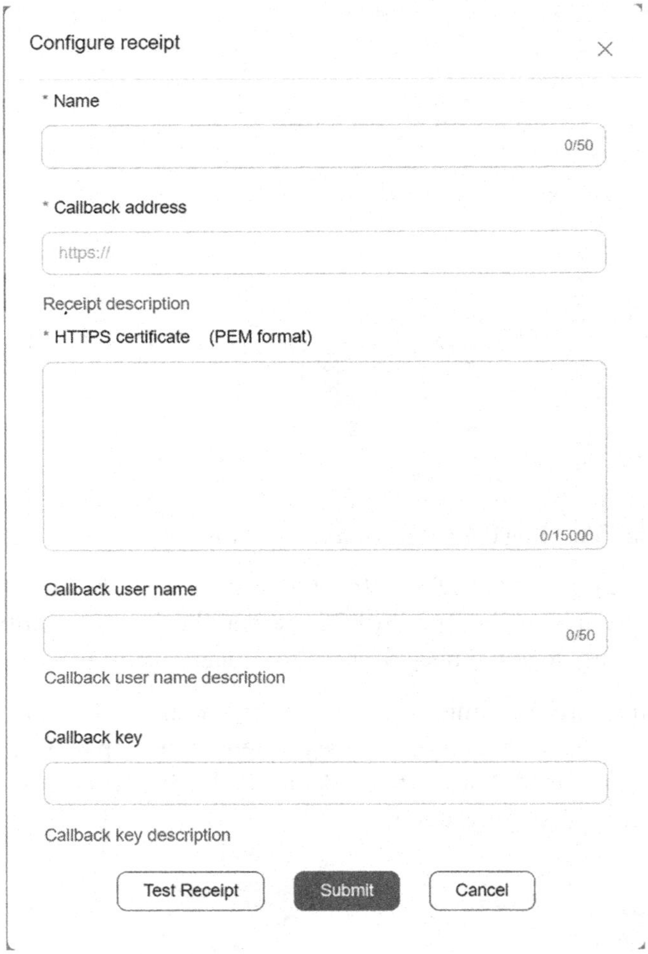

FIGURE 6.33   Setting receipt parameters.

```
        "ABvGXK23N4PQZa-5vLguUNAuw4C2HzhOftO3iNNm
TX _ ikhWZBH7JV91o5LgYzdX0b0x7ERlxjGdLNx5iFUHy74nv4I1z
DkQLb4VMZD _ 5yLhrZAz9YjNkEGxRgTanCS _ pQQ"
    ]
  }
}
```

After the Push Kit server collects the sending result from the device, it includes the **bi_tag** field in the receipt message returned to the app server. The app server identifies the field and analyzes the message delivery status. The following is an example of a receipt message sent by the Push Kit server to the app server:

```
{
  "statuses":[
    {
      "biTag":"pushReceipt",
      "requestId":"15857304718050125201030l",
      "appid":"101778417",

      "token":"ABvGXK23N4PQZa-5vLguUNAuw4C2HzhOft
O3iNNmTX _ ikhWZBH7JV91o5
        LgYzdX0b0x7ERlxjGdLNx5iFUHy74nv4I1zDkQLb4VMZD _
5yLhrZAz9YjNkEGx
          RgTanCS _ pQQ",
      "status":0,
      "timestamp":1585730472701
    }
  ]
}
```

Next, code the app server to receive receipt messages and obtain the message sending status on the device using the **biTag** and **status** fields in the receipt messages. We have now covered the message receipt function, using sample code to illustrate how the sending process works. You can reference materials on the HUAWEI Developers website to get more detailed information regarding the meaning and value of each field in the message receipt.

6.8 SUMMARY

In this chapter, you've been introduced to Push Kit, namely the preparations required for integrating the kit, as well as how to obtain the push token, subscribe to and unsubscribe from a push topic, push messages, and obtain message receipts. In the next chapter, we'll delve into Location Kit and learn how to add location-related functions to the Pet Store app.

CHAPTER 7

Location Kit

7.1 ABOUT THE SERVICE

Before integrating Location Kit, it's useful for us to learn about the functions and principles behind it. Location Kit provides four major capabilities: fused location, activity identification, geofence, and geocoding.

- Fused location: combines the GNSS, Wi-Fi, and base station location information to help your app quickly obtain the device location.

- Activity identification: detects the user activity status[1] using the cellular network and built-in sensors such as accelerometers and magnetometers, helping your app adjust its service profile accordingly.

- Geofence: provides for easy geofence creation. When a user enters, leaves, or stays within a geofence that you have set, Location Kit will send a notification to your app, so that it can perform preprogrammed actions.

- Geocoding: converts location information to a structured address or vice versa.

The overall architecture for Location Kit consists of three layers: application layer, on-device service layer, and on-cloud service layer, as shown in Figure 7.1.

DOI: 10.1201/9781003206699-7

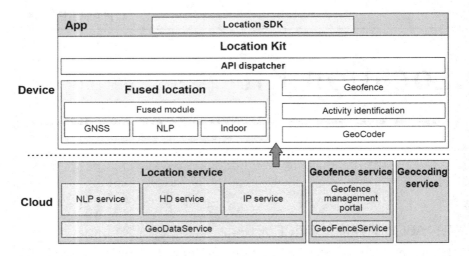

FIGURE 7.1   Overall architecture for Location Kit.

- Application layer: provides the location capabilities of Location Kit. Your app integrates the Location SDK to call various function APIs in Location Kit.

- On-device service layer: provides on-device capabilities of Location Kit, which currently include fused location, activity identification, geofence, and geocoding. Fused location supports different location methods, including the GNSS location, Network Location Provider (NLP) location, and indoor location.

- On-cloud service layer: This layer contains on-cloud capabilities provided by Location Kit, namely the location, geofence, and geocoding capabilities. The on-cloud location capabilities mainly consist of NLP location, high-precision location, IP address location, and location big data.

Fused location, activity identification, geofence, and geocoding will be detailed in later sections.

7.1.1 Fused Location

Location Kit utilizes GNSS, base station, Wi-Fi, and Bluetooth functions to provide the fused location. Location is by either GNSS or NLP methods.

1. GNSS location: calculates the device location based on location information received from navigation satellites, providing for highly responsive and accurate location services without an Internet connection. However, this method is comparatively less power-efficient and can only be used in areas with navigation satellite coverage.

2. NLP location: scans for base station and Wi-Fi signals near the device to obtain the base station ID or Wi-Fi hotspot ID, interacts with the location server to obtain the location information of the base station or Wi-Fi hotspot, and then uses the information to calculate the device location.

Location Kit also delivers an even higher degree of location precision by combining these two methods, specifically using the NLP location to calibrate the device location pinpointed via GNSS. This capability, which is accurate to 1 meter, is ideal for scenarios that require pinpoint location accuracy and is available in areas with both navigation satellite and Internet coverage.

Fused location offers five location modes.

1. Accurate (**PRIORITY_HIGH_ACCURACY**): Location Kit preferentially uses the GNSS method to locate the device. If the device is in an area without navigation satellite coverage, Location Kit will automatically switch to the NLP method to locate the device.

2. Balanced (**PRIORITY_BALANCED_POWER_ACCURACY**): Location Kit determines the optimal location method according to the remaining battery on the device. When the battery level is high, Location Kit will use the GNSS method to locate the device; otherwise, it will use the NLP method.

3. Low power consumption (**PRIORITY_LOW_POWER**): Location Kit directly uses the NLP method to locate the device.

4. Zero power consumption (**PRIORITY_NO_POWER**): Also known as passive location, Location Kit directly obtains the cached device location from HMS Core (APK), rather than requesting the device location via the GNSS or NLP methods.

5. High precision (**PRIORITY_HD_ACCURACY**): Location Kit obtains the device location via the GNSS method, and then calibrates

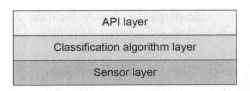

FIGURE 7.2   Principles behind activity identification.

the location using the NLP method to achieve location accuracy down to the meter. This mode is currently available only in the Chinese mainland on HUAWEI P40 series phones.

7.1.2 Activity Identification

Activity identification is a capability that utilizes the user's device to identify their activity. The architecture for activity identification in Location Kit consists of three layers, as shown in Figure 7.2.

Huawei phones collect location data using the cellular network and built-in sensors such as accelerometers and magnetometers, calculate and classify the collected data, and then call relevant APIs to obtain the user's activity status. Lastly, the Location SDK integrated into your app will call the relevant APIs to obtain your user's activity status.

7.1.3 Geofence

The geofence function enables you to encircle a specific area by setting virtual geographical boundaries. When a user device enters, leaves, or stays within this area, as determined by the fused location, your app will receive a geofence event. After your app delivers a geofence, Location Kit will query the user's device location and use it to determine whether or not to report a geofence event. If you are interested in a specific place, set it as a POI and specify a radius (R) to create a geofence, as shown in Figure 7.3. The area within the circle represents the effective area of the geofence.

Location Kit will trigger a geofence event when the user enters, leaves, or stays within the encircled area.

7.1.4 Geocoding

Location Kit offers both forward geocoding and reverse geocoding.

1. Forward geocoding: converts a structured address into specific longitude-latitude coordinates. For example, it can convert the

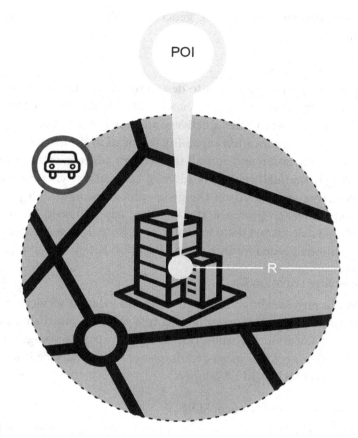

FIGURE 7.3   Creating a geofence.

structured address "101, Ruanjian Avenue, Yuhuatai District, Nanjing, Jiangsu Province, China" into the longitude-latitude coordinates "(118.777726, 31.966673)."

2. Reverse geocoding: converts specific longitude-latitude coordinates into a structured address. For example, it can convert the longitude-latitude coordinates "(116.480881, 39.989410)" into the structured address "6, Futongdong Avenue, Chaoyang District, Beijing, China."

Location Kit is able to provide these geocoding services by calling the native **Geocoder** class in Android. You can call the **getFromLocationName()** and **getFromLocation()** methods for the **Geocoder** class to call the forward and reverse geocoding services, respectively, in Location Kit.

7.2 PREPARATIONS

In Section 3.3, we've learned how to design the functions for filling in the delivery address and viewing the location details for the Pet Store app. When the user wants to enter a delivery address in the Pet Store app, the app can use the fused location capability in Location Kit to quickly obtain the user's exact location and autofill the delivery address, freeing the user from having to manually enter the address. You can also create a geofence in the Pet Store app, based on the geographical location of a pet store. When users enter the geofence, the Pet Store app will send them timely messages that help attract them to visit the pet store. This section describes the preparations needed for integrating Location Kit into your app.

7.2.1 Enabling Location Kit

Location Kit provides basic and high-precision location services. Huawei will automatically enable corresponding free plans on your behalf. To use paid APIs of Location Kit, subscribe to relevant pay-as-you-go plans in AppGallery Connect. For more details, please refer to Service Pricing and Subscription on HUAWEI Developers.

7.2.2 Integrating the Location SDK

Before integrating the Location SDK into the Pet Store app, you'll need to download the **agconnect-services.json** file for the Pet Store app from AppGallery Connect and add it to the project's **app** directory. Then, open the **build.gradle** file in the **app** directory and add the following dependency to the **dependencies** closure:

```
implementation 'com.huawei.hms:location:{version}'
```

In the snippet, *{version}* indicates the version number of the Location SDK. For the latest version, see Version Change History for Location Kit at https://developer.huawei.com/consumer/en/doc/development/HMS-Guides/versionUpdatas. The sample code is as follows:

```
dependencies {
// Integrate the Location SDK.
```

```
implementation 'com.huawei.hms:location:4.0.2.300'
}
```

7.3 DEVELOPING THE FUSED LOCATION FUNCTION

Fused location in Location Kit offers both basic and high-precision location capabilities. The high-precision location capability is accurate to the meter and is currently available only on HUAWEI P40 series phones. Support on more phone models has been planned for the near future (visit the HUAWEI Developers website to learn about the latest supported phone models). The basic location capability, which offers a relatively high degree of precision and responsiveness, is sufficient enough to meet the majority of location-related use cases. If you need to track a user in motion, you can also call the location update request API in Location Kit to continuously obtain the user's device location.

The functional design of the app requires that the user's delivery address is autofilled for them. To do this, you'll need to call the location update request API to obtain the user's location, then call the reverse geocoding capability to convert the obtained location into a structured address, and finally fill in the address as the delivery address.

7.3.1 Configuring Location Permissions

Location information falls under the scope of private user data, thus your app must obtain all relevant permissions before it can utilize the continuous location function in Location Kit. These permissions include:

1. Approximate location permission.

   ```
   <uses-permission android:name="android.permission.ACCESS_
   COARES _ LOCATION"/>
   ```

2. Precise location permission.

   ```
   <uses-permission android:name="android.permission.ACCESS_
   FINE _ LOCATION"/>
   ```

3. Background location permission. If your app needs to obtain the device location when running in the background in Android Q (API Level: 29) or later, you also need to declare the background location permission for your app.

```
<uses-permission android:name="android.permission.ACCESS_
BACKGROUND _ LOCATION" />
```

Since the Pet Store app does not need to continuously obtain user location updates when it runs in the background, you'll only need to declare the approximate location permission and precise location permission in the **AndroidManifest.xml** file.

```
<uses-permission       android:name="android.permission.
ACCESS _ COARES _ LOCATION"/>
<uses-permission       android:name="android.permission.
ACCESS _ FINE _ LOCATION"/>
```

Both are dangerous permissions. In Android 6.0 and later, you will also need to dynamically apply for these permissions after declaring them. The following is the sample code for dynamically applying for these permissions in the **MainAct.java** class:

```
private void checkPermission() {
// Dynamically apply for location permissions.
if(ActivityCompat.checkSelfPermission(this,
Manifest.permission.ACCESS _ FINE _ LOCATION) != Package
Manager.PERMISSION _ GRANTED|| ActivityCompat.checkSelf
Permission(this, Manifest.permission.ACCESS _ COARSE _
LOCATION) != PackageManager.PERMISSION _ GRANTED) {
// List of requested location permissions.
String[] strings = {Manifest.permission.ACCESS _ FINE _
LOCATION, Manifest.permission.ACCESS _ COARSE _ LOCATION};
// Dynamically apply for location permissions.
ActivityCompat.requestPermissions(this, strings, 1);}
}
```

7.3.2 Coding Practice

This section details the procedures for calling fused location and reverse geocoding capabilities in Location Kit, which help you quickly obtain the user device location and convert it into a structured address. Figure 7.4 shows the development process.

The detailed steps are as follows:

1. Build the request body **LocationRequest**. The Pet Store app needs to obtain the precise location both indoors and outdoors, so use the GNSS location method with **Priority** set to

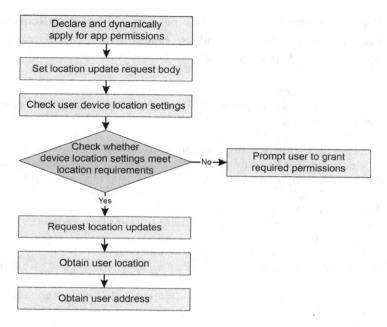

FIGURE 7.4   Fused location development process.

PRIORITY_HIGH_ACCURACY and the number of location updates to **1** in the request body. Build the request body in the **AddressAct.java** class. The sample code is as follows:

```
// Create a request body.
private LocationRequest mLocationRequest;
mLocationRequest = new LocationRequest();
// Set the number of location updates to 1.
mLocationRequest.setNumUpdates(1);
// Set the location method.
mLocationRequest.setPriority(LocationRequest.
PRIORITY _ HIGH _ ACCURACY);
```

2. Check the device location settings. To do this, call the **checkLocationSettings(Location-SettingsRequest)** API in the **AddressAct.java** class. This API will check device location settings, such as whether the location and Bluetooth switches are turned on. If the device location settings do not meet the location update requirements, the app will display a popup message requesting the user to change their location settings as needed.

For the Pet Store app, you'll only need to add **LocationRequest** to **LocationSettingsRequest** and use **false** for the other parameters. The sample code is as follows:

```
// Create a builder.
LocationSettingsRequest.Builder builder = new Location
SettingsRequest.Builder();
// Add the location request.
builder.addLocationRequest(mLocationRequest);
// Specify whether the location information is mandatory.
builder.setAlwaysShow(false);
// Specify whether Bluetooth is mandatory.
builder.setNeedBle(false);
LocationSettingsRequest    locationSettingsRequest    =
builder.build();
  // Check the device location settings.)
settingsClient.checkLocationSettings(location
SettingsRequest)
  .addOnSuccessListener(new  OnSuccessListener<Location
SettingsResponse>() {
@Override
public  void  onSuccess(LocationSettingsResponse  loca-
tionSettingsResponse) {
// The device location settings meet the location update
requirements.
Log.i(TAG, "checkLocationSettings successful");
}}).addOnFailureListener(new OnFailureListener() {
@Override
public void onFailure(Exception e) {
  // If the device location settings do not meet the
location update requirements, obtain the error code and
perform relevant operations.
  int statusCode = ((ApiException) e).getStatusCode();
  switch (statusCode) {
  case LocationSettingsStatusCodes.RESOLUTION _ REQUIRED:
  try {
    ResolvableApiException rae = (ResolvableApiException)
e;
    // Call startResolutionForResult to display a
popup message requesting the user to enable relevant
permissions.
    rae.startResolutionForResult(AddressAct.this, 0);
  } catch (IntentSender.SendIntentException sie) {
    // Failed to show the popup message.
    Log.e(TAG, "start activity failed");
```

```
        }
    break;
}} });
```

3. Send the location update request. Before doing so, you'll need to complete a series of steps, which include configuring permissions, building the request body, and checking the device settings. Then, in the **AddressAct.java** class, you'll need to call the **requestLocationUpdates(LocationRequest, LocationCallback, Looper)** API in the customized **LocationCallback** to obtain the callback result. The sample code is as follows:

```
LocationCallback mLocationCallback;
mLocationCallback = new LocationCallback() {
@Override
    public void onLocationResult(LocationResult location
Result) {
    // Create a location result callback.
    if (locationResult != null) {
      Log.i(TAG, "onLocationResult locationResult is not
null");
      // Obtain the location information.
      List<Location>  locations  =  locationResult.get
Locations();
        if (!locations.isEmpty()) {
        // Obtain the latest location information.
        Location location = locations.get(0);
          Log.i(TAG, "Location[Longitude,Latitude,Accuracy]:" +
            location.getLongitude() + ","+ location.getLati-
tude() + "," +
            location.getAccuracy());
          // Perform reverse geocoding to obtain the structured
address.
            final Geocoder geocoder = new Geocoder(AddressAct.
this, SIMPLIFIED _ CHINESE);
      // Call the reverse geocoding capability in a sub-thread
to obtain location information.
      new Thread(() -> {
      try {
        List<Address>  addrs  =  geocoder.getFromLocation(-
location.getLatitude(),
          location.getLongitude(), 1);
      // Update the UI using the handler after the address
information has been successfully updated.
        for (Address address : addrs) {
```

```
Message msg = new Message();
   msg.what = GETLOCATIONINFO;
   msg.obj = addrs.get(0).getAddressLine(0);
   handler.sendMessage(msg);
  }
} catch (IOException e) {
  Log.e(TAG, "reverseGeocode wrong " +e.getMessage())}).
start()} }}
};
// Initiate the location update request.
fusedLocationProviderClient
.requestLocationUpdates(mLocationRequest,      mLoca-
tionCallback, Looper.getMainLooper())
  .addOnSuccessListener(newOnSuccessListener<Void>()
{
    @Override
    public void onSuccess(Void aVoid) {
    // The API call is successful.
    Log.i(TAG, "onLocationResult onSuccess");
    }});
```

4. Stop requesting location updates. If location updates are no longer required, call the **removeLocationUpdates()** API to stop the requests. Since the number of location updates for the Pet Store app has been set, manually stopping requests is not necessary. The Location SDK will automatically stop requesting location updates, based on the preset number of location updates.

5. Test the developed function. To do this, touch the location icon in the Pet Store app to obtain the current location. If the address is obtained, as shown in Figure 7.5, location updates have been requested successfully. The address can be manually modified as needed.

7.4 DEVELOPING THE MOCK LOCATION FUNCTION

Location Kit provides a mock location function for debugging, which can be used to set a mock location for devices. After you set this location, the called **requestLocationUpdates** API will obtain the mock location, rather than the device's actual location. This function is mainly intended for such scenarios as setting virtual locations in games, debugging map apps, and developing VR-based features.

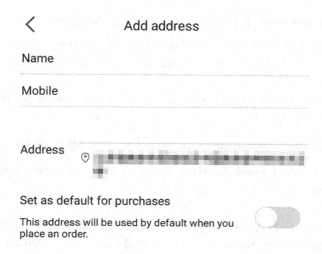

FIGURE 7.5   Location result.

7.4.1 Selecting an App to Use for the Mock Location

First, you'll need to enable **Developer options** on the device and select your app to use for the mock location. The steps are as follows:

1. Go to **Settings>System & updates** on the device to access the **System & updates** screen.

2. Touch **Developer options** to access the **Developer options** screen.

3. Touch **Select mock location app** to access the **Select application** screen, and then select your app.

If you do not see **Developer options** on the **System & updates** screen, go to **Settings>About phone** and touch **Build number** seven consecutive times to have it displayed.

7.4.2 Coding Practice

This section outlines how to code your app to use the mock location function.

1. Declare permissions in the **AndroidManifest.xml** file.

```
<uses-permission
android:name="android.permission.ACCESS _
MOCK _ LOCATION"
tools:ignore="MockLocation,ProtectedPermissions" />
```

2. Call the **setMockMode(boolean isMockMode)** API to set the mock mode.

```
// Set the mock mode to true to enable the mock loca-
tion function.
fusedLocationProviderClient.setMockMode(true)
.addOnSuccessListener(new OnSuccessListener<Void>()
{ @Override
  public void onSuccess(Void aVoid){
    // The mock mode is enabled successfully.
    Log.i(TAG, "setMockMode onSuccess");}
}).addOnFailureListener(new OnFailureListener(){
  @Override
  public void onFailure(Exception e)
  {
```

```
// Failed to enable the mock mode.
Log.i(TAG, "setMockMode onFailure:" + e.getMessage());
}});
```

3. Call the **setMockLocation(Location mockLocation)** API to set a mock location.

```
// Set a mock location.
fusedLocationProviderClient.setMockLocation
(mockLocation)
.addOnSuccessListener(new OnSuccessListener<Void>(){
   @Override
   public void onSuccess(Void aVoid) {
   // The mock location is set successfully.
   Log.i(TAG, "setMockLocation onSuccess");}})
   .addOnFailureListener(new OnFailureListener() {
   @Override
   public void onFailure(Exception e) {
   // Failed to set the mock location.
   Log.i(TAG,  "setMockLocation  onFailure:"  +  e.get
Message()) }});
```

4. Disable the mock location function. Once the debugging is complete, disable the mock location function to ensure that the other apps using Location Kit on the device aren't prevented from obtaining the real device location. The sample code is as follows:

```
// Set the mock mode to false to disable the mock loca-
tion function.
fusedLocationProviderClient.setMockMode(false).
addOnSuccessListener(new
   OnSuccessListener<Void>()
{ @Override
   public void onSuccess(Void aVoid){
   // The mock location function is disabled successfully.
   Log.i(TAG, "setMockMode onSuccess");}
}).addOnFailureListener(new OnFailureListener(){
@Override
   public void onFailure(Exception e)
   {
   // Failed to disable the mock location function.
   Log.i(TAG, "setMockMode onFailure:" + e.getMessage());
   }});
```

7.5 DEVELOPING THE ACTIVITY IDENTIFICATION FUNCTION

Location Kit's activity identification function helps you identify the user's activity status, which can be resting, walking, running, cycling, or on-vehicle. The function mainly consists of two APIs:

1. Activity identification API, used to identify the user's current activity status, for example, walking or running.

2. Activity conversion API, used to detect user's activity status conversion. Currently, the API can detect activity conversions between entry and exit, for example, from resting to running.

7.5.1 Configuring the Activity Identification Permissions

User activity status falls under the scope of private user data, so your app must obtain user permission before it can utilize the activity identification function in Location Kit. You'll need to declare all required permissions in the **AndroidManifest.xml** file. The sample code is as follows:

```
<uses-permission android:name="com.huawei.hms.
permission.ACTIVITY_RECOGNITION" />
<uses-permission android:name="android.permission.
ACTIVITY_RECOGNITION" />
```

The activity identification permissions are dangerous permissions, so you'll also need to apply for them to ask the user to grant access to their data. The sample code is as follows:

```
if (Build.VERSION.SDK_INT < Build.VERSION_CODES.Q) {
  // Apply for activity identification permissions in
versions earlier than Android Q.
  if (ActivityCompat.checkSelfPermission(this,
    "com.huawei.hms.permission.ACTIVITY_RECOGNITION")
    != PackageManager.PERMISSION_GRANTED) {
    String permissions[] = {"com.huawei.hms.
permission.ACTIVITY_RECOGNITION"};
    ActivityCompat.requestPermissions(this,
permissions, 1);
    LocationLog.i(TAG, "requestActivityUpdates
ButtonHandler: Apply permission");
```

```
    }
} else {
    // Apply for activity identification permissions in
Android Q.
    if (ActivityCompat.checkSelfPermission(this,
      "android.permission.ACTIVITY_RECOGNITION")
      != PackageManager.PERMISSION_GRANTED) {
      String permissions[] = {"android.permission.
ACTIVITY_RECOGNITION"};
      ActivityCompat.requestPermissions(this,
permissions, 2);
      LocationLog.i(TAG, "requestActivityUpdates
ButtonHandler: Apply permission");
    }
}
```

7.5.2 Coding Practice

This section details how to code your app to use the activity identification function.

1. Request activity identification updates.

    Location Kit provides the **ActivityIdentificationService** class, which enables you to call **ActivityIdentification** to create an **ActivityIdentificationService** instance, and then use a **PendingIntent** object to obtain the callback result. You can customize how the **PendingIntent** object and callback result are obtained. Here, broadcast is used as an example. The sample code is as follows.

    (1) Create an activity identification client.

    ```
    private PendingIntent pendingIntent;
    private ActivityIdentificationService activityIdenti
    ficationService;
    protected void onCreate(Bundle savedInstanceState) {
        a c t i v i t y I d e n t i f i c a t i o n S e r v i c e =
    ActivityIdentification.getService(this);
        pendingIntent = getPendingIntent();
    };
    ```

    (2) Create a **PendingIntent** object to obtain the activity identification result.

```
private PendingIntent getPendingIntent() {
// The LocationBroadcastReceiver class is a custom-
ized static broadcast class.
Intent intent = new Intent(this, LocationBroadcast
Receiver.class);
  intent.setAction(LocationBroadcastReceiver.
ACTION _ PROCESS _ LOCATION);
return PendingIntent.getBroadcast(this, 0, intent,
PendingIntent.FLAG _ UPDATE _ CURRENT);
}
```

(3) Create a listener to listen for activity identification updates to detect current user activity.

You can call the **createActivityIdentificationUpdates (long detectionIntervalMillis, PendingIntent pendingintent)** API to continuously detect the user activity. In the API, **detectionIntervalMillis** indicates the update interval and **PendingIntent** is used to obtain the callback result.

```
activityIdentificationService.createActivityIdentifi
cationUpdates(5000, pendingIntent)
.addOnSuccessListener(new  OnSuccessListener<Void>()
{
    @Override
    public void onSuccess(Void aVoid) {
    // The activity identification update request
is delivered successfully.
    Log.i(TAG, "createActivityIdentificationUpdates
onSuccess");
    }
  })
    .addOnFailureListener(new OnFailureListener() {
    @Override
    public void onFailure(Exception e) {
    // Failed to deliver the activity identification
update request.
    Log.e(TAG,       "createActivityIdentificationUpdates
onFailure:" + e.getMessage());
    }
  });
```

2. Obtain the activity identification result.

The sample code is as follows:

```
public class LocationBroadcastReceiver extends Broad
castReceiver {
```

```
public static final String ACTION _ PROCESS _ LOCATION =
   "com.huawei.hms.location.ACTION _ PROCESS _
LOCATION";
@Override
   public void onReceive(Context context, Intent intent) {
      if (intent != null) {
         final String action = intent.getAction();
         if (ACTION _ PROCESS _ LOCATION.equals(action)) {
// Obtain the activity identification result.
ActivityIdentificationResponse    activityIdentification-
Response =
   ActivityIdentificationResponse.getDataFrom
Intent(intent);
List<ActivityIdentificationData>        list       =
activityIdentificationResponse.
   getActivityIdentificationDatas();
      }
     }
   }
}
```

3. Stop requesting activity identification updates.

   After using the activity identification function, you'll need to call the **activityIdentificationService.deleteActivityIdentificationUpd ates(pendingIntent)** API to stop requesting activity identification updates. Please note that the **PendingIntent** object must match the object in the **createActivityIdentificationUpdates(long detection-IntervalMillis, PendingIntent callbackIntent)** API.

   The sample code is as follows:

```
activityIdentificationService.deleteActivityIdentificat
ionUpdates(pendingIntent)
   .addOnSuccessListener(new OnSuccessListener<Void>() {
      @Override
      public void onSuccess(Void aVoid) {
         // Requesting activity identification updates is
stopped successfully.
         Log.i(TAG,      "deleteActivityIdentificationUpdates
onSuccess");
      }
   })
   .addOnFailureListener(new OnFailureListener() {
      @Override
      public void onFailure(Exception e) {
```

```
// Failed to stop requesting activity identification
updates.
Log.e(TAG, "deleteActivityIdentificationUpdates onFailure:"
+ e.getMessage());
    }});
```

4. Request activity conversion updates.

You can call the **createActivityConversionUpdates(request, pendingIntent)** API to obtain the activity conversion result.

(1) Set parameters for requesting activity conversion updates. For example, to detect when the user enters or exits the resting status, use the following code:

```
ActivityConversionInfo activityConversionInfo1 = new
    ActivityConversionInfo(DetectedActivity.STILL,
    ActivityConversionInfo.ENTER _ ACTIVITY _
CONVERSION);
ActivityConversionInfo activityConversionInfo2 = new
    ActivityConversionInfo(STILL,    ActivityConversion
Info. EXIT _ ACTIVITY _ CONVERSION);
List<ActivityConversionInfo> activityConversionInfos
= new ArrayList<>();
activityConversionInfos.add(activityConversionInfo1);
activityConversionInfos.add(activityConversionInfo2);
ActivityConversionRequest    request    =    new
ActivityConversionRequest();
request.setActivityConversions(activity
ConversionInfos);
```

(2) Create a listener to listen for activity conversion updates. The sample code is as follows:

```
Task<Void> task = activityIdentificationService.
    createActivityConversionUpdates(request,
pendingIntent);
task.addOnSuccessListener(new    OnSuccessListener
<Void>(){
  @Override
  public void onSuccess(Void aVoid) {
    Log.i(TAG,      "createActivityConversionUpdates
onSuccess");
  }
}).addOnFailureListener(new OnFailureListener() {
  @Override
  public void onFailure(Exception e) {
```

```
      Log.e(TAG,      "createActivityConversionUpdates
   onFailure:" + e.getMessage());
     }
   });
```

(3) Obtain the result via the **PendingIntent** method. The sample code is as follows:

```
public   class   LocationBroadcastReceiver   extends
BroadcastReceiver {
  public   static   final   String  ACTION _ PROCESS _
LOCATION =
     "com.huawei.hms.location.ACTION _
PROCESS _ LOCATION";
  @Override
  public  void  onReceive(Context  context,  Intent
intent) {
    if (intent != null) {
      final String action = intent.getAction();
      if (ACTION _ PROCESS _ LOCATION.equals(action)) {
        ActivityConversionResponse    activityConver-
sionResponse =
          ActivityConversionResponse.getData
FromIntent(intent);
        List<ActivityConversionData> list =
          activityConversionResponse   .getActivity
ConversionDatas();
      }
     }
    }
   }
}
```

5. Stop requesting activity conversion updates.

If requesting activity conversion updates is no longer needed, call **deleteActivityConversionUpdates(PendingIntent pendingIntent)** to stop it. The sample code is as follows:

```
activityIdentificationService.deleteActivity
ConversionUpdates(pendingIntent)
  .addOnSuccessListener(new OnSuccessListener<Void>() {
  @Override
  public void onSuccess(Void aVoid) {
    Log.i(TAG,      "deleteActivityConversionUpdates
onSuccess");
  }
  })
```

```
.addOnFailureListener(new OnFailureListener() {
  @Override
  public void onFailure(Exception e) {
    Log.e(TAG,        "deleteActivityConversionUpdates
onFailure:" +
      e.getMessage());
  }
});
```

7.6 DEVELOPING THE GEOFENCE FUNCTION

The geofence function lets you detect the distance between the user's current location and a potential place of interest. You can specify when to trigger the geofence, such as when the user enters or exits the geofence, or stays within the geofence for a specified period. Currently, Location Kit supports only circular geofences, and up to 100 geofences per app.

7.6.1 Creating a Geofence

This section details the process for creating a geofence.

1. Declare app permissions.

2. Create a geofence service client. After integrating Location Kit into your app, you'll be able to create a geofence service client using **LocationServices**.

3. Create a geofence instance. You'll need to add the geofence to the geofence list and add the geofence ID to the corresponding geofence ID list.

4. Create and add a geofence request. Location Kit provides the **GeofenceRequest.Builder** class, with which you can build a geofence request body efficiently.

5. Create a **PendingIntent** method, which is used to send a geofence event to your app when the user enters or leaves the geofence.

6. Deliver the geofence.

7. Process the geofence events. When receiving a geofence event, which is sent via **PendingIntent**, your app will process it with the programmed action.

8. Remove the geofence when it is no longer required.

7.6.2 Coding Practice

Figure 7.6 shows the geofence triggering screen in the Pet Store app. Users interested in a pet store can touch the heart icon to follow it. The Pet Store app will then deliver a geofence with the followed pet store at the center,

FIGURE 7.6   Pet store location screen.

encircled by a 1-km radius. When the user enters the geofence, the Pet Store app will send them a notification containing the latest or most relevant promotions for the pet store. If the user unfollows the pet store, the Pet Store app will automatically remove the delivered geofence.

The following details the process for coding the Pet Store app to use the geofence function:

1. Declare app permissions. The geofence function requires the same permissions as listed for the fused location function in Section 7.3.

2. Create a geofence service client in **PetStoreSearchDetailActivity. java**. The sample code is as follows:

```
geofenceService = LocationServices.getGeofenceService
(this);
```

3. Create a geofence instance. In the Pet Store app, set the pet store followed by a user as a POI, use the longitude-latitude coordinates of the pet store as the geofence center, and set the geofence radius to 1 kilometer. The sample code is as follows:

```
geofenceList.add(new Geofence.Builder()
    .setUniqueId("mGeofence")
    .setValidContinueTime(validTime)
    // Pass the longitude-latitude coordinates of the
geofence and its radius in meters.
    .setRoundArea(latitude, longitude, radius)
    // Trigger a callback when the user enters or leaves
the geofence.
    .setConversions(Geofence.ENTER _ GEOFENCE _
CONVERSION )
    .build());
// Add the geofence ID to the geofence ID list.
idList.add("mGeofence");
```

4. Create a geofence request.

```
/**
* Create a request for adding a geofence.
*/
private GeofenceRequest getAddGeofenceRequest() {
  GeofenceRequest.Builder builder = new GeofenceRequest.
Builder();
    // Trigger a callback immediately after the geofence
is added, if the user is already within the geofence.
```

```
builder.setInitConversions(GeofenceRequest.
ENTER _ INIT _ CONVERSION);
  builder.createGeofenceList(geofenceList);
  return builder.build();
}
```

5. Create a **PendingIntent** method for obtaining the geofence status. The sample code is as follows:

```
private PendingIntent getPendingIntent() {
    // The GeoFenceBroadcastReceiver class is a custom-
ized static broadcast class. For details about how to
implement this class, please refer to the sample code.
    Intent        intent      =      new          Intent(this,
GeoFenceBroadcastReceiver.class);
    intent.setAction(GeoFenceBroadcastReceiver.
ACTION _ PROCESS _ LOCATION);
    return  PendingIntent.getBroadcast(this,  0,  intent,
PendingIntent.FLAG _ UPDATE _ CURRENT);
}
```

6. Deliver the geofence.

```
/**
* Send the request to add a geofence.
*/
private void requestGeoFenceWithNewIntent() {
ToastUtil.getInstance().showShort(-
PetStoreSearchDetailActivity.this, "Add to favorites");
    // Set the color of a touched button.
    isClickedCollection = true;
mTvPetStoreCollection.setTextColor(getResources().
getColor(R.color.Blue _ 600));
    Log.i(TAG, "begin to create Geofence");
    pendingIntent = getPendingIntent();
    geofenceList = new ArrayList<>();
    double latitude = mPlace.latLng.latitude;
    double longitude = mPlace.latLng.longitude;
    // Set the geofence radius to 1 kilometer.
    float radius = 1000;
    // Deliver a geofence based on the location of the
place of interest.
    geofenceList.add(new   Geofence.Builder().setUniqueId(-
mPlace.getSiteId())
      .setValidContinueTime(1000000)
      // Pass the longitude-latitude coordinates of the
geofence and its radius in meters.
      .setRoundArea(latitude, longitude, radius)
```

```
    // Trigger a callback when the user enters the
geofence.
    .setConversions(Geofence.ENTER _ GEOFENCE _
CONVERSION)
    .build());
  geofenceService.createGeofenceList(getAdd
GeofenceRequest(), pendingIntent)
    .addOnCompleteListener(new
OnCompleteListener<Void>() {
    @Override
    public void onComplete(Task<Void> task) {
      if (task.isSuccessful()) {
        Log.i(TAG, "add geofence success! ");
      } else {
        Log.w(TAG, "add geofence failed : " + task.
getException().
        getMessage());
      }
    }
  });
}
```

7. Process the geofence events. When a geofence event is triggered in the app, Location Kit will broadcast the event via the **PendingIntent** method passed during geofence creation. The Pet Store app will then receive and process the event. The sample code is as follows:

```
public void onReceive(Context context, Intent intent) {
  if (intent != null) {
    final String action = intent.getAction();
    if (ACTION _ PROCESS _ LOCATION.equals(action)) {
    GeofenceData geofenceData = GeofenceData.getData
FromIntent(intent);
      if (geofenceData != null) {
        int errorCode = geofenceData.getErrorCode();
        int conversion = geofenceData.getConversion();
        List<Geofence>     list     =     geofenceData.
getConvertingGeofenceList();
        Location mLocation = geofenceData.getConverting
Location();
        boolean status = geofenceData.isSuccess();
        // Print the geofence event information.
        StringBuilder sb = new StringBuilder();
        String next = "\n";
```

```
    sb.append("errorcode: " + errorCode + next);
    sb.append("conversion: " + conversion + next);
    for (int i = 0; i < list.size(); i++) {
        sb.append("geoFence id :" + list.get(i).getU-
niqueId() + next);
    }
    sb.append("location is :"+mLocation.getLongitude()
+ " " +
        mLocation.getLatitude() + next);
    sb.append("is successful :" + status);
    Log.i(TAG, sb.toString());
    // Push notifications to the notification panel
of the user device.
    showNotification(context);
    Toast.makeText(context, "Entered the geofence" +
sb.toString(),
        Toast.LENGTH _ LONG).show();
}}}}
```

When the user enters the geofence, a message will be pushed to the notification panel, as shown in Figure 7.7.

8. Remove the geofence when it is no longer required.

```
private void removeGeoFenceWithID() {
  Log.i(TAG, "have clicked collection button" +
isClickedCollection);
  ToastUtil.getInstance().showShort(-
PetStoreSearchDetailActivity.this, "Remove from
favorites");
  // Restore the favorites button to its normal color,
after removing the pet store from favorites.
  mTvPetStoreCollection.setTextColor(getResources().
getColor(R.color.Deep _ Orange _ A700));
  isClickedCollection = false;
  // Remove the geofence.
  idList = new ArrayList<>();
  idList.add(mPlace.getSiteId());
  geofenceService.deleteGeofenceList(idList).
addOnCompleteListener
    (new OnCompleteListener<Void>() {
    @Override
    public void onComplete(Task<Void> task) {
      if (task.isSuccessful()) {
        Log.i(TAG, "delete geofence with ID success! ");
```

```
    } else {
       Log.w(TAG, "delete geofence with ID failed ");
    }
  }
});
}
```

FIGURE 7.7 Geofence event notification.

7.7 SUMMARY

This chapter stepped us through the process of integrating Location Kit. We've learned how the kit can help obtain and autofill an address that corresponds to the user's real-time location to provide your users more convenience. Furthermore, it described how your app can deliver geofences, based on POIs set for users, to send out relevant and engaging service information for a user in the vicinity.

In the next chapter, we'll introduce how to integrate Site Kit into the Pet Store app, which enables users to search for pet stores through the app with newfound ease.

NOTE

1 Location Kit is currently capable of identifying the following activity statuses: resting, walking, running, cycling, and on-vehicle.

CHAPTER 8

Site Kit

8.1 ABOUT THE SERVICE

This section outlines the core principles behind Site Kit.

Site Kit provides a myriad of different capabilities, including place search, geocoding, and time zone search, and can be accessed through either the Site SDK or RESTful APIs. Figure 8.1 shows the system architecture of Site Kit.

1. Site SDK

   After integrating the Site SDK into your app, your app will obtain the following capabilities:

   (1) Keyword search: searches for places based on entered keywords.

   (2) Nearby place search: searches for places, such as hotels and scenic spots, which are close to a specified location.

   (3) Place search suggestion: returns a list of places that are relevant to the user input.

   (4) Place detail search: searches for detailed information related to a specific place.

   These capabilities require synergy among the Site SDK, HMS Core (APK), and Huawei Site Server. The client consists of the Site SDK and HMS Core (APK), while the Huawei Site Server provides a range of capabilities, including authentication and search engine.

DOI: 10.1201/9781003206699-8

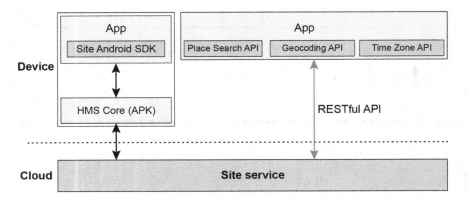

FIGURE 8.1   System architecture of Site Kit.

After integrating the Site SDK into your app, the Site SDK will communicate with the Huawei Site Server via HMS Core (APK) to implement all corresponding place search functions.

2. RESTful API

Your app can call the RESTful APIs provided by the Huawei Site Server to implement the same place search capabilities as those offered by the Site SDK. In calling the RESTful APIs, your app can also implement the following functions:

(1) Forward and reverse geocoding: converts structured addresses into geographic longitude-latitude coordinates, and vice versa.

(2) Time zone search: obtains the time zone for a specific place, based on its coordinates.

Let's use the geocoding function to demonstrate how this process works. This function requires close collaboration between the geocoding API and Huawei Site Server. To use the geocoding API, you'll need to build a valid JSON request body and send a correct POST request to

NOTE

The geocoding function in Site Kit uses the same data source as that for the geocoding function in Location Kit. The difference is that Location Kit uses the native Android APIs in providing services, whereas Site Kit uses RESTful APIs. You can choose to use the geocoding function in either Location Kit or Site Kit.

the Huawei Site Server. After verifying and processing the request, the Huawei Site Server will then return a JSON-format response that contains the geocoding result.

8.2 PREPARATIONS

In Section 3.4, we designed functions for browsing nearby pet stores, viewing place details, and searching for nearby places via the Pet Store app. In this section, we'll walk you through how to integrate Site Kit into the Pet Store app and implement all of these functions via Site Kit. To prepare to integrate Site Kit, you'll need to register as a Huawei developer, create an app, and configure the signing certificate fingerprint in AppGallery Connect. You'll also need to download the **agconnect-services.json** file for your app from AppGallery Connect and copy the file to the project's **app** directory. The detailed steps were explained in earlier chapters. Once you've done all of that, all you'll need to do is integrate the Site SDK.

Open the Pet Store app project, and add the dependency on the Site SDK to the **build.gradle** file in the **app** directory. The sample code is as follows:

```
implementation 'com.huawei.hms:site: 4.0.2.300'
```

Here, the Site SDK version is 4.0.2.300. You can refer to the *Site Kit Development Guide* on the HUAWEI Developers website to view the latest Site SDK version. After configuring the dependency, click **Sync Now** in the upper right corner and wait for the synchronization to complete, as shown in Figure 8.2.

To use the functions in Site Kit such as geocoding, you'll need to apply for an API key. You can obtain the API key that is automatically generated when you create your app in AppGallery Connect, or instead, obtain the API key by creating a credential on the HUAWEI Developers website.

1. Obtain the API key in AppGallery Connect.

    After creating an app, sign in to AppGallery Connect, click **My projects**, and click the app in your project. Then, go to **Project settings > General information**. In the **App information** area, click the copy icon next to the **API key** field to copy the API key to the clipboard, as shown in Figure 8.3.

FIGURE 8.2   Synchronizing the project.

FIGURE 8.3   Obtaining the API key in AppGallery Connect.

FIGURE 8.4   Enabling Site Kit.

2. Obtain the API key on the HUAWEI Developers website.

Sign in to the HUAWEI Developers website, and click **Console**. On the page displayed, click **API Library** in the left navigation tree, click the **Site Kit** card in the right area, and then click **Enable** to enable Site Kit, as shown in Figure 8.4.

Click **Credentials** in the left navigation tree, and select the desired project (**HMSPetStoreApp** in this case). Then, click **Create credential**, and select **API key** from the drop-down list. A dialog box will be displayed, indicating that the API key has been created, as shown in Figure 8.5. You can click **Restrict** in the dialog box, and set the API key usage restrictions on the page displayed, to further enhance security. If you only call the RESTful APIs from Site Kit into your web app, it is recommended that you directly apply for an API key on the HUAWEI Developers website. This will free you from needing to create an app in AppGallery Connect.

We'll show you how to use the obtained API key in Section 8.4. Since the development preparations that include enabling Site Kit in AppGallery Connect and configuring obfuscation scripts have been detailed in earlier chapters, let's now directly address the different functions in Site Kit.

NOTE

If the API key contains special characters, you'll need to URL-encode it. For example, if the original API key is **ABC/ DFG+**, the encoding result will be **ABC%2FDFG%2B**.

FIGURE 8.5   Creating an API key.

8.3 PLACE SEARCH

In this section, you'll learn how to use the place search function. As noted earlier, Site Kit provides both the Site SDK and RESTful APIs for you to implement place search functions, which include keyword search, place search suggestion, place detail search, and nearby place search. The methods for using each of these functions are similar. The procedure for using the Site SDK is as follows:

1. Create a **SearchService** object and instantiate it through **SearchServiceFactory.create()**.

2. Create a place search request object.

3. Create a **SearchResultListener** object, which will be used to listen for the search result. In the object, the **onSearchResult** API will return the search result, and the **onSearchError** API will return the search status.

4. Initiate a place search request through **SearchService**.

The subsequent sections will delve into how to implement these functions.

8.3.1 Keyword Search

You can specify keywords and geographic areas, with which users search for a myriad of different places, including scenic attractions, businesses, and schools. The procedure for doing so is as follows:

1. Declare a **SearchService** object and instantiate it through **SearchServiceFactory**. To create a **SearchService** object, you'll need to pass the **Context** parameter and API key.

```
// Declare a SearchService
object.
private SearchService search
Service;
// Instantiate the SearchService
object.
searchService = SearchServiceFactory.create(this, System
Util.getApiKey());
```

NOTE

It is recommended that you pass the **Context** parameter of the **Activity** type when creating a **SearchService** object. This ensures that the system will prompt the user to update their HMS Core (APK) to a supported version.

2. Create a **TextSearchRequest** object, which is the request body for place search by keyword. In the object, the **query** parameter is mandatory, while the other parameters are optional. The sample code is as follows:

```
// Create a request body.
TextSearchRequest request = new TextSearchRequest();
// Set the keyword Paris.
request.setQuery("Paris");
Coordinate location = new Coordinate(48.893478, 2.334595);
request.setLocation(location);
// Set the search radius to 1000 meters.
request.setRadius(1000);
// Set the POI type to address.
request.setPoiType(LocationType.ADDRESS);
request.setCountryCode("FR");
request.setLanguage("fr");
request.setPageIndex(1);
request.setPageSize(5);
```

Table 8.1 describes the parameters in the **TextSearchRequest** object.

3. Create a **SearchResultListener** object, which will be used to listen for the search result. The **onSearchResult** API will return a **TextSearchResponse** object containing the keyword search result,

TABLE 8.1   Parameters in the TextSearchRequest object

Parameter	Mandatory	Type	Description
countryCode	No	String	Country code, which complies with ISO 3166-1 alpha-2. This parameter is used to specify the country where places are searched.
language	No	String	Language in which the search result is displayed.
location	No	Coordinate	Longitude-latitude coordinates to which the search result needs to be biased.
pageIndex	No	Integer	Current page number.
pageSize	No	Integer	Number of records on each page.
poiTypes	No	LocationType	POI type for places being searched.
query	Yes	String	Search keyword.
radius	No	Integer	Search radius.

and the **onSearchError** API will return the search exception information containing the result code. The sample code is as follows:

```
// Create a search result listener.
SearchResultListener<TextSearchResponse>    resultLis-
tener = new SearchResultListener
  <TextSearchResponse>() {
  // Return the search result upon a successful search.
  @Override
  public void onSearchResult(TextSearchResponse results)
  {
    }
  // Return the result code and description upon a
search exception.
  @Override
  public void onSearchError(SearchStatus status) {
    }
};
```

4. Call the **textSearch()** API using the **SearchService** object, with the **TextSearchRequest** and **SearchResultListener** objects passed as parameters to the API.

```
// Call the keyword search API.
searchService.textSearch(request, resultListener);
```

5. Obtain a **TextSearchResponse** object containing the search result and a **Site** object that contains a list of places through the **SearchResultListener** object, and then parse the specific address.

```
// Create a search result listener.
SearchResultListener<TextSearchResponse> resultListener =
new SearchResultListener
  <TextSearchResponse>() {
  // Return the search result upon a successful search.
  @Override
  public void onSearchResult(TextSearchResponse results) {
    List<Site> sites = results.getSites();
    if (results == null || results.getTotalCount() <= 0
|| sites ==
      null || sites.size() <= 0) {
      return;
    }
    for (Site site : sites) {
      Log.i("TAG", String.format("siteId: '%s', name: %s\r\n",
        site.getSiteId(), site.getName()));
    }
  }
  // Return the result code and description upon a search
exception.
  @Override
  public void onSearchError(SearchStatus status) {
      Log.i("TAG", "Error : " + status.getErrorCode() + " " +
        status.getErrorMessage());
  }
};
```

As shown in Figure 8.6, the details for a place are shown in the keyword search results in logs. These include the ID, name, structured address, POI type, and longitude-latitude coordinates for the place.

FIGURE 8.6   Place details in the keyword search results.

8.3.2 Place Search Suggestion

This function returns a list of suggestions when the user enters search keywords, which makes it quick and easy for them to search for potential places of interest. The procedure for doing so is as follows:

1. Declare a **SearchService** object and instantiate it through **Search ServiceFactory**. To create a **SearchService** object, you'll need to pass the **Context** parameter and API key.

```
// Declare a SearchService object.
private SearchService mSearchService;
// Instantiate the SearchService object.
mSearchService = SearchServiceFactory.create(this, System
Util.getApiKey());
```

2. In the **PetStoreSearchActivity.java** file, create a **Query SuggestionRequest** object for place search suggestion, and set the search keyword to **petstore**, search radius to 50 kilometers, and current user location to the preset longitude-latitude coordinates.

```
QuerySuggestionRequest request = new QuerySuggestion
Request();
// Set the search keyword to petstore.
request.setQuery("petstore");
// Set the search radius to 50 kilometers.
request.setRadius(50000);// Search radius.
// Set the current location to the preset longitude-latitude
coordinates.
request.setLocation(SPConstants.COORDINATE);
```

Table 8.2 describes the parameters in the **QuerySuggestion Request** object.

3. Create a **SearchResultListener** object, which will be used to listen for the search result. The **onSearchResult** API will return a **QuerySuggestionResponse** object containing the place search suggestion result, and the **onSearchError** API will return the search exception information containing the result code.

```
private SearchResultListener searchResultListener = new
SearchResultListener
    <QuerySuggestionResponse>() {
    @Override
```

TABLE 8.2   Parameters in the QuerySuggestionRequest Object

Parameter	Mandatory	Type	Description
bounds	No	CoordinateBounds	Coordinate bounds to which the search result needs to be biased.
countryCode	No	String	Country code, which complies with ISO 3166-1 alpha-2. This parameter is used to specify the country where places are searched.
language	No	String	Language in which the search result is displayed.
location	No	Coordinate	Longitude-latitude coordinates to which the search result needs to be biased.
poiTypes	No	List<LocationType>	POI type for places being searched.
query	Yes	String	Search keyword.
radius	No	Integer	Search radius, in meters.

```
    public    void    onSearchResult(QuerySuggestionResponse
    results) {
        }
    }
    @Override
    public void onSearchError(SearchStatus status) {
        }
};
```

4. Call the **querySuggestion()** API using the **SearchService** object, with the created **QuerySuggestionRequest** and **searchResultListener** objects passed as parameters to the API.

```
mSearchService.querySuggestion(request,  searchResult
Listener);
```

5. Obtain the place search suggestion result and display it in **ListView**. Save the obtained **Site** object containing the **SiteId**, **Name**, **FormatAddress**, and **Location** parameters to the **Place** object for further use in the place detail search function.

```
    private SearchResultListener searchResultListener = new
SearchResultListener
        <QuerySuggestionResponse>() {
        @Override
        public  void  onSearchResult(QuerySuggestionResponse
results) {
```

```
     if (results != null) {
       List<Site> sites = results.getSites();
       generatePlaces(sites);
     }
   }
   @Override
   public void onSearchError(SearchStatus status) {
     LogM.e(TAG, "failed " + status.getErrorCode() + " "
+ status.getErrorMessage());
   }
};
  // Save the obtained Site object to the customized
Place object.
   private void generatePlaces(List<Site> resultList) {
     mPlaces.clear();
     for (Site bean : resultList) {
       Place place = new Place();
       place.setSiteId(bean.getSiteId());
       place.setName(bean.getName());
       place.setFormatAddress(bean.getFormatAddress());
       Coordinate coordinate = bean.getLocation();
       place.setLatLng(new     LatLng(coordinate.getLat(),
coordinate.getLng()));
       mPlaces.add(place);
     }
     // Instruct the main thread to update the UI.
     Message message = Message.obtain();
     message.what = GETAUTOCOMPLETE _ SUCCESS;
     mHandler.sendMessage(message);
}
```

Figure 8.7 shows the displayed results for place search suggestion.

8.3.3 Place Detail Search

This function obtains the corresponding details for a place, such as the detailed address and POI type, based on the place's unique ID (**SiteId**). The procedure is as follows:

1. Declare a **SearchService** object and instantiate it through **SearchServiceFactory**. To create a **SearchService** object, you'll need to pass the **Context** parameter and API key.

```
// Declare a SearchService object.
private SearchService mSearchService;
```

FIGURE 8.7   Place search suggestion.

```
// Instantiate the SearchService object.
mSearchService   =   SearchServiceFactory.create(this,
SystemUtil.getApiKey());
```

2. In the **PetStoreSearchDetailActivity.java** class, create a **Detail SearchRequest** object for place detail search, with **SiteId** in the **Place** object passed as a parameter to the object.

```
DetailSearchRequest request = new DetailSearchRequest();
request.setSiteId(id);
```

   Table 8.3 describes the parameters in the **DetailSearchRequest** object.

3. Create a **SearchResultListener** object, which will be used to listen for the search result. The **onSearchResult** API will return a **DetailSearchResponse** object containing the place detail search result, and the **onSearchError** API will return the search exception information containing the result code. Here, the Pet Store app reads the name and structured address of a pet store and displays them on the store details screen.

```
private SearchResultListener<DetailSearchResponse> result
Listener =
  new SearchResultListener<DetailSearchResponse>() {
  @Override
  public    void    onSearchResult(DetailSearchResponse
results) {
    Site site;
    if (results == null || (site = results.getSite()) ==
null) {
      return;
    }
    mTvPetStoreName.setText(site.getName());
    mTvPetStoreDescription.setText
      (site.getFormatAddress());
  }
  @Override
  public void onSearchError(SearchStatus
```

TABLE 8.3   Parameters in the DetailSearchRequest object

Parameter	Mandatory	Type	Description
siteId	Yes	String	ID of a place.
language	No	String	Language in which the search result is displayed.

```
      status) {
      LogM.e(TAG, "failed " + status.
        getErrorCode() + " " +
        status.getErrorMessage());
    }
  };
```

4. Call the **detailSearch()** API using the **SearchService** object, with the created **DetailSearchRequest** and **searchResultListener** objects passed as parameters to the API.

```
mSearchService.detailSearch(request,
searchResultListener);
```

Figure 8.8 shows an actual example of place detail search results.

8.3.4 Nearby Place Search

This function obtains a list of places near the passed location. The procedure is as follows:

1. Declare a **SearchService** object and instantiate it through **Search ServiceFactory**. To create a **SearchService** object, you'll need to pass the **Context** parameter and API key.

```
// Declare a SearchService object.
private SearchService mSearchService;
// Instantiate the SearchService object.
mSearchService   =   SearchServiceFactory.create(this,
SystemUtil.getApiKey());
```

2. In the **PetStoreNearbySearchActivity.java** file, create a **Nearby SearchRequest** object for nearby place search, with the longitude-latitude coordinates of the selected pet store passed as parameters to the object.

```
NearbySearchRequest request = new NearbySearchRequest();
  LatLng latLng = mCurrentPlace.getLatLng();
  double lat = latLng.latitude;
  double lng = latLng.longitude;
  Coordinate location = new Coordinate(lat, lng);
  request.setLocation(location);
```

Table 8.4 describes the parameters in the **NearbySearchRequest** object.

FIGURE 8.8   Place detail search.

TABLE 8.4   Parameters in the NearbySearchRequest object

Parameter	Mandatory	Type	Description
language	No	String	Language in which the search result is displayed.
location	Yes	Coordinate	Current user location.
pageIndex	No	Integer	Current page number.
pageSize	No	Integer	Number of records on each page.
poiTypes	No	List<LocationType>	POI type.
query	No	String	Search keyword.
radius	No	Integer	Search radius.

3. Create a **SearchResultListener** object, which will be used to listen for the search result. The **onSearchResult** API will return a **NearbySearchResponse** object, containing the place search suggestion result, and the **onSearchError** API will return the search exception information containing the result code.

```
SearchResultListener<NearbySearchResponse> resultLis-
tener =
    new SearchResultListener<NearbySearchResponse>() {
    // Return the search result upon a successful search.
    @Override
    public    void    onSearchResult(NearbySearchResponse
    results) {
    }
    // Return the result code and description upon a
    search exception.
    @Override
    public void onSearchError(SearchStatus status) {
    }
};
```

4. Call the **nearbySearch** API using the **SearchService** object, with the created **NearbySearchRequest** and **searchResultListener** objects passed as parameters to the API.

```
searchService.nearbySearch(request, searchResultListener);
```

5. Call the **onSearchResult** callback method to obtain the **NearbySearchResponse** object that contains the search result, and display the processing result in **BottomSheet**.

```
@Override
public    void    onSearchResult(NearbySearchResponse
results) {
    if (null != query && (TextUtils.isEmpty(mSearchText)
      || !query.equals(mSearchText))) {
      return;
    }
    List<Site> sites;
    if (null != results && null != (sites = results.
getSites()) &&
      sites.size() > 0) {
    // Obtain and display the search result.
  resolveResult(sites, query);
    } else {
      hideBottomSheet();
    }
  }
  // Return the result code and description upon a
search exception.
  @Override
  public void onSearchError(SearchStatus status) {
    if (null == query || TextUtils.isEmpty(mSearchText)
      || !query.equals(mSearchText)) {
      return;
    }
    hideBottomSheet();
  }
};
```

Here, no search keyword was specified. Thus, the Pet Store app directly obtains places located close to a pet store, as shown in Figure 8.9.

8.4 GEOCODING

In earlier chapters, we used the geocoding function in Location Kit to develop the automatic delivery address fill-in function for the Pet Store app. The geocoding functions in Site Kit and Location Kit use the same data source. Therefore, we do not need to integrate the geocoding function from Site Kit into the Pet Store app.

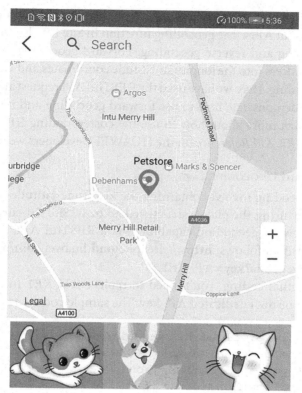

Triple Two Coffee

West Midlands, England DY5 1 the United Kingdom

Retail Travel

The Merryhill Centre, Dudley, England DY5 1SW the United Kingdom

FIGURE 8.9 Nearby place search.

Site Kit differs from Location Kit in that it provides the geocoding function via RESTful APIs. The geocoding function in Site Kit also includes forward geocoding and reverse geocoding. Forward geocoding converts the structured address into the longitude-latitude coordinates and vice versa for reverse geocoding. Here we have used the RESTful API request and response examples to demonstrate how to use forward geocoding and reverse geocoding. To learn more about how to use the corresponding RESTful APIs, view the *Site Kit API Reference* on the HUAWEI Developers website.

8.4.1 Forward Geocoding

Forward geocoding involves obtaining the longitude-latitude coordinates for a place by using the place's structured address. Site Kit currently provides the forward geocoding capability via a RESTful API. The request URL format is as follows: **https://siteapi.cloud.huawei.com/mapApi/v1/siteService/geocode?key=***API KEY*.

During actual coding, you'll need to replace *API KEY* in the request URL with your own dedicated API key. The sample code is as follows:

```
https://siteapi.cloud.huawei.com/mapApi/v1/
siteService/geocode?key=API KEY
Content-Type: application/json
Accept: application/json
{
  "address": "Cleary Garden,Queen Victoria St,London",
  "language": "en",
}
```

Table 8.5 describes the parameters in the forward geocoding request.

TABLE 8.5   Parameters in the forward geocoding request

Parameter	Mandatory	Type	Description
address	Yes	String(<=512)	Detailed address for a place.
bounds	No	CoordinateBounds	Coordinate bounds to which the search result needs to be biased.
language	No	String(<=6)	Language in which the search result is displayed. If this parameter is not passed, the local language for the place will be used.

The response to the POST request for the URL is similar to the following:

```json
{
  "returnCode": "0",
  "sites": [
    {
      // Structured address of a place.
      "formatAddress": "Queen Victoria Street,City of
London,EC4V 4,City of
      London,London,England,the United Kingdom",
      // Place details.
      "address": {
        "country": "the United Kingdom",
        "countryCode": "GB",
        "locality": "City of London",
        "adminArea": "England",
        "subAdminArea": "London",
        "thoroughfare": "Queen Victoria Street"
      },
      "viewport": {},
      // Place name.
    "name": "Cleary Garden",
      // Unique place ID.
      "siteId": "NzNjNTViMjZjN2VjNTY2NzNkZmY0MGZhY
zcxOWUyNjdmNjFiYTFjNzA4Yz
      YwNDAwNjBiZjllYzM2MWVjNDIyNQ",
      "location": {
        "lng": -0.0953,
        "lat": 51.512
      }
    }
  ],
  "returnDesc": "OK"
}
```

In the code snippet, **returnCode** indicates the API call result code, **SiteId** indicates the unique place ID, and **location** indicates the longitude-latitude coordinates of the place. For details about the other parameters in the response, please refer to the *Site Kit API Reference* on the HUAWEI Developers website.

8.4.2 Reverse Geocoding

Reverse geocoding obtains the structured address of a place by using the place's longitude-latitude coordinates. Site Kit currently provides the reverse geocoding capability via a RESTful API. Use the following request URL format, replacing *API KEY* with your own dedicated API key:

```
https://siteapi.cloud.huawei.com/mapApi/v1/
siteService/ reverseGeocode?key=API KEY
```

The following sample code obtains the structured address corresponding to the longitude-latitude coordinates (77.2155, 18.0527):

```
POST https://siteapi.cloud.huawei.com/mapApi/v1/
siteService/reverseGeocode?key=API KEY HTTP/1.1
Content-Type: application/json
Accept: application/json
{
  "location": {
    "lng": 77.2155,
    "lat": 18.0527
  },
  "language": "en",
  "returnPoi": true
}
```

Table 8.6 describes the parameters in the reverse geocoding request.

The response to the POST request for the URL is similar to the following. In the information, **returnCode** indicates the API call result code,

TABLE 8.6   Parameters in the reverse geocoding request

Parameter	Mandatory	Type	Description
location	Yes	Coordinate	Longitude-latitude coordinates for a place.
language	No	String(<=6)	Language in which the search result is displayed. If this parameter is not passed, the local language for the place will be used.
returnPoi	No	Boolean	Indicates whether to return the place name of a POI. The default value is **true**.

and **formatAddress** indicates the structured address for the place. For details about the other parameters in the response, please refer to the *Site Kit API Reference* on the HUAWEI Developers website.

```
{
  "returnCode": "0",
  "sites": [
    {
      "formatAddress": "Bhalki, Bidar, Karnataka,
Indian Ocean",
      "address": {
        "country": "India",
        "countryCode": "IN",
        "subLocality": "Bhalki",
        "locality": "Bidar",
        "adminArea": "Karnataka"
      },
      "viewport": {
        "southwest": {
          "lng": 77.19028253443632,
          "lat": 18.037237269564656
        },
        "northeast": {
          "lng": 77.19406155017738,
          "lat": 18.040830530700358
        }
      },
      "name": "",
      "siteId": "OTU3MjkxMjg5Zjk0MGYzM2RkYjZhNjYxMDU
2ZGIwZmFjODEyMDhh
        Mjc4MDFhMzg4N2QzYzkwNzQ5Njc4NjA1Mw",
      "location": {
        "lng": 77.19217202301087,
        "lat": 18.039033909306255
      }
    }
    // A maximum of 11 records can be returned.
    ......
  "returnDesc": "OK"
}
```

8.5 TIME ZONE SEARCH

If your app is designed for the global market, it will need to obtain the time zone for the current device location. This can endow your app with customized time-related services, such as local time querying, and time difference querying. Site Kit offers a time zone search function that obtains the time zone for a specific place from its longitude-latitude coordinates. This function is implemented via a RESTful API. The API format is as follows:

```
https://siteapi.cloud.huawei.com/mapApi/v1/
timezoneService/getTimezone?key=API KEY
```

During actual coding, you'll need to replace *API KEY* in the request URL with your own dedicated API key. The following sample code obtains the time zone of the longitude-latitude coordinates (30.23235, 12.242585):

```
POST https://siteapi.cloud.huawei.com/mapApi/v1/
timezoneService/getTimezone?key=API KEY
HTTP/1.1
Content-Type: application/json
Accept: application/json
{
  "location": {
    "lng": "30.23235",
    "lat": "12.242585"
  },
  "timestamp": 1577435043,
  "language": "en"
}
```

Table 8.7 describes the parameters in the time zone search request.

TABLE 8.7   Parameters in the time zone search request

Parameter	Mandatory	Type	Description
location	Yes	Coordinate	Longitude-latitude coordinates for a place.
timestamp	No	Long	Number of seconds elapsed between 00:00:00 on January 1, 1970 (UTC) and the current time.
language	No	String($<=6$)	Language in which the search result is displayed. If this parameter is not passed, the local language for the place will be used.

The response to the preceding POST request is similar to the following, where **returnCode** indicates the API call result code, and **timeZoneName** indicates the time zone of the place. For details about the other parameters in the response, please refer to the *Site Kit API Reference* on the HUAWEI Developers website.

```
{
"returnCode": "0",
"timeZoneName": "Eastern African Time",
"rawOffset": 10800,
"timeZoneId": "Africa/Khartoum",
"dstOffset": 0,
"returnDesc": "OK"
}
```

8.6 SUMMARY

This chapter provided an overview of how to integrate Site Kit into your app, as well as how the Site SDK can be used in conjunction with the Android and RESTful APIs offered by Site Kit. In coding practice, we explained how the keyword search, place search suggestion, place detail search, and nearby place search functions work, while also delving into the geocoding and time zone search functions in Site Kit.

In the next chapter, we'll introduce HUAWEI Map Kit and detail how the kit can be harnessed to develop map-related functions within your app.

CHAPTER 9

Map Kit

- Map display: displays buildings, roads, water systems, POIs, and other key attributes.

- Map interaction: provides support for UI controls, gestures, map events, and other features.

- Map drawing: adds markers, ground overlays, and other shapes to generated maps.

- Map style customization: customizes the map style.

- Route planning: implements route planning between the point of departure and destination, via three distinct travel modes.

9.1 ABOUT THE SERVICE

Map Kit incorporates a myriad of different functions, split into the following three categories: in-app map, route planning, and web map. Figure 9.1 shows the service principles behind Map Kit.

1. In-app map

This service provides a range of enriching functions, including map display, interaction, drawing, and style customization. The service client consists of the Map SDK and HMS Core (APK). The Huawei Map Server provides authentication and map obtaining, while the integrated Map SDK communicates with the Huawei Map Server via HMS Core (APK) to implement in-app map functions.

DOI: 10.1201/9781003206699-9

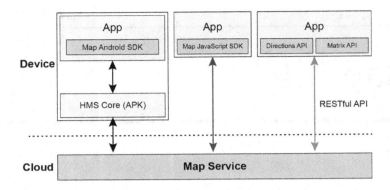

FIGURE 9.1   Service principles behind Map Kit.

2. Route planning

This service helps determine optimal routes for users, based on the specified departure place, waypoints, destination, and other preferences. It comes with RESTful APIs, including both Directions APIs and Matrix APIs. In order to use the Directions APIs, you'll need to build a valid JSON body and send a valid POST request to the Huawei Map Server. After verifying the request, the Huawei Map Server will return a JSON body that contains the planned routes. The Matrix APIs can be seen as enhanced Directions APIs, allowing for multiple groups of departure places and destinations through a single request. After verifying the request, the Huawei Map Server returns planned routes between the departure places and destinations.

3. Web map

This service implements map-related functions on web pages. Such functions include basic map display, map controls, map interaction, map drawing, place search, and route planning. The Map JavaScript SDK and Huawei Map Server work in concert to implement web map functions. For more details,

> **NOTE**
>
> Map Kit provides map services in the background of your app. It is not a map app for end users. Huawei will automatically enable corresponding free plans on your behalf. To use paid APIs of Map Kit, subscribe to relevant pay-as-you-go plans in AppGallery Connect. For more details, please refer to Service Pricing and Subscription on HUAWEI Developers.

please refer to the development documentation on the HUAWEI Developers website.

9.2 PREPARATIONS

As planned, let's develop the Pet Store app to ensure that users can view geographic locations for pet stores on maps within the app, which, in turn, helps them locate and plan their route to the nearest pet stores. Next, we'll explain how to integrate Map Kit into the Pet Store app to implement these functions.

To prepare to integrate Map Kit, you'll need to register as a Huawei developer, create an app, and configure the signing certificate fingerprint in AppGallery Connect. The detailed steps were explained in earlier chapters. To use Map Kit, you'll need to declare the following permissions in the **AndroidMainfest.xml** file:

```
<uses-permission android:name="android.permission.
INTERNET"/>
<uses-permission android:name="android.permission.
ACCESS_NETWORK_STATE"/>
<uses-permission android:name="com.huawei.Appmarket.
service.commondata.permission.GET_COMMON_DATA"/>
```

To obtain the current device location, you'll also need to declare the following permissions in the file. (In Android 6.0 or later, you'll also need to apply for them to ask the user to grant access to their data.)

```
<uses-permission android:name="android.permission.
ACCESS_COARSE_LOCATION"/>
<uses-permission android:name="android.permission.
ACCESS_FINE_LOCATION"/>
```

After that, you'll need to enable Map Kit in AppGallery Connect. The procedure is as follows:

Sign in to AppGallery Connect, click **My projects**, and click the Pet Store app in the project. Then, go to **Project settings > Manage APIs**, as shown in Figure 9.2.

On the **Manage APIs** page, toggle on the **Map Kit** switch, as shown in Figure 9.3.

Now, we'll show you how to integrate the Map SDK.

FIGURE 9.2   Manage APIs page.

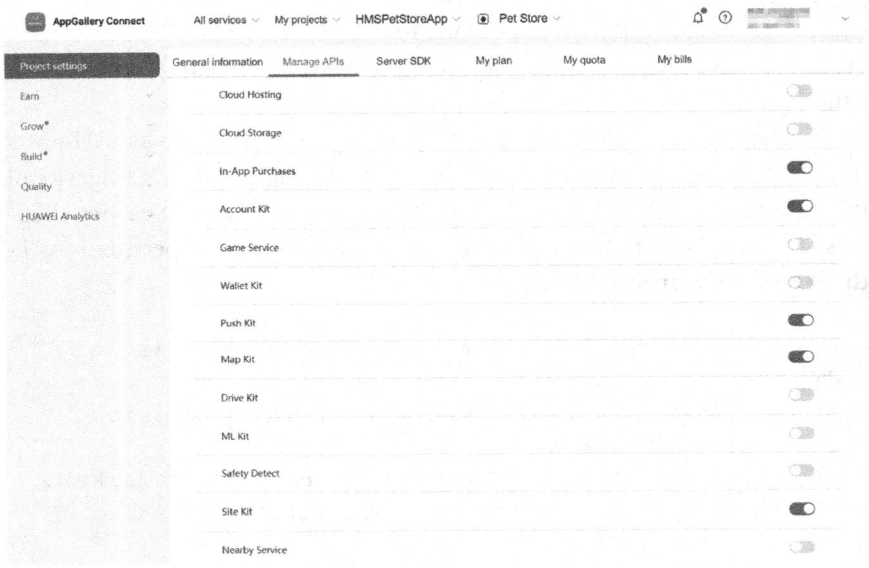

FIGURE 9.3   Enabling Map Kit.

Open the **build.gradle** file in the **app** directory for your project, and add the build dependency on the Map SDK in the **dependencies** closure.

```
implementation 'com.huawei.hms:maps: 4.0.1.300'
```

In the code above, version 4.0.1.300 is used as an example. For details about the latest version, please refer to our documentation on the HUAWEI Developers website. After configuring the dependency, click **Sync Now** in the upper right corner and wait for synchronization to complete, as shown in Figure 9.4.

To use the route planning function in Map Kit, you'll need to apply for an API key for your app. For details about how to do so, please refer to Chapter 8.

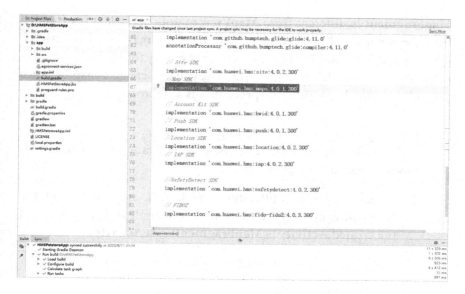

FIGURE 9.4   Integrating the Map SDK.

9.3 CREATING A MAP

This section illustrates the process of how to load a map in the Pet Store app using a map container.

9.3.1 Creating a Map Instance

Just as text can only be displayed via the **TextView** control, a map can only be displayed via a map container. The Map SDK for Android currently supports two types of map containers: **MapFragment** and **MapView**.

- **MapFragment**: A subclass of the Android **Fragment** class. It can serve as a map container and provide an entry for accessing a **HuaweiMap** object.

- **MapView**: A subclass of the Android **Fragment** class. It can also serve as a map container and provide an entry for accessing a **HuaweiMap** object. It's important to note that when using **MapView**, you'll need to call the following lifecycle methods for **MapView** in the respective lifecycle methods for **Activity**: **onCreate()**, **onStart()**, **onResume()**, **onPause()**, **onStop()**, **onDestroy()**, **onSaveInstanceState(Bundle outState)**, and **onLowMemory()**.

MapFragment is different from **MapView** mainly because it is extended from **Fragment** and its lifecycle is automatically managed by **Activity**, whereas **MapView** needs to be bound with **Activity** for lifecycle management. No matter which container you use, you can create a map instance via coding or the layout file. The procedure is as follows:

1. Creating a map instance via coding

    The following uses **MapFragment** as an example to demonstrate how to create a map instance:

    (1) Declare the **OnMapReadyCallback** API and implement the **OnMapReady** method. The following sample code assumes that the created **Activity** is **MapFragmentCodeActivity**:

    ```
    public    class    MapFragmentCodeActivity    extends
    AppCompatActivity implements
      OnMapReadyCallback {
      @Override
      protected void onCreate(Bundle savedInstanceState)
    {
        super.onCreate(savedInstanceState);
        setContentView(R.layout.activity _ map _
    fragment _ code);
      }
      @Override
      public void onMapReady(HuaweiMap huaweiMap) {
      }
    }
    ```

    (2) Call the **MapFragment.newInstance()** method to instantiate **MapFragment**, and call the **MapFragment.getMapAsync()** method to execute the **onMapReady** callback method. The sample code is as follows:

    ```
    private MapFragment mMapFragment;
    private HuaweiMap hMap;
    @Override
    protected void onCreate(Bundle savedInstanceState) {
        super.onCreate(savedInstanceState);
        setContentView(R.layout.activity _ map _
    fragment _ code _ demo);
        HuaweiMapOptions huaweiMapOptions = new Huawei
    MapOptions();
    ```

```
    // Obtain a MapFragment object through the
HuaweiOptions object.
    mMapFragment = MapFragment.newInstance(huaweiMap
Options);
    // Obtain a FragmentManager instance.
    FragmentManager fragmentManager = getFragment
Manager();
    // Obtain a FragmentTransaction instance.
    FragmentTransaction fragmentTransaction=fragment
Manager.beginTransaction();
    // Add the mMapFragment object to the layout file.
    fragmentTransaction.add(R.id.frame _ mapfragment-
codedemo, mMapFragment);
    // Submit your modification.
    fragmentTransaction.commit();
    mMapFragment.getMapAsync(this);
}
```

(3) Call the **HuaweiMap** object via the **onMapReady** method. The object can then be used to control the map.

```
@Override
public void onMapReady(HuaweiMap map) {
    hMap = map;
    // Set the center of the initialized map.
    hMap.moveCamera(CameraUpdateFactory.
newLatLngZoom(new LatLng(48.893478,
    2.334595), 10));
}
```

2. Creating a map instance via the layout file

In contrast with the coding mode, this mode reduces your coding workload by letting you set map attributes in the XML layout file. The following uses **MapFragment** as an example to demonstrate how to create a map instance through the layout file:

(1) Add a **MapFragment** object to the layout file for **Activity**, add the map namespace **xmlns:map=http://schemas.android.com/apk/res-auto** to the **MapFragment** block, and set the map attributes. The sample code is as follows:

```
<fragment xmlns:android="http://schemas.android.com/
apk/res/android"
    xmlns:map="http://schemas.android.com/apk/res-auto"
    android:id="@+id/mapfragment _ mapfragmentdemo"
```

```
class="com.huawei.hms.maps.MapFragment"
android:layout _ width="match _ parent"
android:layout _ height="match _ parent"
map:cameraTargetLat="48.893478"
map:cameraTargetLng="2.334595"
map:cameraZoom="10" />
```

The most common map attributes are listed below:

– **mapType**: map type, which can be **none** or **normal**.

– **cameraTargetLng** and **cameraTargetLat**: longitude and latitude of the center of the map.

– **cameraZoom**: map zoom level around the center of the screen.

– **cameraBearing**: map rotation angle in degrees, clockwise from the north.

– **cameraTilt**: camera angle in degrees, from the nadir (directly facing the Earth).

– **uiZoomControls**: indicates whether to display the zoom icons. The zoom icons are displayed by default.

– **uiCompass**: indicates whether to enable the compass. The compass is enabled by default.

– **uiZoomGestures**, **uiScrollGestures**, **uiRotateGestures**, and **uiTiltGestures**: indicate whether to enable the zoom gestures, scroll gestures, rotation gestures, and tilt gestures, respectively. By default, these gestures are enabled.

– **zOrderOnTop**: indicates whether to place the map view on top of all other map layers. By default, the map view is placed on top of all other map layers.

(2) Declare the **OnMapReadyCallback** API and implement the **OnMapReady** method. Call the **HuaweiMap** object via the **onMapReady** method. The object can then be used to control the map.

```
public class MapFragmentDemoActivity extends App
CompatActivity implements
```

```
OnMapReadyCallback {
  private HuaweiMap hMap;
@Override
protected void onCreate(Bundle savedInstanceState) {
  super.onCreate(savedInstanceState);
  setContentView(R.layout.activity _ map _ fragment _
demo);
}
@Override
public void onMapReady(HuaweiMap map) {
  hMap = map;
  // Set the center of the initialized map.
  hMap.moveCamera(CameraUpdateFactory.
newLatLngZoom(new LatLng(48.893478,
    2.334595), 10));}
}
}
```

(3) Load **MapFragment** in the **onCreate** method for **Activity**, and call the **getMapAsync()** method for **MapFragment** to execute the **onMapReady** callback method.

```
public    class    MapFragmentDemoActivity    extends
AppCompatActivity implements
  OnMapReadyCallback {
    private Huawei hMap;
    @Override
    protected void onCreate(Bundle savedInstanceState) {
      super.onCreate(savedInstanceState);
      setContentView(R.layout.activity _ map _
fragment _ demo);
      private MapFragment mMapFragment = (MapFragment)
      getFragmentManager().findFragmentById(R.
id.mapfragment _ mapfragmentdemo);
      mMapFragment.getMapAsync(this);
    }
@Override
public void onMapReady(HuaweiMap map) {
  hMap = map;
  // Set the center of the initialized map.
  hMap.moveCamera(CameraUpdateFactory.
newLatLngZoom(new LatLng(48.893478,
    2.334595), 10));}
}
```

9.3.2 Setting the Map Type

Map Kit supports two types of maps, which can be set by calling the **setMapType** method of the **HuaweiMap** object:

- **MAP_TYPE_NORMAL**: standard map, which shows roads, artificial structures, and natural features such as rivers.

- **MAP_TYPE_NONE**: empty map that does not display any data.

The default display is a standard map suitable for most scenarios and daily life. An empty map will not display any ground objects, so use it when you want to display only certain drawn markers or shapes on the map other than the geographic location information.

To set a standard map, call **setMapType(HuaweiMap.MAP_TYPE_NORMAL)** for the **HuaweiMap** object. Figure 9.5 shows a standard map.

To set an empty map, call **setMapType(HuaweiMap.MAP_TYPE_NONE)** for the **HuaweiMap** object. Figure 9.6 shows an empty map.

9.3.3 Setting the Padding

Map Kit implements maps the same way a camera works. The map camera area will center on the target location and be padded. Map controls (such as the compass, zoom control, and my-location icon) are placed at the border of the map camera area. By default, the compass is placed in the upper right corner of the map camera area; the zoom control and my-location icon are placed in the lower right corner of the map camera area. When laying out the map, you can adjust the padding between map controls and map bounds to prevent the controls from covering important information on the map.

To do this, you'll need to call the **HuaweiMap.setPadding(int left, int top, int right, int bottom)** method. The parameters for this method are as follows:

- **left**: a meaningless parameter. Set it to **0**.

- **top**: padding between the compass and the top bound of the map camera area, in pixels.

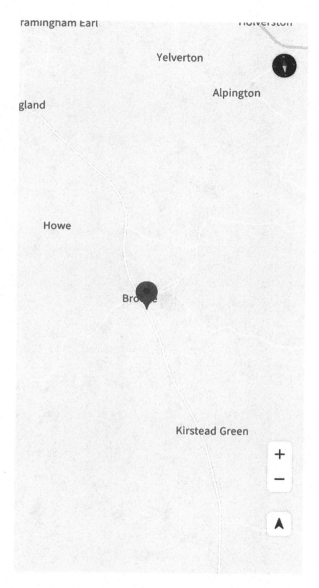

FIGURE 9.5 Standard map.

FIGURE 9.6   Empty map.

- **right**: padding between the compass, zoom control, and my-location icon and the right bound of the map camera area, in pixels.

- **bottom**: padding between the zoom control and my-location icon and the bottom bound of the map camera area, in pixels.

Figures 9.7 and 9.8 show the maps with the default and custom padding, respectively.

Please note that after you set the padding, the map center will shift accordingly. For example, if the **HuaweiMap.setPadding(0, 0, 100, 100)** method is called, the map center will shift to the upper left corner.

9.3.4 Coding Practice

In this section, you'll step through the process for creating a map in the Pet Store app. Here, we use **MapView** as the map container for creating a map via the layout file. The procedure is as follows:

1. Add a **MapView** object to the layout file for **PetStoreSearch DetailActivity.java**.

```
<com.huawei.hms.maps.MapView
   android:id="@+id/mapview _ mapviewdemo"
   android:layout _ width="match _ parent"
   android:layout _ height="match _ parent"
<!-Set the map type to normal.-->
   map:mapType="normal"
<!-Set the compass to be visible.-->
   map:uiCompass="true"
<!-Set the zoom button to be visible.-->
   map:uiZoomControls="true"
<!-Set not to place the map layer on the top.-->
   map:zOrderOnTop="false" />
```

2. Implement the **OnMapReadyCallback** API and override the **onMap Ready** method to ensure that the map can be used in the app.

```
public    class    PetStoreSearchDetailActivity    extends
AppCompatActivity implements
   OnMapReadyCallback {
@Override
public void onMapReady(HuaweiMap map) {
}
}
```

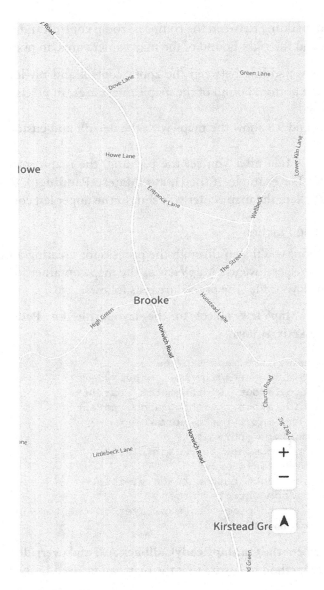

FIGURE 9.7   Default padding.

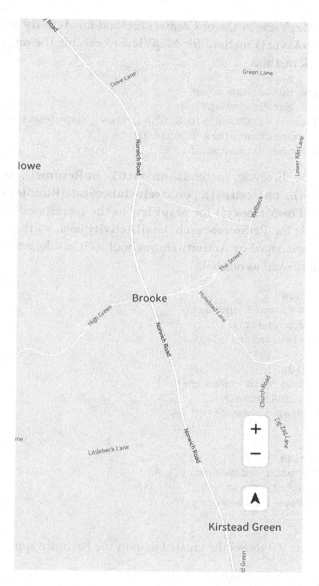

FIGURE 9.8   Custom padding.

3. Load **MapView** in the **onCreate()** method for **Activity** and call the **getMapAsync()** method for **MapView** to execute the **onMapReady** callback method.

```
private HuaweiMap hMap;
private MapView mMapView;
mMapView = findViewById(R.id.mapview _ mapviewdemo);
mMapView.onCreate(new Bundle());
mMapView.getMapAsync(this);
```

4. Call the lifecycle methods **onStart()**, **onResume()**, **onPause()**, **onStop()**, **onDestroy()**, **onSaveInstanceState(Bundle outState)**, and **onLowMemory()** for **MapView** in the corresponding lifecycle methods for **PetStoreSearchDetailActivity.java**, so that **MapView** can be managed by **Activity** throughout its lifecycle, and be created and destroyed as needed.

```
@Override
protected void onStart() {
  super.onStart();
  mMapView.onStart();
}
@Override
protected void onResume() {
  super.onResume();
  mMapView.onResume();
}
...
@Override
public void onLowMemory() {
  super.onLowMemory();
  mMapView.onLowMemory();
}
```

Figure 9.9 shows the created map in the Pet Store app.

9.4 INTERACTING WITH THE MAP

After accessing the in-app map, a user is free to perform a range of different interactions such as swiping and touching. This section describes how to set the map interaction operations.

The process is remarkably simple and the settings are explained in the following sections, so we won't code them here.

FIGURE 9.9   Created map.

9.4.1 Map Camera

Map Kit implements maps like a camera. You can control the visible region of a map by changing camera settings such as focal length and angle to shoot different areas on the map, as shown in Figure 9.10.

Table 9.1 describes the map camera attributes.

Figure 9.11 shows a map camera view with **target** set to **(0.0, 0.0)**, **zoom** to **3**, **tilt** to **0°**, and **bearing** to **0°**.

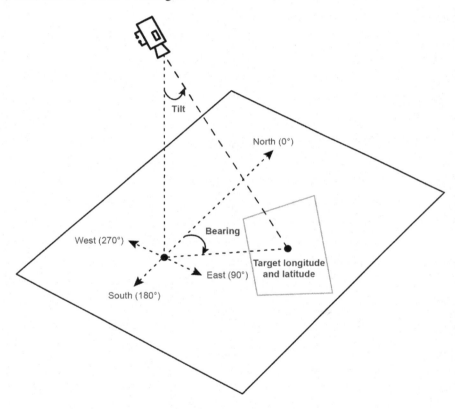

FIGURE 9.10   Map camera movements.

TABLE 9.1   Map camera attributes

Attribute	Description
Target	Longitude-latitude coordinates for the map center.
bearing	Map rotation angle in degrees, clockwise from the north.
Tilt	Camera angle in degrees, from the nadir (directly facing the Earth).
Zoom	Map zoom level around the center of the screen.

CameraPosition:{bearing=0.0,zoom=3.0,tilt=0.0,target=latitude:
0.0 longitude: 0.0}

FIGURE 9.11   Original map camera view.

The following sample code shifts the map camera view, with **target** set to **(52.541326999999995, 1.3710089999999966)**, **zoom** to **14**, **tilt** to **45°**, and **bearing** to **245°**:

```
CameraPosition build =
  new CameraPosition.Builder().target(new
LatLng(52.541326999999995, 1.3710089999999966)).
zoom(18).tilt(45).bearing(80).build();
CameraUpdate cameraUpdate = CameraUpdateFactory.
newCameraPosition(build);
// Move the map camera in non-animation mode.
hmap.moveCamera(cameraUpdate);
```

Figure 9.12 shows this new map camera view.

9.4.2 UI Controls and Gestures

Map Kit allows you to set built-in UI controls and map gestures as needed to customize the way users interact with the maps in your app. The UI controls and map gestures are detailed below.

1. UI controls

    UI controls include the zoom control, compass, and my-location icon. You can call the **getUiSettings()** method of the **HuaweiMap** class to obtain a **UiSettings** object, through which you'll be able to control the visibility of relevant UI controls. Figure 9.13 shows the UI controls on Huawei maps.

    (1) Zoom control

    Map Kit displays a built-in zoom control by default. To hide the zoom control, set the code as follows:

    ```
    // Set not to display the zoom control.
    hMap.getUiSettings().setZoomControlsEnabled(false);
    ```

    (2) Compass

    Map Kit displays a compass in the upper right corner of the map by default. If the compass is enabled, and the map is not oriented due north, the compass icon will display in the upper right corner of the map. The user can touch the compass icon to reorient the map due north. If the compass is enabled and the

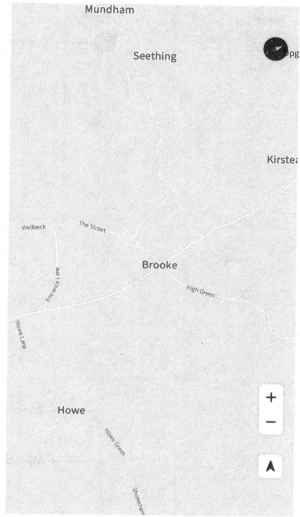

CameraPosition:
{bearing=245.0,zoom=14.0,tilt=45.0,target=latitude:
52.541326999999995 longitude: 1.3710089999999966}

FIGURE 9.12   New map camera view.

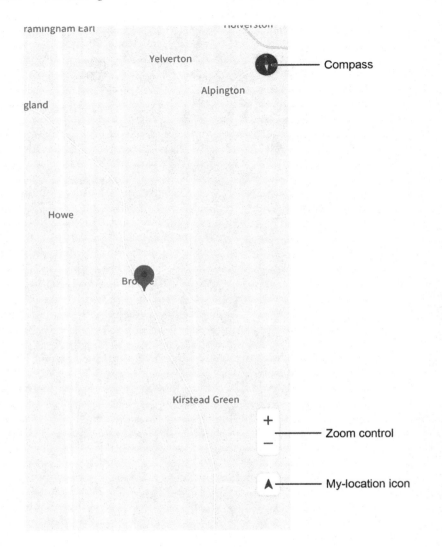

FIGURE 9.13   UI controls on Huawei maps.

map is oriented due north, the compass icon will be hidden. If the compass is disabled, the compass icon will not display under any circumstances. The sample code for disabling the compass is as follows:

```
// Set not to display the compass.
hMap.getUiSettings().setCompassEnabled(false);
```

(3) My-location icon

Before enabling the my-location icon, you'll need to declare the relevant location permissions. The Android OS provides two location permissions: **ACCESS_COARSE_LOCATION** (approximate location permission) and **ACCESS_FINE_LOCATION** (precise location permission). These permissions are declared in the **AndroidManifest.xml** file. The sample code is as follows:

```
<uses-permission    android:name="android.permission.
ACCESS _ COARES _ LOCATION"/>
<uses-permission    android:name="android.permission.
ACCESS _ FINE _ LOCATION"/>
```

After adding the code to the **AndroidManifest.xml** file, you'll still need to apply for them to ask the user to grant access to their data (according to requirements for dangerous permissions in Android 6.0). The sample code is as follows:

```
if (Build.VERSION.SDK _ INT >= Build.VERSION _ CODES.M) {
  Log.i(TAG, "sdk >= 23 M");
  if (ActivityCompat.checkSelfPermission(this,
    Manifest.permission.ACCESS _ FINE _ LOCATION)    !=
PackageManager.PERMISSION _ GRANTED
    || ActivityCompat.checkSelfPermission(this,
      Manifest.permission.ACCESS _ COARSE _ LOCATION) !=
    PackageManager.PERMISSION _ GRANTED) {
    String[] strings =
      {Manifest.permission.ACCESS _ FINE _ LOCATION,
Manifest.permission.
        ACCESS _ COARSE _ LOCATION};
    ActivityCompat.requestPermissions(this, strings, 1);
  }
}
```

After declaring the required permissions, code the **onMapReady** method in **PetStoreSearchDetailActivity.java** to enable the my-location icon. The sample code is as follows:

```
@RequiresPermission(allOf = {ACCESS _ FINE _ LOCATION,
ACCESS _ WIFI _ STATE})
@Override
public void onMapReady(HuaweiMap map){
  hMap = map;
```

```
  hMap.setMyLocationEnabled(true);  //  Enable  the
  my-location layer.
    hMap.getUiSettings().setMyLocationButtonEnabled(-
  true);// Enable the my-location icon.
  }
```

Once this function has been enabled, the my-location icon will display in the lower right corner of the map by default, and the user's current location will display as a purple dot. When the user touches this icon, the user's current location (if obtained) will center on the screen, as shown in Figure 9.14.

To hide the my-location icon, call the **getUiSettings(). setMyLocationButtonEnabled(false)** method for the **HuaweiMap** object.

2. Map gestures

You can also define gestures for users to interact with the maps in your app, for example, pinching out on the map with two fingers to increase the zoom level, or sliding the map with one finger to move the map. By default, Map Kit enables all map gestures, including zoom gestures, scroll gestures, tilt gestures, and rotation gestures. The **UiSettings** object can be used to enable or disable map gestures. To disable these gestures, you can use the sample code below.

(1) Disabling the zoom gestures:

```
hMap.getUiSettings().setZoomGesturesEnabled(false);
```

(2) Disabling the scroll gestures:

```
hMap.getUiSettings().setScrollGesturesEnabled(false);
```

(3) Disabling the tilt gestures:

```
hMap.getUiSettings().setTiltGesturesEnabled(false);
```

(4) Disabling the rotation gestures:

```
hMap.getUiSetting.setRotateGesturesEnabled(false);
```

9.4.3 Map Events

Map Kit supports a myriad of different events: map touch, map long-press, POI touch, and camera movement. You can set listeners to listen for

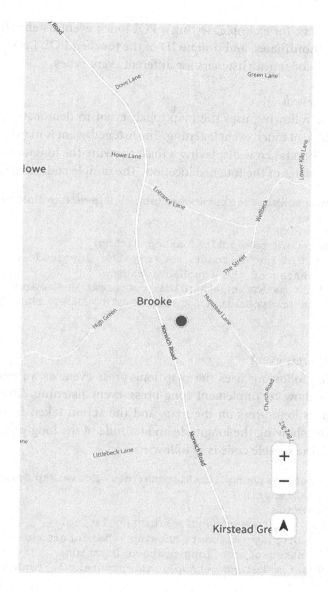

FIGURE 9.14   Viewing my location.

relevant events, for example, setting a POI touch event listener to obtain the name, coordinates, and unique ID of the touched POI. Let's learn the sample code for setting listeners for different event types.

1. Touch event

The following uses the map touch event to demonstrate how to implement touch event listening. The listened event is map touch, and the action taken is displaying a toast showing the longitude-latitude coordinates of the touched location. The sample code is as follows:

```
hMap.setOnMapClickListener(new    HuaweiMap.OnMapClick
Listener() {
    @Override
public void onMapClick(LatLng latLng) {
    // Display a toast  showing  the  longitude-latitude
coordinates of the touched location.
    Toast.makeText(getApplicationContext(), "onMapClick:" +
      latLng.toString(), Toast.LENGTH _ SHORT).show();
    }
});
```

2. Long-press event

The following uses the map long-press event as an example to detail how to implement long-press event listening. The listened event is long press on the map, and the action taken is displaying a toast showing the longitude and latitude of the long-pressed location. The sample code is as follows:

```
hMap.setOnMapLongClickListener(new  HuaweiMap.OnMapLong
ClickListener() {
    @Override
public void onMapLongClick(LatLng latLng) {
    // Display a toast  showing  the  longitude-latitude
coordinates of the long-pressed location.
    Toast.makeText(getApplicationContext(),  "onMapLong-
Click:" +
      latLng.toString(), Toast.LENGTH _ SHORT).show();
    }
});
```

3. POI touch event

If you are interested in a POI, you can set a listener to listen for touch events corresponding to the POI. In the example, the listened event is POI touch, and the action taken is displaying a toast showing the POI information. The sample code is as follows:

```
hMap.setOnPoiClickListener(new      HuaweiMap.OnPoiClick
Listener() {
    @Override
    public void onPoiClick(PointOfInterest pointOfIn-
terest) {
        // Display a toast showing the POI information.
        Toast.makeText(getApplication(), "Name:" + pointOf
Interest.
            name + "\nPlaceId:" + pointOfInterest.placeId +
            "\nLocation:\n" + pointOfInterest.latLng.toString(),
            Toast.LENGTH _ LONG).show();
    }
});
```

The preceding sample code sets a pet store as a POI. Figure 9.15 shows the POI touch event.

4. Camera moving event

Map camera movements refer to any changes in various attributes, including position, zoom level, and tilt angle. After a listener is set for camera moving events, the application layer can listen for the camera moving status. The sample code is as follows:

```
@Override
public void onMapReady(HuaweiMap huaweiMap) {
  Log.i(TAG, "onMapReady: ");
hMap = huaweiMap;
// Set a listener to listen for the start of camera
moving.
hMap.setOnCameraMoveStartedListener(this);
// Set a listener to listen for the end of camera moving.
hMap.setOnCameraIdleListener(this);
  // Set a listener to listen for camera moving.
  hMap.setOnCameraMoveListener(this); }
// Set the callback to be executed when the camera
starts moving.
@Override
public void onCameraMoveStarted(int reason) {
  Log.i(TAG, "onCameraMoveStarted: successful");
}
// Set the callback to be executed when the camera
stops moving.
```

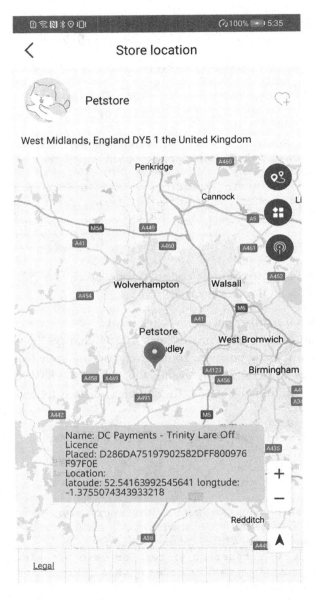

FIGURE 9.15 Listening for POI touch events.

```
@Override
public void onCameraIdle() {
  Log.i(TAG, "onCameraIdle: successful");
}
// Set the callback to be executed during camera moving.
@Override
public void onCameraMove() {
  Log.i(TAG, "onCameraMove: successful");
}
```

The following sample code listens for the map zoom level during camera moving:

```
hMap.setOnCameraMoveListener(new HuaweiMap.OnCameraMove
Listener() {
@Override
// Set the callback to be executed during camera moving.
public void onCameraMove() {
Toast.makeText(getApplication(), "Current  Zoom  is  " +
hMap.getCameraPosition().zoom,
  Toast.LENGTH _ LONG).show();
}
});
```

In this example, the toast "Current Zoom is 17.092348" displays during camera moving, as shown in Figure 9.16.

5. Marker touch event

Once we've added a marker for a pet store as demonstrated in Section 9.5, the following sample code centers the marker when touched:

```
hMap.setOnMarkerClickListener(newHuaweiMap.OnMarkerClick
Listener() {
  @Override
public boolean onMarkerClick(Marker marker) {
  // Move the marker to the center of the map.
    hMap.moveCamera(CameraUpdateFactory.newLatLng(-
marker.getPosition))
    return false;
  }
});
```

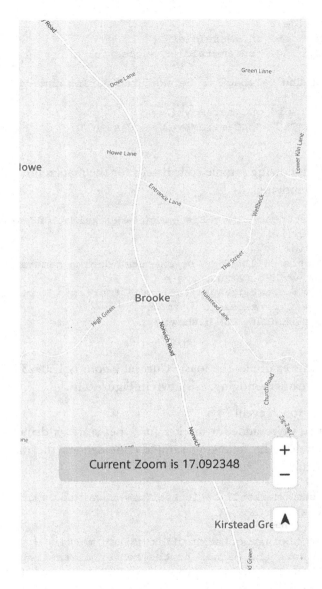

FIGURE 9.16   Listening for camera moving.

6. Information window touch event

Once we've added an information window for a pet store as demonstrated in Section 9.5, the following sample code sets a listener to listen for the information window touch event:

```
hMap.setOnInfoWindowClickListener(new          HuaweiMap.
OnInfoWindowClickListener() {
  @Override
public void onInfoWindowClick(Marker marker) {
    // Display a toast showing the marker information.
    Toast.makeText(getApplicationContext(),  "onInfoWin-
dowClick:" +
      marker.getTitle(), Toast.LENGTH _ SHORT).show();
  }
});
```

9.5 DRAWING ON THE MAP

This section steps you through the process of drawing markers, ground overlays, and shapes on a map. Map Kit enables you to draw the following elements on the map:

- Markers: A marker is used to mark a POI. You can add a marker at a specified location on the map, to identify a place, store, or building.

- Information windows: An information window is a part of the marker and is displayed above the marker by default. It is used to display information relating to the marker.

- Ground overlays: A ground overlay is an image overlapping the bottom map layer.

- Shapes: Supported shapes include polylines, polygons, and circles. You can use a polyline to draw the user motion track over a period of time, or use a polygon or circle to mark an area of interest.

The subsequent sections will detail how to draw these elements on the map.

NOTE

The functions in this chapter can be coded independently, and thus, this chapter does not include any coding practice.

9.5.1 Markers

Map Kit enables you to add and cluster markers on the map and add information windows for them.

1. Adding a marker

   The following sample code adds a simple marker with the default icon on the map:

```
// Define a marker variable.
private Marker mMarker;
// Set marker attributes.
MarkerOptions options = new MarkerOptions()
    .position(new LatLng(48.893478, 2.334595))
    .title("Hello Huawei Map")
    .snippet("This is a snippet!");
// Add the marker on the map.
mMarker = hMap.addMarker(options);
}
```

You can use a custom image to replace the default icon or modify marker attributes to change the marker icon. Table 9.2 describes the custom marker attributes.

TABLE 9.2   Custom marker attributes

Attribute	Description
Position	Longitude-latitude coordinates of a marker on the map. This is the only mandatory attribute for a **Marker** object.
Rotation	Rotation angle of a marker on the map.
Title	String to be displayed in the information window, when the user touches a marker.
Snippet	Other text to be displayed in the title text box.
Icon	Image used to replace the default marker icon.
Visible	Indicates whether a marker is visible. By default, a marker is visible.
Zindex	Z-index of a marker. A marker with a comparatively large z-index will overlap a marker with a comparatively small z-index. The default value is **0**.
Anchor	Anchor point of a marker.
Draggable	Indicates whether a marker can be dragged. By default, a marker cannot be dragged.
Alpha	Transparency of a marker. The value range is [0, 1]. The value **0** indicates that the marker is completely transparent, and **1** indicates that the marker is opaque. The default value is **1**.
Flat	Indicates whether a marker is flat on the map.
Infowindowanchor	Anchor point coordinates of the information window for a marker.

The Pet Store app requires markers to mark the pet stores on the map. Hence, we'll need to code **Marker** in the **PetStoreSearchDetailActivity.java** class to implement the function for adding markers.

(1) Define a **MarkerOptions** object to set the marker attributes, including the coordinates, anchor point, and icon.

```
/**
 * Obtain a MarkerOptions object.
 *
 * @param position Coordinates of a marker.
 * @param name Pet store name.
 * @return MarkerOptions
 */
private    MarkerOptions    getMarkerOptions(LatLng
position, String name) {
    MarkerOptions markerOptions = new MarkerOptions().
position(position)
        .anchorMarker(0.5f,  0.9f)
        .icon(BitmapDescriptorFactory.fromBitmap
(getMarkerBitmap(name)));
        return markerOptions;
    }
```

(2) Add the marker on the map.

```
hMap.addMarker(getMarkerOptions(latLng, p.getName())).
setTag(p.getSiteId());
```

Figure 9.17 shows the added marker.

2. Clustering markers

Map Kit lets you to effectively manage map markers at different zoom levels. When the user zooms in more, all markers are displayed on the map. When the user zooms out, the markers are clustered to ensure a clean, orderly display.

The following sample code implements the marker clustering function:

```
@Override
  public void onMapReady(HuaweiMap map) {
    hMap = map;
  // Move the camera view to a certain location.
    hMap.moveCamera(CameraUpdateFactory.newLatLngZoom(
```

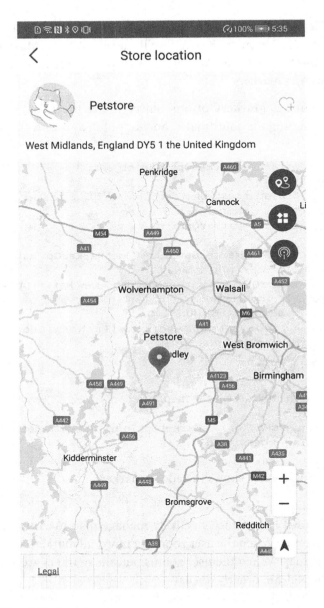

FIGURE 9.17 Added marker.

```
        new LatLng(48.893478, 2.334595),10));
     // Add six markers around the location, and set
clusterable to true for these markers.
     hMap.addMarker(new MarkerOptions().position(new LatLng
(48.891478,
        2.334595)).title("Marker1").clusterable(true));
     hMap.addMarker(new MarkerOptions().position(new LatLng
(48.892478,
        2.334595)).title("Marker2").clusterable(true));
     hMap.addMarker(new MarkerOptions().position(new LatLng
(48.893478,
        2.334595)).title("Marker3").clusterable(true));
     hMap.addMarker(new MarkerOptions().position(new LatLng
(48.894478,
        2.334595)).title("Marker4").clusterable(true));
     hMap.addMarker(new MarkerOptions().position(new LatLng
(48.895478,
        2.334595)).title("Marker5").clusterable(true));
     hMap.addMarker(new MarkerOptions().position(new LatLng
(48.896478,
        2.334595)).title("Marker6").clusterable(true));
     hMap.setMarkersClustering(true);
   }
```

Figure 9.18 shows the marker clustering effects in practice. Figure 9.18 (a) shows the markers at a high zoom level, while Figure 9.18 (b) shows the clustered marker at a low zoom level.

3. Adding an information window

Map Kit allows you to create both default and custom information windows. The procedure is as follows:

(1) Add an information window.

The easiest way to add an information window for a marker is to set the **title(String title)** and **snippet(String snippet)** attributes for the corresponding **Marker** object. After the attributes are set, an information window will display when the user touches the marker. You can set the **title** and **snippet** attributes of a **Marker** object using either of the following methods:

Method 1: Use **MarkerOptions** to set the marker attributes. The sample code is as follows:

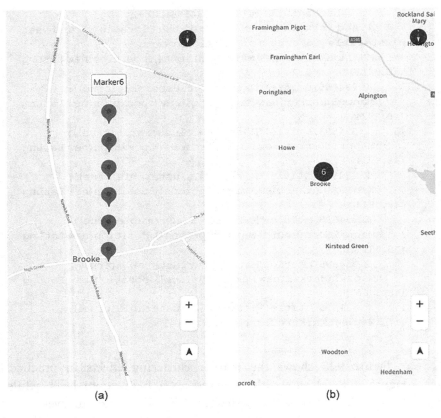

(a)　　　　　　　　　　(b)

FIGURE 9.18　Marker clustering effects.

```
private Marker mMarker;
MarkerOptions options = new MarkerOptions().position(-
new LatLng(52.541327, 1.371009));
  options.title("Title: PetStore");
  options.snippet("Snippet: This is a petstore.");
  mMarker = hMap.addMarker(options);
```

Method 2: Use the **Marker.setTitle(String title)** and **Marker. setSnippet(String snippet)** methods to set or modify the marker attributes. The sample code is as follows:

```
mMarker    =    hMap.addMarker(new    MarkerOptions().
position(new LatLng(52.541327, 1.371009)));
mMarker.setTitle("Title: PetStore");
mMarker.setSnippet("Snippet: This is a petstore.");
```

FIGURE 9.19   Default information window.

Both methods achieve the same effect. After the marker is added on the map, an information window will display when the user touches the marker, as shown in Figure 9.19.

(2) Display or hide an information window.

An information window is a response to the touch on a marker, automatically displaying when the user touches a marker on the map and hiding when the user touches other areas on the map. You can also call **showInfoWindow()** for a **Marker** object to display the information window, or call **hideInfoWindow()** for the **Marker** object to hide it.

The sample code for displaying the information window is as follows:

```
private void showInfoWindow() {
  boolean isInfoWindowShown = mMarker.
    isInfoWindowShown();
  if (!isInfoWindowShown) {
    // Display the information window.
    mMarker.showInfoWindow();
  }
}
```

The sample code for hiding the information window is as follows:

```
private void hideInfoWindow() {
  boolean isInfoWindowShown = mMarker.isInfoWindow
Shown();
  if (isInfoWindowShown) {
    // Hide the information window.
    mMarker.hideInfoWindow();
  }
}
```

(3) Customize an information window.

Map Kit allows you to customize the information window for a marker. To do this, you'll need to customize the **CustomInfoWindowAdapter** class to implement the **InfoWindowAdapter** API, and call the API using the **setInfoWindowAdapter()** method for the **HuaweiMap** object. The procedure is as follows:

a. Create the **custom_info_window.xml** file, which is used as the custom layout file for the information window.

```
<?xml version="1.0" encoding="utf-8"?>
<LinearLayout     xmlns:android="http://schemas.
android.com/apk/res/android"
```

```xml
      android:layout_width="wrap_content"
      android:layout_height="wrap_content"
      android:orientation="horizontal">
    <ImageView
      android:id="@+id/img_marker_icon"
      android:layout_width="50dp"
      android:layout_height="50dp"
      android:layout_marginRight="5dp"
      android:adjustViewBounds="true"
      android:src="@mipmap/ic_launcher" />
    <LinearLayout
      android:layout_width="wrap_content"
      android:layout_height="wrap_content"
      android:orientation="vertical">
    <TextView
      android:id="@+id/txtv_titlee"
      android:layout_width="wrap_content"
      android:layout_height="wrap_content"
      android:text="PetStore"
      android:ellipsize="end"
      android:singleLine="true"
      android:textColor="#ff000000"
      android:textSize="14sp"
      android:textStyle="bold" />
    <TextView
      android:id="@+id/txtv_snippett"
      android:layout_width="wrap_content"
      android:layout_height="wrap_content"
      android:text="This is a petstore"
      android:ellipsize="end"
      android:singleLine="true"
      android:textColor="#ff7f7f7f"
      android:textSize="14sp" />
  </LinearLayout>
</LinearLayout>
```

b. Implement the **HuaweiMap.InfoWindowAdapter** API, which provides an adapter for the custom marker window view. The **HuaweiMap.InfoWindowAdapter** API provides two methods: **getInfoWindow(Marker)** and **getInfoContents (Marker)**. The **getInfoWindow(Marker)** method is used to customize the window background. The default background is used when **null** is returned. The **getInfoContents(Marker)** method is used to customize the window content. Likewise, the default content is used when **null** is returned. The sample code is as follows:

```
private class CustomInfoWindowAdapter implements
HuaweiMap.InfoWindowAdapter {
  private final View mWindow;
CustomInfoWindowAdapter() {
    // Convert the custom layout file into a view.
    mWindow = getLayoutInflater().inflate(R.layout.
custom _ info _ window, null);
  }
  // Customize an information window.
  @Override
  public View getInfoWindow(Marker marker) {
    return null;
  }
  // Customize the information window content.
  @Override
  public View getInfoContents(Marker marker) {
    return mWindow;
  }
}
```

c. Set a custom information window adapter for **HuaweiMap**. The sample code is as follows:

```
@Override
public void onMapReady(HuaweiMap map) {
  if (map == null) {
    return;
  }
  // Set a custom information window for the marker.
  hMap.setInfoWindowAdapter(new
    CustomInfoWindowAdapter());
  hMap.addMarker(new MarkerOptions().position
    (hMap.getCameraPosition().target));
}
```

Figure 9.20 shows what this custom information window looks like in practice.

FIGURE 9.20 Custom information window.

9.5.2 Ground Overlay

A ground overlay is an image overlapping the bottom map layer. You can opt to add a ground overlay on the map to mark a specific place.

1. Adding a ground overlay

    (1) Use the **BitmapDescriptorFactory** class to create a **Bitmap Descriptor** object. The sample code is as follows:

    ```
    // Obtain an image from the asset directory.
    BitmapDescriptor descriptor = BitmapDescriptorFactory.
    fromAsset("images/
      avocado.jpg");
    // Load a bitmap image.
    BitmapDescriptor descriptor = BitmapDescriptorFactory.
    fromBitmap(bitmap);
    // Obtain an image from the internal storage based
    on its file name.
    BitmapDescriptor descriptor = BitmapDescriptorFactory.
    fromFile(fileName);
    // Load an image from its absolute path.
    BitmapDescriptor descriptor = BitmapDescriptorFactory.
    fromPath(path);
    // Load an image from the resource file.
    BitmapDescriptor descriptor = BitmapDescriptorFactory.
    fromResource(R.drawable.
      makalong);
    ```

    (2) Create a **GroundOverlayOptions** object to set the **position** and **image** attributes of the ground overlay. The sample code is as follows:

    ```
    GroundOverlayOptions options = new GroundOverlay
    Options().position(new
      LatLng(48.956074, 2.27778), 200, 200).image(descriptor);
    ```

    (3) Call the **addGroundOverlay(GroundOverlayOptions options)** method for the **HuaweiMap** object to add the ground overlay. The sample code is as follows:

    ```
    private GroundOverlay mGroundOverlay;
    // Add a ground overlay on the map.
    mGroundOverlay = hMap.addGroundOverlay(options);
    ```

    Figure 9.21 shows the added ground overlay on the map.

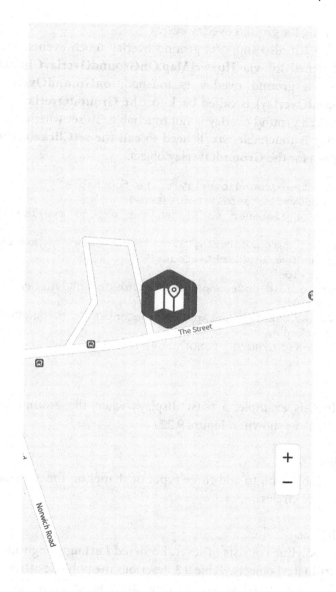

FIGURE 9.21   Ground overlay.

2. Listening for ground overlay events

Map Kit also supports ground overlay touch events, which can be listened for via **HuaweiMap.OnGroundOverlayClickListener**. When a ground overlay is touched, **onGroundOverlayClick(-GroundOverlay)** is called back for the **GroundOverlay** object. By default, a ground overlay is not touchable. To set whether a ground overlay is touchable, you'll need to call the **setClickable(boolean)** method for the **GroundOverlay** object.

```
// Set the ground overlay to be touchable.
mGroundOverlay.setClickable(true);
// Set a listener to listen for ground overlay touch
events.
hMap.setOnGroundOverlayClickListener(new       HuaweiMap.
OnGroundOverlayClickListener() {
  @Override
  public void onGroundOverlayClick(GroundOverlay groun-
dOverlay) {
    Toast.makeText(getApplicationContext(), "GroundOverlay
is clicked.",
      Toast.LENGTH _ LONG).show();
  }
});
```

In this example, a toast displays when the ground overlay is touched, as shown in Figure 9.22.

9.5.3 Shapes

Map Kit enables you to add three types of shapes on the map: polylines, polygons, and circles.

1. Polylines

A polyline consists of several ordered **LatLng** (longitude-latitude coordinates) objects. Table 9.3 describes the polyline attributes.

The following describes the procedures for creating a polyline and listening for polyline touch events:

(1) Create a polyline object.

You can add a polyline using the **addPolyline** method. To change the shape of an added polyline, you'll need to call the **setPoints()** method of the polyline object and pass a new list of

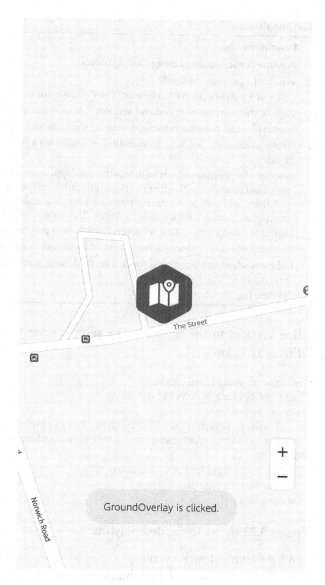

FIGURE 9.22   Ground overlay touch event.

TABLE 9.3   Polyline attributes

Attribute	Description
Points	Polyline vertices defined using **LatLng** objects.
Width	Width of a polyline, in pixels.
Color	Color of a polyline, in ARGB format. The default color is black.
Start/End Cap	Caps of the polyline start and end vertices. The default cap is **ButtCap**.
Joint type	Joint type of all polyline vertices, except for the start and end vertices.
Stroke Pattern	Stroke pattern of a polyline. By default, the strokes for a polyline are solid.
Z-Index	Z-index of a polyline, which indicates the overlapping order of the polyline compared with other overlays (ground overlays, circles, polylines, and polygons). An overlay with a larger z-index will overlap an overlay with a smaller z-index. The default value is **0**.
Visibility	Indicates whether a polyline is visible. By default, a polyline is visible.
Geodesic	Indicates whether to draw each segment of a polyline as a geodesic.
Clickability	Indicates whether a polyline is touchable. By default, a polyline is not touchable.
Tag	Polyline tag.

polyline vertices to the method. The sample code for adding a polyline is as follows:

```
// Define a Polyline object.
private Polyline mPolyline;
// Add a polyline.
  mPolyline = hMap.addPolyline(new PolylineOptions()
    .add(new LatLng(47.1606, 2.4000), new LatLng(47.2006,
2.000),
      new LatLng(47.3000, 2.1000))
    .color(Color.BLUE)
    .width(8));
```

Figure 9.23 shows the added polyline.

(2) Listen for polyline touch events.

You can call the **setClickable(boolean)** method for a **Polyline** object to specify whether the corresponding polyline is touchable. To listen for polyline touch events, call the **setOnPolylineClickListener(OnPolylineClickListener)** method for the **HuaweiMap** object.

```
// Set the polyline to be touchable.
```

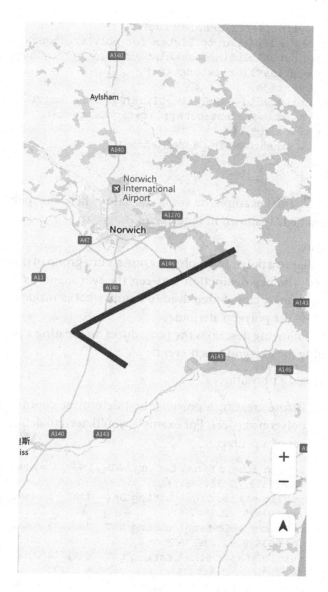

FIGURE 9.23   Polyline.

```
mPolyline.setClickable(true);
// Set a listener to listen for polyline touch events.
hMap.setOnPolylineClickListener(new          HuaweiMap.
OnPolylineClickListener() {
  @Override
  public void onPolylineClick(Polyline polyline) {
    Toast.makeText(getApplicationContext(), "Polyline
is clicked.",
      Toast.LENGTH _ LONG).show();
  }
});
```

In this example, a toast displays when the polyline is touched, as shown in Figure 9.24.

2. Polygons

Similar to a polyline, a polygon consists of a group of ordered coordinates. The key distinction between the two shapes is that a polygon contains a closed area used to define what is inside it. Table 9.4 describes the polygon attributes.

The following describes the procedures for creating a polygon and listening for polygon touch events:

(1) Create a polygon.

   a. Before creating a polygon, first determine coordinates of the polygon vertices. For example, you'll need to define five vertices of a pentagon.

```
public static final LatLng LAT _ LNG _ 1 = new LatLng(
47.893478, 2.334595);
public static final LatLng LAT _ LNG _ 2 = new LatLng
(47.894478, 2.336595);
public static final LatLng LAT _ LNG _ 3 = new LatLng
(47.893478, 2.339595);
public static final LatLng LAT _ LNG _ 4 = new LatLng
(47.893278, 2.342595);
public static final LatLng LAT _ LNG _ 5 = new LatLng
(47.890078, 2.334595);
```

   b. Add a polygon, and place the polygon in the center of the map.

```
hMap.addPolygon(
new PolygonOptions().add(LAT _ LNG _ 1, LAT _ LNG _ 2,
LAT _ LNG _ 3, LAT _ LNG _ 4,
LAT _ LNG _ 5).fillColor(Color.GREEN));
```

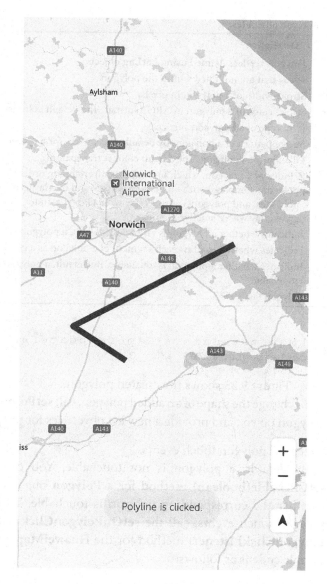

FIGURE 9.24   Polyline touch event.

TABLE 9.4   Polygon attributes

Attribute	Description
Points	Polygon vertices defined using **LatLng** objects.
Holes	Areas that are not filled within the polygon.
Stroke Width	Stroke width of a polygon in pixels.
Stroke Color	Stroke color of a polygon in ARGB format. The default color is black.
Joint type	Joint type of all polygon vertices.
Stroke Pattern	Stroke pattern of a polygon. By default, the strokes for a polygon are solid.
Fill Color	Fill color of a polygon. The default color is transparent.
Z-Index	Z-index of a polygon, which indicates the overlapping order of the polygon, compared with other overlays (ground overlays, circles, polylines, and polygons). An overlay with a larger z-index will overlap an overlay with a smaller z-index.
Visibility	Indicates whether a polygon is visible. By default, a polygon is visible.
Geodesic	Indicates whether to draw each segment of a polygon as a geodesic.
Clickability	Indicates whether a polygon is touchable. By default, a polygon is not touchable.
Tag	Polygon tag.

```
hMap.moveCamera(CameraUpdateFactory.
newLatLngZoom(LAT _ LNG _ 3, 15));
```

Figure 9.25 shows the created polygon.

To change the shape of an added polygon, call **setPoints()** for the **Polygon** object, and provide a new list of vertices for the polygon.

2   Listen for polygon touch events.

By default, a polygon is not touchable. You can call the **setClickable(boolean)** method for a **Polygon** object to specify whether the corresponding polygon is touchable. To listen for polygon touch events, call the **setOnPolygonClickListener(On PolygonClickListener)** method for the **HuaweiMap** object. The sample code is as follows:

```
// Set the polygon to be touchable.
mPolygon.setClickable(true);
// Set a listener to listen for polygon touch events.
hMap.setOnPolygonClickListener(new          HuaweiMap.
OnPolygonClickListener() {
    @Override
    public void onPolygonClick(Polygon polygon) {
```

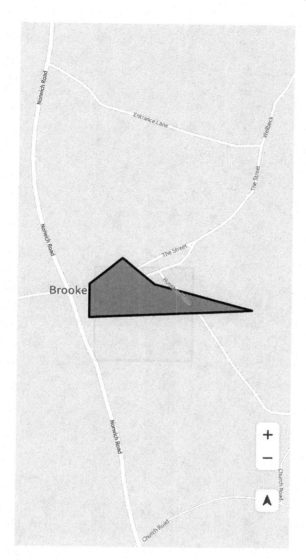

FIGURE 9.25   Polygon.

```
        Toast.makeText(getApplicationContext(),
    "Polygon is clicked.",
        Toast.LENGTH _ LONG).show();
    }
});
```

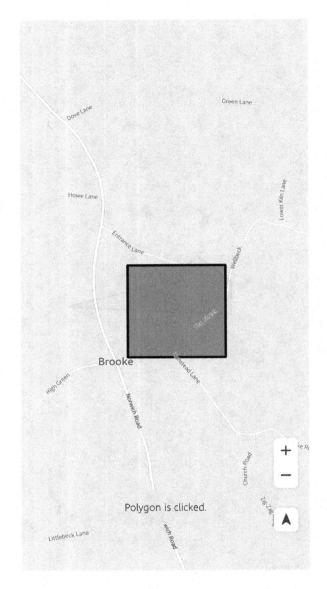

FIGURE 9.26   Polygon touch event.

TABLE 9.5   Circle attributes

Attribute	Description
Center	Center of a circle, which is defined using a **LatLng** object. This attribute is mandatory.
Radius	Radius of a circle, in meters.
Stroke Width	Stroke width of a circle in pixels.
Stroke Color	Stroke color of a circle in ARGB format. The default color is black.
Stroke Pattern	Stroke pattern of a circle. By default, the circle strokes are solid.
Fill Color	Fill color of a circle. The default color is transparent.
Z-Index	Z-index of a circle, which indicates the overlapping order of the circle compared with other overlays (ground overlays, circles, polylines, and polygons). An overlay with a larger z-index will overlap an overlay with a smaller z-index.
Visibility	Indicates whether a circle is visible. By default, a circle is visible.
Tag	Circle tag.

In this example, a toast displays when the polygon is touched, as shown in Figure 9.26.

3. Circles

Map Kit supports both solid (default) and hollow circles. Table 9.5 describes the circle attributes.

The following describes the procedures for creating a circle and listening for circle touch events:

(1) Create a circle object with the center coordinates and radius specified. The sample code is as follows:

```
private Circle mCircle;
mCircle = hMap.addCircle(new CircleOptions()
    .center(new LatLng(31.97846, 118.76454))
    .radius(500)
    .fillColor(Color.GREEN));
```

Figure 9.27 shows the added circle.

To change the center and radius of an added circle, you can call the **setCenter()** and **setRadius()** methods for the circle object.

(2) Listen for circle touch events.

By default, a circle is not touchable. You can call the **Circle. setClickable(boolean)** method to specify whether a circle is

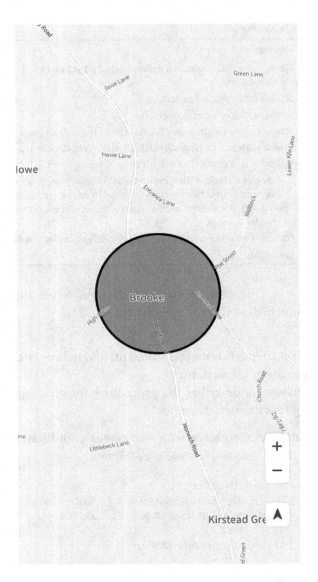

FIGURE 9.27 Circle.

touchable. Call the **setOnCircleClickListener(Huaweimap. OnCircleClickListener)** method for the **HuaweiMap** object to listen for circle touch events. When a circle is touched, the

onCircleClick(Circle) method calls the circle object. The sample code is as follows:

```
// Set the circle to be touchable.
  mCircle.setClickable(true);
  // Set a listener to listen for circle touch events.
  hMap.setOnCircleClickListener(newHuaweiMap.OnCircle
ClickListener() {
    @Override
    public void onCircleClick(Circle circle) {
      Toast.makeText(getApplicationContext(), "Circle
is clicked.",
        Toast.LENGTH _ LONG).show();
  }
});
```

In this example, a toast displays when the circle is touched, as shown in Figure 9.28.

(3) Set a hollow circle. The sample code is as follows:

```
mCircle.setFillColor(Color.TRANSPARENT);  // Set  the
fill color of a circle to transparent.
mCircle.setStrokeColor(int  strokeColor);  // Set  the
stroke color of a circle.
mCircle.setStrokeWidth(float strokeWidth); // Set the
stroke width of a circle.
```

Figure 9.29 shows the added hollow circle.

9.5.4 Tile Overlay

A tile overlay is a set of images displayed on the map, equivalent to a large ground overlay that covers the entire map. It consists of square tiles organized into grids. When the map is moved to a new location, or the zoom level changes, Map Kit will determine the new tiles that need to be displayed.

The number of tiles is determined by the map zoom level; the unique ID for a tile is co-determined by the tile location coordinates (x, y) and map zoom level. The tile with location coordinates (0, 0) will always display in the northeast corner. The value of **x** increases from west to east, while **y** increases from north to south. The **x** and **y** coordinates of the origin are used to index tiles. The following are some examples.

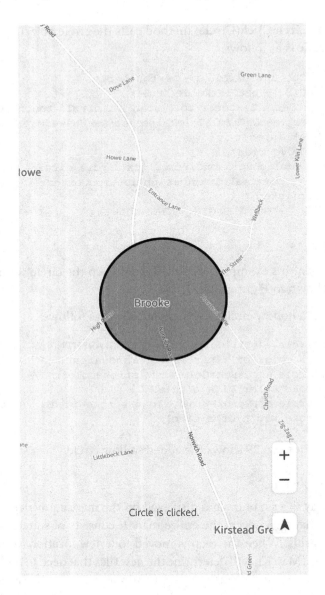

FIGURE 9.28   Circle touch event.

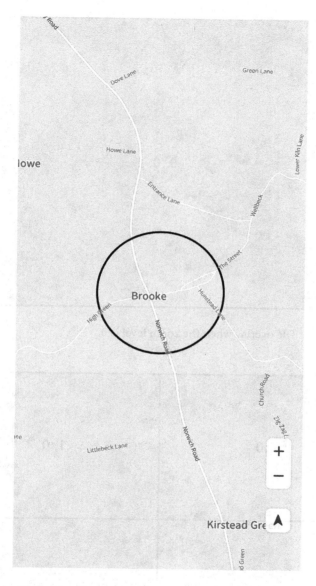

FIGURE 9.29   Hollow circle.

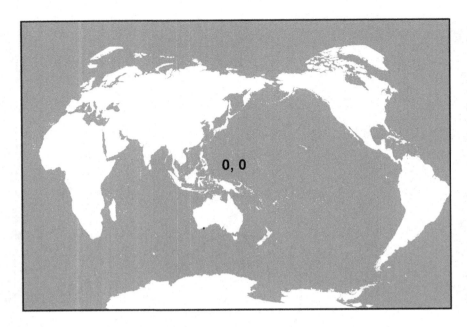

FIGURE 9.30 Tile overlay when the zoom level is 0.

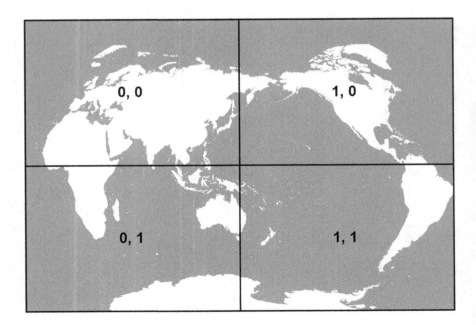

FIGURE 9.31 Tile overlay when the zoom level is 1.

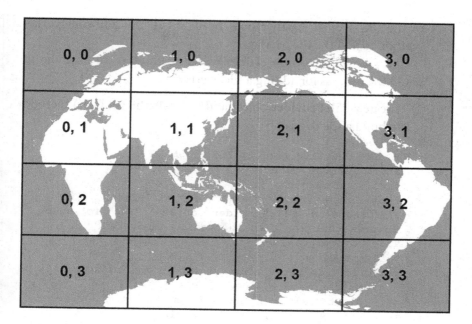

FIGURE 9.32   Tile overlay when the zoom level is 2.

If the zoom level is 0, the entire world map will be displayed in a single tile, where the number of tiles is 1 and the tile coordinates are (0, 0), as shown in Figure 9.30.

Each increase in the zoom level doubles the magnification. For instance, if the zoom level is 1, the map will be rendered as 2×2 grids (4 tiles), as shown in Figure 9.31. Each tile can be referenced through the coordinates (x, y) and zoom level.

When the zoom level is 2, the world map is rendered as 4×4 grids (16 tiles), as shown in Figure 9.32.

When the zoom level is 3, the world map is rendered as 8×8 grids (64 tiles), and so on up to level 20. Please note that Map Kit supports zoom levels 3–20, so the above zoom levels of 0, 1, and 2 were for illustration only.

1. Adding a tile overlay

   A tile is the minimum unit of a tile overlay. You can use the **TileProvider** (local) or **UrlTileProvider** (web) methods to obtain the tile image, and then create a **TileOverlayOptions** object to set fade-in effect, transparency, overlapping order, and other attributes of the tile overlay. Lastly, you'll need to call the **addTileOverlay** method to add the tile overlay.

The following uses the **TileProvider** method as an example to detail the process for adding a tile overlay:

(1) Create a **TileProvider** object and override the **getTile()** method to build a tile overlay.

```
// Set the tile size to 256 × 256.
int mTileSize = 256;
final int mScale = 1;
final int mDimension = mScale * mTileSize;
// Create a TileProvider object. The following
assumes that the tile is locally generated.
TileProvider mTileProvider = new TileProvider() {
  @Override
  public Tile getTile(int x, int y, int zoom) {
      Matrix matrix = new Matrix();
      float scale = (float) Math.pow(2, zoom) * mScale;
      matrix.postScale(scale, scale);
      matrix.postTranslate(-x * mDimension, -y *
mDimension);
      // Generate a Bitmap image.
    final Bitmap bitmap=Bitmap.createBitmap(mDimension,
mDimension,
      Bitmap.Config.RGB _ 565);
      bitmap.eraseColor(Color.parseColor("#024CFF"));
      ByteArrayOutputStream stream = new ByteArray
OutputStream();
      bitmap.compress(Bitmap.CompressFormat.PNG, 100,
stream);
      return new Tile(mDimension, mDimension, stream.
toByteArray());
      } };
```

(2) Create a **TileOverlayOptions** object to set the tile overlay attributes, such as the transparency and fade-in and fade-out animations for changes in transparency.

```
TileOverlayOptions options = new TileOverlayOptions().
tileProvider(mTileProvider).transparency(0.5f).
fadeIn(true);
```

TABLE 9.6   Methods for setting tile overlay attributes

Attribute	Method	Description
Tile Provider	tileProvider(TileProvider tileProvider)	Sets the tile provider for a tile overlay.
FadeIn	fadeIn(boolean fadeIn)	Sets whether a tile overlay fades in. By default, the tile overlay fades in.
Z-Index	zIndex(float zIndex)	Sets the z-index of a tile overlay. The default value is **0**.
Transparency	transparency(float transparency)	Sets the transparency of a tile overlay. By default, the tile overlay is opaque.
Visibility	visible(boolean visible)	Sets whether a tile overlay is visible. By default, the tile overlay is visible.

Table 9.6 shows you the methods used to set tile overlay attributes.

(3) Use the **addTileOverlay(TileOverlayOptions options)** method of the **HuaweiMap** object to add a tile overlay. This method will return a **TileOverlay** object.

```
mTileOverlay = hMap.addTileOverlay(options);
```

Figure 9.33 shows the added tile overlay.

2. Modifying a tile overlay

You can modify the attributes of an added tile overlay to suit your needs. The sample code is as follows:

```
// Set the transparency of the tile overlay.
if (null != mTileOverlay) {
  mTileOverlay.setTransparency(0.3f);
}
// Set the tile overlay not to fade in.
if (null != mTileOverlay) {
  mTileOverlay.setFadeIn(false);
}
// Set the tile overlay not to be visible.
if (null != mTileOverlay) {
  mTileOverlay.setVisible(false);
}
```

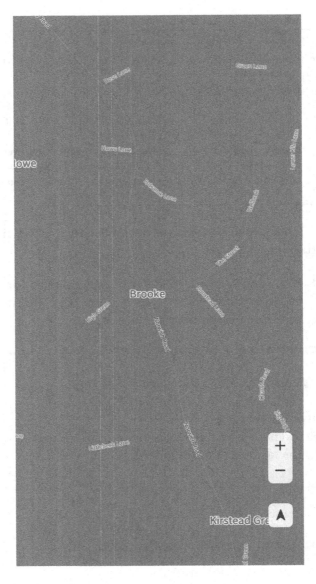

FIGURE 9.33   Tile overlay.

3. Removing a tile overlay

You can also remove a tile overlay that is no longer required. The sample code is as follows:

```
if (null != mTileOverlay) {
  mTileOverlay.remove();
}
```

If the tiles on a tile overlay become obsolete (e.g., the tiles change), you can call the **clearTileCache()** method to forcibly refresh the tile overlay and reload all of the tiles on it.

```
if (null != mTileOverlay) {
  mTileOverlay.clearTileCache();
}
```

9.6 CUSTOMIZING THE MAP STYLE

This section details the process for adding a custom map to your app. Map Kit provides you with a range of customizations for your app map to display roads, parks, businesses, and other POIs.

9.6.1 Use Example

The following uses a simple example to illustrate map style customization:

1. Define the JSON file **mapstyle_simple.json** in the **res/raw** directory. The file contains two character strings **landcover.natural** and **water**, which indicate the land and water system, respectively. This map style file will color the land green and water system dark blue on the map.

```
[
  {
    "mapFeature": "landcover.natural",
    "options": "geometry.fill",
    "paint": {
      "color": "#8FBC8F"
    }
  },
  {
    "mapFeature": "water",
```

```
    "options": "geometry.fill",
    "paint": {
      "color": "#4682B4"
    }
  }
]
```

2. Use the **loadRawResourceStyle()** method to load the JSON file as a **MapStyleOptions** object, and pass the object to the **HuaweiMap. setMapStyle()** method.

```
HuaweiMap hMap;
MapStyleOptions style;
style = MapStyleOptions.loadRawResourceStyle
  (this, R.raw.mapstyle _ simple);
hMap.setMapStyle(style);
```

3. View the effects of the custom map style, as shown in Figure 9.34.

9.6.2 Style Reference

The JSON file defines the map style with four parameters: **mapFeature**, **options**, **paint**, and **visibility**.

1. **mapFeature**: map element whose style needs to be changed. Such elements include buildings, water systems, and roads. When this parameter is set to **all**, the changed style will be applied to all map elements.

2. **options**: element options, for example, the building outline or fill and POI icon or text style. When this parameter is not set, all elements are included by default. The element options are as follows:

   – **geometry.fill**: geometric filling.

   – **geometry.stroke**: geometric stroke.

   – **geometry.icon**: geometric icon.

   – **labels.text.fill**: text filling.

   – **labels.text.stroke**: text stroke.

3. **paint**: drawing attributes.

   – **color**: color in hexadecimal format, for example, #FFFF00 (yellow).

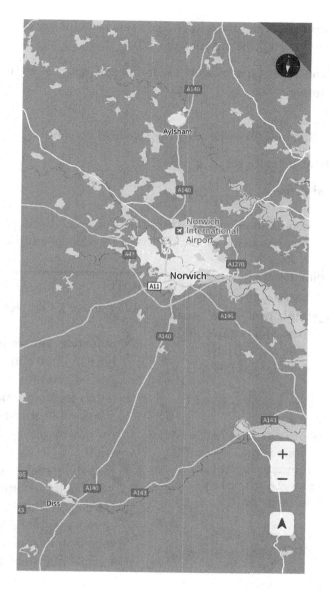

FIGURE 9.34   Custom map style.

- **weight**: stroke width. The value is an integer ranging from 0 to 8. The default value is **0**. A larger value indicates a wider stroke.

- **saturation**: degree of saturation. The value is an integer ranging from −100 to 100. The default value is **0**.

- **lightness**: brightness level. The value is an integer ranging from −100 to 100. The default value is **0**.

- **icon-type**: type of icon used. Current options are **night** and **simple**.

4. **visibility**: indicates whether a map element is visible.

- **true** (default): yes

- **false**: no

For details about map elements that can be modified, please refer to the documentation on the HUAWEI Developers website.

9.6.3 Coding Practice

Here, we'll define two style files: **mapstyle_simple.json** and **mapstyle_night.json**, for simple mode and night mode, respectively.

The sample code is as follows:

```
// Load the simple-mode
style file.
MapStyleOptions styleSimple
= MapStyleOptions.
loadRawResourceStyle(this,
R.raw.mapstyle_simple);
// Set the map style.
hMap.
setMapStyle(styleSimple);
// Load the night-mode
style file.
MapStyleOptions styleNight
= MapStyleOptions.
loadRawResourceStyle(this, R.raw.mapstyle_night);
// Set the map style.
hMap.setMapStyle(styleNight);
```

NOTE

Obtain these JSON files at:

- **mapstyle_simple.json**: https://github.com/-HMS-Core/hms-mapkit-demo-java/blob/master/mapsample/app/src/main/res/raw/mapstyle_simple.json
- **mapstyle_night.json**: https://github.com/-HMS-Core/hms-mapkit-demo-java/blob/master/mapsample/app/src/main/res/raw/mapstyle_night.json

Figure 9.35 shows the simple-mode map, and Figure 9.36 shows the night-mode map.

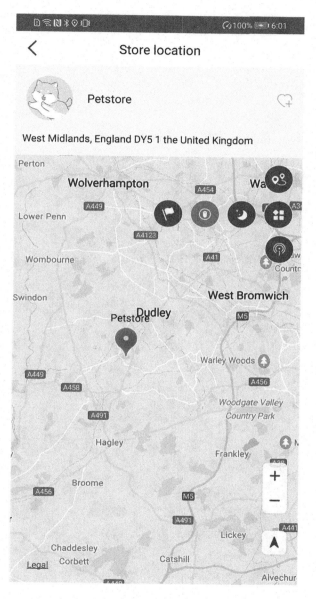

FIGURE 9.35   Simple-mode map.

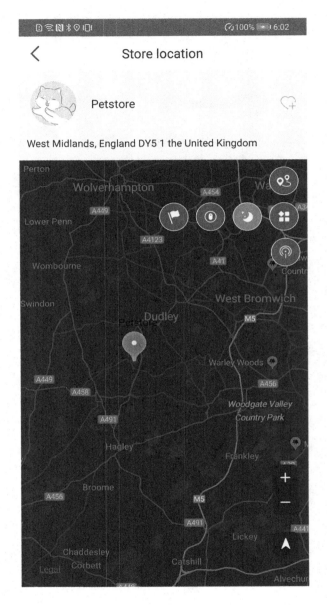

FIGURE 9.36   Night-mode map.

9.7 PLANNING ROUTES

This section details the route planning function of Map Kit. Estimated time of arrival (ETA) is a key factor for consideration during route planning, along with user travel preferences. For example, if the user prefers to avoid highways, the route planning algorithm will decrease the relative weight of highways to ensure that planned routes cover as few highways as possible. Furthermore, the function allows for multiple routes to be planned, from which the user can select their preferred route.

9.7.1 Overview

Map Kit provides two types of APIs for route planning: Directions APIs for planning routes between two points, and Matrix APIs for planning routes between multiple departure places and destinations. The following uses Directions APIs to illustrate how to use the route planning function.

Route planning APIs offer capabilities related to searching for routes and calculating route distances via RESTful. The route search result is returned in JSON format and is then used for route planning. Map Kit supports three route types: walking, cycling, and driving.

1. Walking route planning is restricted to a distance of 100 km.

2. Cycling route planning is restricted to a distance of 100 km.

3. Driving route planning:

   - Returns up to 3 routes per request.

   - Supports up to 5 waypoints.

   - Supports planned future travel.

   - Returns routes that take real-time traffic conditions into account.

9.7.2 Coding Practice

The procedure for developing the route planning function includes four steps as outlined in Figure 9.37.

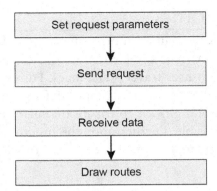

FIGURE 9.37   Route planning development process.

1. Setting the request parameters
   The sample code is as follows:

```
JSONObject json = new JSONObject();
try {
// Set the longitude-latitude coordinates of the depar-
ture place.
  origin.put("lat", latLngOrigin.latitude);
origin.put("lng", latLngOrigin.longitude);
// Set the longitude-latitude coordinates of the
destination.
  destination.put("lat", latLngDestination.latitude);
  destination.put("lng", latLngDestination.longitude);
  json.put("origin", origin);
  json.put("destination", destination);
} catch (JSONException e) {
  e.printStackTrace();
}
```

The departure place and destination are mandatory for route planning. To plan driving routes, the user can also specify waypoints and choose whether to return multiple routes. For the Pet Store app, set the departure place to the current user location, and the destination to the location of the target pet store in a JSON-format request body. The sample code is as follows:

```
{
  "origin": {
    "lng": -4.66529,
    "lat": 54.216608
```

```
  },
  "destination": {
    "lng": -4.66552,
    "lat": 54.2166
  }
}
```

Table 9.7 describes the parameters in the route planning request body.

TABLE 9.7   Parameters in the route planning request body

Parameter	Type	Description
Origin	Coordinate	Longitude and latitude of the departure place.
destination	Coordinate	Longitude and latitude of the destination.
waypoints	Coordinate[]	Waypoints. Up to 5 waypoints can be specified.
viaType	Boolean	Waypoint type. The options are as follows: • **false** (default): stopover • **true**: pass by
optimize	Boolean	Indicates whether to optimize the waypoints. The options are as follows: • **false** (default): no • **true**: yes
alternatives	Boolean	Indicates whether to return multiple planned routes. The options are as follows: • **false** (default): no • **true**: yes This parameter is unavailable when waypoints are set.
Avoid	Int[]	Indicates the road types that should be avoided. The options are as follows: • **1**: toll roads • **2**: highways If this parameter is not included in the request, the fastest route by time will be returned by default.
departAt	Long	Estimated departure time, in seconds elapsed since 00:00:00 on January 1, 1970 (UTC). The value must be either the current time or a future time.
trafficMode	Int	Time estimation model. The options are as follows: • **0** (default): Best guess. • **1**: Traffic conditions are worse than the historical average. • **2**: Traffic conditions are better than the historical average.

(Continued)

TABLE 9.7 CONTINUED   Parameters in the route planning request body

Parameter	Type	Description
Origin	Coordinate	Longitude and latitude of the departure place.
destination	Coordinate	Longitude and latitude of the destination.
waypoints	Coordinate[]	Waypoints. Up to 5 waypoints can be specified.
viaType	Boolean	Waypoint type. The options are as follows: • **false** (default): stopover • **true**: pass by
optimize	Boolean	Indicates whether to optimize the waypoints. The options are as follows: • **false** (default): no • **true**: yes
alternatives	Boolean	Indicates whether to return multiple planned routes. The options are as follows: • **false** (default): no • **true**: yes This parameter is unavailable when waypoints are set.
Avoid	Int[]	Indicates the road types that should be avoided. The options are as follows: • **1**: toll roads • **2**: highways If this parameter is not included in the request, the fastest route by time will be returned by default.
departAt	Long	Estimated departure time, in seconds elapsed since 00:00:00 on January 1, 1970 (UTC). The value must be either the current time, or a future time.
trafficMode	Int	Time estimation model. The options are as follows: • **0** (default): Best guess. • **1**: Traffic conditions are worse than the historical average. • **2**: Traffic conditions are better than the historical average.

2. Sending the request

After constructing the JSON body, you'll need to send a POST request containing the API key. If you do not have an API key, apply for one on the HUAWEI Developers website. For more details, please refer to Section 9.2.

If the API key contains special characters, you'll need to URL-encode it first. The request APIs for planning driving, walking, and cycling routes are as follows:

– Driving: https://mapapi.cloud.huawei.com/mapApi/v1/route
Service/driving?key=*API KEY*

– Walking: https://mapapi.cloud.huawei.com/mapApi/v1/route Service/walking?key=*API KEY*

– Cycling: https://mapapi.cloud.huawei.com/mapApi/v1/route Service/bicycling?key=*API KEY*

The following sample code sends a request to plan the driving route:

```
String url = https://mapapi.cloud.huawei.com/mapApi/v1/
routeService/driving?key=API KEY;
RequestBody requestBody = RequestBody.create(MediaType.
parse("Application/json;    charset=utf-8"),    String.
valueOf(json));
Request request=newRequest.Builder().url(url).post(request
Body).build();
Response response = getNetClient().initOkHttpClient().
newCall(request).execute();
```

3. Receiving data

The obtained data is a JSON body, and the planned route consists of multiple polylines. The method for obtaining the data is as follows:

```
String result = response.body().string()
```

The sample code for obtaining data is as follows:

```
{
  "routes": [
    {
      "paths": [
        {
          "duration": 9,
          "durationInTraffic": 0,
          "distance": 9,
          "startLocation": {
            "lng": -4.665290197110473,
            "lat": 54.21660781838372
          },
          "steps": [
            {
              "duration": 0,
              "orientation": 1,
              "distance": 0,
              "startLocation": {
```

```json
        "lng": -4.665290197110473,
        "lat": 54.21660781838372
      },
      "action": "straight",
      "endLocation": {
        "lng": -4.665290833333334,
        "lat": 54.216608055555554
      },
      "polyline": [
        {
          "lng": -4.66529,
          "lat": 54.216608
        },
        {
          "lng": -4.665291,
          "lat": 54.216608
        }
      ],
      "roadName": "Poortown Road"
    },
    {

      "duration": 9,
      "orientation": 1,
      "distance": 9,
      "startLocation": {
        "lng": -4.665290833333334,
        "lat": 54.216608055555554
      },
      "action": "unknown",
      "endLocation": {
        "lng": -4.6654460345493955,
        "lat": 54.21666592137546
      },
      "polyline": [
        {
          "lng": -4.665291,
          "lat": 54.216608
        },
        {
          "lng": -4.665405,
          "lat": 54.21665
        },
        {
          "lng": -4.665446,
          "lat": 54.216666
        }
```

```
            ],
            "roadName": "Poortown Road"
          }
        ],
        "endLocation": {
          "lng": -4.654460345493955,
          "lat": 54.21666592137546
        }
      }
    ],
    "bounds": {
      "southwest": {
        "lng": -4.655219444444445,
        "lat": 54.21584277777778
      },
      "northeast": {
        "lng": -4.662165833333333,
        "lat": 54.21669555555555
      }
    }
  }
],
"returnCode": "0",
"returnDesc": "OK"
}
```

4. Drawing routes

(1) Clear old tracks.

```
private void removePolylines() {
  for (Polyline polyline : mPolylines) {
    polyline.remove();
  }
  mPolylines.clear();
  mPaths.clear();
  mLatLngBounds = null;
}
```

(2) Request data preprocessing.

```
private void generateRoute(String json) {
  try {
    JSONObject jsonObject = new JSONObject(json);
    JSONArray routes=jsonObject.optJSONArray("routes");
    if (null == routes || routes.length() == 0) {
```

```
        return;
    }
    JSONObject route = routes.getJSONObject(0);
    // Obtain bounds where the route is located.
    JSONObject bounds = route.optJSONObject("bounds");
    if (null != bounds && bounds.has("southwest") &&
bounds.has("northeast")) {
        JSONObject southwest = bounds.optJSONObject
("southwest");
        JSONObject northeast = bounds.optJSONObject
("northeast");
        LatLng sw = new LatLng(southwest.optDouble("lat"),
            southwest.optDouble("lng"));
        LatLng ne = new LatLng(northeast.optDouble("lat"),
            northeast.optDouble("lng"));
        mLatLngBounds = new LatLngBounds(sw, ne);
    }
    // Obtain the route.
    JSONArray paths = route.optJSONArray("paths");
    for (int i = 0; i < paths.length(); i++) {
        JSONObject path = paths.optJSONObject(i);
        List<LatLng> mPath = new ArrayList<>();
        JSONArray steps = path.optJSONArray("steps");
        for (int j = 0; j < steps.length(); j++) {
            JSONObject step = steps.optJSONObject(j);
            JSONArray polyline = step.optJSONArray
("polyline");
            for (int k = 0; k < polyline.length(); k++) {
                if (j > 0 && k == 0) {
                    continue;
                }
                JSONObject line = polyline.getJSONObject(k);
                double lat = line.optDouble("lat");
                double lng = line.optDouble("lng");
                LatLng latLng = new LatLng(lat, lng);
                mPath.add(latLng);
            }
        }
        mPaths.add(i, mPath);
    }
    mHandler.sendEmptyMessage(ROUTE _ PLANNING _
COMPLETE _ SUCCESS);
    } catch (JSONException e) {
        log.e(TAG, "JSONException" + e.toString());
    }
}
```

(3) Draw the route.

```
private void renderRoute(List<List<LatLng>> paths,
LatLngBounds latLngBounds) {
  if (null == paths || paths.size() <= 0 || paths.get(-
0).size() <= 0) {
    return;
  }
  // Draw a route on the map using polylines.
  for (int i = 0; i < paths.size(); i++) {
    List<LatLng> path = paths.get(i);
    PolylineOptions options = new PolylineOptions().
color(Color.BLUE).width(5);
    for (LatLng latLng : path) {
      options.add(latLng);
    }
    Polyline polyline = hMap.addPolyline(options);
    mPolylines.add(i, polyline);
  }

  addOriginMarker(paths.get(0).get(0));
  if (null != latLngBounds) {
    CameraUpdate cameraUpdate = CameraUpdateFactory.
      newLatLngBounds(latLngBounds, 80);
    hMap.moveCamera(cameraUpdate);
  } else {
    LatLngBounds.Builder boundsBuilder = new LatLng
Bounds.Builder();
    // Save the longitude-latitude coordinates of the
departure place and destination.
    boundsBuilder.include(latLngOrigin);  // Include
the departure place.
    boundsBuilder.include(latLngDestination);//
Include the destination.
    hMap.moveCamera(CameraUpdateFactory.
newLatLngBounds(boundsBuilder.build(),
      SystemUtil.dp2px(PetStoreSearchDetailActivity.
this, 80)));
  }
}
```

(4) Add a marker for the departure place.

```
private void addOriginMarker(LatLng latLng) {
  if (null != mMarkerOrigin) {
    mMarkerOrigin.remove();
  }
```

```
mMarkerOrigin = hMap.addMarker(new MarkerOptions().
position(latLng)
    .anchor(0.5f, 0.9f)
    .anchorMarker(0.5f, 0.9f));
}
```

Figure 9.38 shows how the planned route looks in practice.

FIGURE 9.38   Planned route.

9.8 SUMMARY

In this chapter, you've learned how to:

1. Integrate Map Kit into your app, create map instances and select map types, and display the current user location.

2. Interact with the map, move the map camera to adjust the visible map area, and listen for map events.

3. Add markers, information windows, ground overlays, and shapes on the map, as well as customize the map style.

4. Build a route planning function into your app, and in doing so, enable users to plot walking, cycling, and driving routes.

Now that you have an in-depth understanding of Map Kit and all that it offers, you will be able to quickly build map-related services into your app at minimal cost and provide your users with a wealth of interactive and responsive operations.

CHAPTER 10

Safety Detect

10.1 ABOUT THE SERVICE

As shown in Figure 10.1, Safety Detect helps you boost security by building SysIntegrity, AppsCheck, URLCheck, and UserDetect into your app.

1. **SysIntegrity**: checks whether devices running your app are secure, for example, if they are rooted or unlocked. For payment scenarios, an app initiating a payment request can check the system integrity by first calling the **SysIntegrity** API. If the device is rooted, the app warns the user or blocks the request to prevent malicious attacks from occurring.

2. **AppsCheck**: obtains a list of malicious apps on the user device. With this list, you can either warn the user of potential risks or intercept their access to such apps.

3. **URLCheck**: checks whether a requested URL is malicious, for example, a phishing URL. You can either warn the user of the risk or block the URL.

4. **UserDetect**: checks whether your app is interacting with a fake user. This prevents a range of malicious behavior, including spam registrations, credential stuffing attacks, activity bonus hunting, and content crawling.

DOI: 10.1201/9781003206699-10

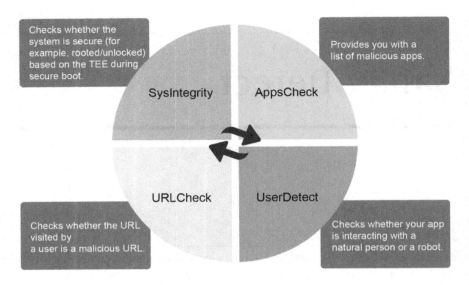

FIGURE 10.1   Overview of safety detect.

FIGURE 10.2   Safety detect use cases.

10.2 PREPARATIONS

In our Pet Store app, SysIntegrity and UserDetect are used in member payments and sign-ins respectively. To implement these features, let's first make preparations as outlined in previous chapters: register as a Huawei developer, create the Pet Store app in AppGallery Connect, and configure a certificate fingerprint for it. Next, we'll enable Safety Detect, integrate the Safety Detect SDK, and configure the obfuscation scripts.

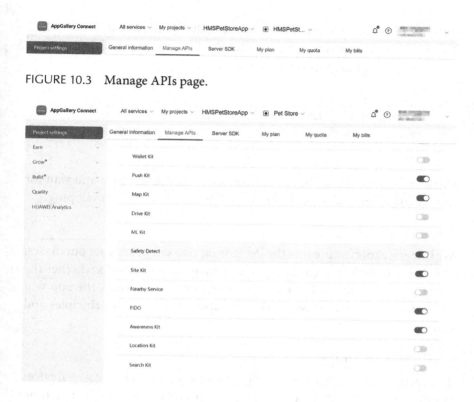

FIGURE 10.3　Manage APIs page.

FIGURE 10.4　Enabling safety detect.

10.2.1　Enabling Safety Detect

Sign in to AppGallery Connect, click **My projects**, find and click the project that contains our app, and go to **Project settings > Manage APIs**, as shown in Figure 10.3.

Toggle on the **Safety Detect** switch, as shown in Figure 10.4.

10.2.2　Integrating the Safety Detect SDK

Before integrating the SDK, download the **agconnect-services.json** file for your app from AppGallery Connect and save the file to the **app** directory of your project, as detailed in earlier chapters. Then, configure the dependency on the Safety Detect SDK. To do this, open the **build.gradle** file in the **app** directory of your project, and add the following build dependency in the **dependencies** block:

```
implementation 'com.huawei.hms:safetydetect:{version}'
```

Here, *{version}* indicates the version number of the Safety Detect SDK. The example version number is **4.0.2.300**. You can find the latest version number on the HUAWEI Developers website.

```
dependencies {
// Integrate the Safety Detect SDK.
implementation 'com.huawei.hms:safetydetect:4.0.2.300'
}
```

Click **Sync Now** in the upper right corner of Android Studio and wait for the synchronization to complete. Once it has, we can start developing.

10.3 SYSINTEGRITY

We integrate this feature into the Pet Store app to safeguard user purchases. When a user makes a payment, the **SysIntegrity** API checks whether the user's device is secure. For example, if the device is rooted, the app will remind the user of the risk. Let's learn about SysIntegrity principles and coding.

10.3.1 Service Process

The SysIntegrity feature is available for many devices. On Huawei devices running EMUI 9.1 or later, SysIntegrity provides check results based on the Trusted Execution Environment (TEE). When enabled, it checks the device environment and securely stores the results in the TEE. On other Huawei devices or non-Huawei devices, the check results are saved on the server and secured through a digital certificate, as shown in Figure 10.5.

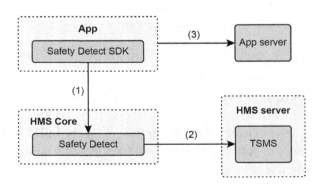

FIGURE 10.5 SysIntegrity service process.

1. Your app integrated with the Safety Detect SDK calls the **SysIntegrity** API of Safety Detect to request a check.

2. Safety Detect checks system security and sends the result to the Trusted Security Management Service (TSMS) server. The server signs the result using the X.509 digital certificate and sends it as a JSON Web Signature (JWS) string to your app.

3. Your app sends the signed check result to the app server for verification.

10.3.2 Coding Practice

Let's practice the implementation, as shown in Figure 10.6.

1. Obtain a nonce value.

   When calling the **SysIntegrity** API of Safety Detect, you need to pass a nonce value that serves as a temporary request ID. The value will be contained in the check result. You can check the nonce value to verify that the returned result corresponds to your request, which prevents replay attacks.

   Note that a nonce value can be used only once, and must contain at least 16 bytes. It is recommended that you derive it from the data sent to your server. For example, you can set the value to be the user name plus the current timestamp:

```
byte[] nonce = (name+ System.currentTimeMillis()).get
Bytes();
```

2. Call the **SysIntegrity** API.

   The **SysIntegrity** API has two input parameters: the nonce value and your app ID. Obtain the app ID from the **agconnect-services. json** file under the **app** directory of your project.

   When a user purchases a membership in the Pet Store app, the app calls the **SysIntegrity** API to check whether the payment environment has any risks. When coding, call the **detectSysIntegrity** API of the **SafetyDetectUtil** class with the **onAdapterItemClick** method in the **MemberCenterAct.java** class. Here's the code:

```
private void onAdapterItemClick(int position) {
// Call the SysIntegrity API to check for risks in the
payment environment.
```

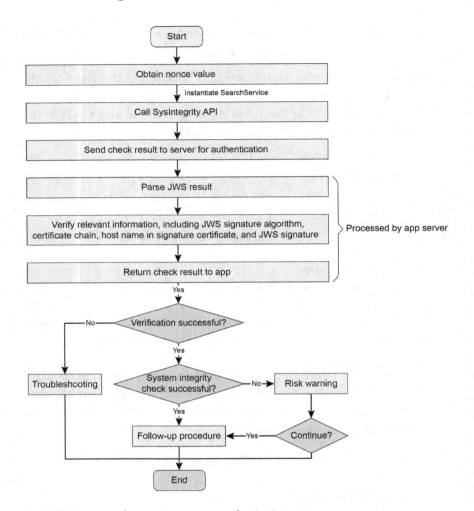

FIGURE 10.6 Implementation process for SysIntegrity.

```
SafetyDetectUtil.detectSysIntegrity(this, new ICallBack
<Boolean>() { @Override
public void onSuccess(Boolean baseIntegrity) { if
(baseIntegrity) {
// Proceed with the purchase if the system integrity is
not corrupted.
buy(productInfo);
} else {
// If the system integrity is corrupted, display a pop-up
to warn the user and ask the user whether to continue.
```

```
showRootTipDialog(productInfo);
}
}
    ...
});
}
```

In the Pet Store app, the system integrity check function is implemented in the **SafetyDetectUtil.java** class. The key check logic of this class is encapsulated in the **detectSysIntegrity** method:

```
public static void detectSysIntegrity(final Activity
activity, final ICallBack
<? super Boolean> callBack) {
// Generate a nonce value.
byte[] nonce = ("Sample" + System.currentTimeMillis()).
getBytes(StandardCharsets.UTF_8);
// Read the app_id field from the agconnect-services.
json file in the app directory.
String appId = AGConnectServicesConfig.fromContext(-
activity). getString("client/app_id");
// Obtain the Safety Detect client, call the sysInteg-
rity API, and add a listening event.
SafetyDetect.getClient(activity)
.sysIntegrity(nonce, appId)
.addOnSuccessListener(new OnSuccessListener<SysIntegri
tyResp>() { @Override
public void onSuccess(SysIntegrityResp response) {
// The Safety Detect API responds successfully. You can
use the getResult method of the
// SysIntegrityResp class to obtain the check result.
String jwsStr = response.getResult();
VerifyResultHandler verifyResultHandler =
new VerifyResultHandler(jwsStr, callBack);
// Send the check result to your server for verification.
verifyJws(activity, jwsStr, verifyResultHandler);
}
});
}
```

Call the relevant app server API in the **verifyJws** method to verify the check result. The third parameter in this method is an object of the **VerifyResultHandler** class. It implements a callback API to process the verification result.

3. Verify the check result on the app server.

After receiving the check result from the TSMS server, the app will send the result to the app server. Then, the app server uses the HUAWEI CBG Root CA certificate, which you preset in a server directory, to verify the signature and certificate chain in the check result, so it can determine whether the check result is valid.

The sample code for the app server to read the certificate and verify the JWS string is as follows:

1. Parse the header, payload, and signature from the JWS string.

```
public JwsVerifyResp verifyJws(JwsVerifyReq jwsVeri-
fyReq) {
// Obtain the JWS string sent from the app to the
server.
String jwsStr = jwsVerifyReq.getJws();
// Parse the JWS string by segment. A JWS string has
three fixed segments, which are separated by peri-
ods (.).
String[] jwsSplit = jwsStr.split("\\."); try {
// Perform Base64 decoding on each segment and con-
struct a JWS object for each decoded segment.
JWSObject jwsObject = new JWSObject(new Base64URL(-
jwsSplit[0]),    new    Base64URL(jwsSplit[1]),    new
Base64URL(jwsSplit[2]));
// Verify the JWS string and set the verification
result.
boolean result = VerifySignatureUtil.verifySignature
(jwsObject);
// Construct the response body for check result
verification on the app server.
JwsVerifyResp jwsVerifyResp = new JwsVerifyResp();
jwsVerifyResp.setResult(result);
} catch (ParseException | NoSuchAlgorithmException e)
{ RUN _ LOG.catching(e);
}
return jwsVerifyResp;
}
```

2. Use the **verifySignature** method in the **VerifySignatureUtil** class to verify the JWS signature

NOTE

To download the HUAWEI CBG Root CA certificate, please refer to the *Safety Detect Development Guide* on the HUAWEI Developers website.

algorithm, certificate chain, host name in the signing certificate, and JWS string.

```
public   static   boolean   verifySignature(JWSObject
jws) throws NoSuchAlgorithmException { JWSAlgorithm
jwsAlgorithm = jws.getHeader().getAlgorithm();
// 1. Verify the JWS signature algorithm.
if ("RS256".equals(jwsAlgorithm.getName())) {
// Verify the certificate chain and obtain an instance
of the Signature class based on the signature algo-
rithm to verify the signature.
return verify(Signature.getInstance("SHA256withRSA"),
jws);
}
return false;
}
private static boolean verify(Signature signature,
JWSObject jws) {
// Extract the certificate chain information from
the header parsed from the JWS string and convert
the certificate chain into a proper type for subse-
quent processing.
X509Certificate[] certs = extractX509CertChain(jws);
// 2. Verify the certificate chain.
try { verifyCertChain(certs);
} catch (Exception e) { return false;
}
// 3. Verify the domain name in the signing cer-
tificate (leaf certificate). The domain name must be
sysintegrity.platform.hicloud.com.
try {
new   DefaultHostnameVerifier().verify("sysintegrity.
platform.hicloud.com", certs[0]);
} catch (SSLException e) { return false;
}
// 4. Verify the JWS signature information using the
public key obtained from the signing certificate.
PublicKey pubKey = certs[0].getPublicKey(); try {
// Use the public key obtained from the signing cer-
tificate to initialize the Signature instance.
signature.initVerify(pubKey);
// Extract the input signature from the JWS string
and pass it as a parameter to the Signature instance.
signature.update(jws.getSigningInput());
// Use the Signature instance to verify the signa-
ture information.
```

```
return signature.verify(jws.getSignature().decode());
} catch (InvalidKeyException | SignatureException e)
{ return false;
}
}
```

The **extractX509CertChain** method extracts the certificate chain from the JWS header as follows:

```
private static X509Certificate[] extractX509CertChain(-
JWSObject jws) { List<X509Certificate> certs = new
ArrayList<>();      List<com.nimbusds.jose.util.Base64>
x509CertChain  =  jws.getHeader().getX509CertChain();
try {
CertificateFactory certFactory = CertificateFactory.
getInstance("X.509");     certs.addAll(x509CertChain.
stream().map(cert -> {
try {
return     (X509Certificate)    certFactory.generate
Certificate(new ByteArrayInputStream(cert.decode()));
} catch (CertificateException e) { RUN _ LOG.error("X5c
extract failed!");
}
return null;
}).filter(Objects::nonNull).collect(Collectors.
toList()));
} catch (CertificateException e) { RUN _ LOG.error("X5c
extract failed!");
}
return (X509Certificate[]) certs.toArray();
}
```

The **verifyCertChain** method verifies the certificate chain as follows:

```
private static void verifyCertChain(X509Certificate[]
certs) throws CertificateException, NoSuchAlgorithm
Exception,
InvalidKeyException, NoSuchProviderException, Signature
Exception {
// Verify the validity period and issue of each
certificate.
for (int i = 0; i < certs.length - 1; ++i) { certs[i].
checkValidity();
```

```
PublicKey  pubKey  =  certs[i  +  1].getPublicKey();
certs[i].verify(pubKey);
}
// Use the preset HUAWEI CBG Root CA certificate to
verify the last certificate in the certificate chain.
PublicKey  caPubKey  =  huaweiCbgRootCaCert.getPub-
licKey(); certs[certs.length - 1].verify(caPubKey);
}
```

The HUAWEI CBG Root CA certificate is loaded in the static code snippet of the **VerifySignatureUtil** class as follows:

```
static {
// Load the preset HUAWEI CBG Root CA certificate.
File filepath = "~/certs/Huawei _ cbg _ root.cer";
try  (FileInputStream  in  =  new  FileInputStream
(filepath)) { CertificateFactory cf = CertificateFactory.
getInstance("X.509");     huaweiCbgRootCaCert     =
(X509Certificate) cf.generateCertificate(in);
} catch  (IOException | CertificateException e)  {
RUN _ LOG.error("HUAWEI CBG root cert load failed!");
}
}
```

So far, we've verified the integrity check result on the app server and returned it to the app for further service processing. Our sample code only highlights the key steps. For the complete code, please visit the URL provided in the appendix of this book.

4. Obtain the system integrity check result.

Once API calling is successful, the app can then obtain reliable system integrity check results from the payload of the JWS string. Parse the system integrity check result from the callback API of the **VerifyResultHandler** class as follows:

```
private static final class VerifyResultHandler imple-
ments ICallBack<Boolean> { private final String jwsStr;
private final ICallBack<? super Boolean> callBack;
private VerifyResultHandler(String jwsStr, ICallBack<?
super Boolean> callBack) { this.jwsStr = jwsStr;
this.callBack = callBack;
}
@Override
```

```
public void onSuccess(Boolean verified) { if (verified)
{
// Extract the system integrity check result that has
been verified by the app server.
String payloadDetail = new String(Base64.decode(jwsStr.
split("\\.") [1].getBytes(StandardCharsets.UTF _ 8), Base64.
URL _ SAFE), StandardCharsets.UTF _ 8);
try {
final   boolean  basicIntegrity  =  new   JSONObject(-
payloadDetail). getBoolean("basicIntegrity");
// Obtain the system integrity check result through the
callback method.
callBack.onSuccess(basicIntegrity);
} catch (JSONException e) {
    ...
}
}
    ...
}
}
```

The following is an example of the system integrity check response:

```
{
"advice":"RESTORE _ TO _ FACTORY _ ROM",
"apkCertificateDigestSha256":[ "yT5JtXRgeIgXssx1gQTsMA9G
zM9ER4xAgCsCC69Fz3I="
],
"apkDigestSha256":"6Ihk8Wcv1MLm0O5KUCEVYCI/0KWzA
Hn9DyN38R3WYu8=", "apkPackageName":"com.huawei.hms.safe-
tydetectsample", "basicIntegrity":false,
"nonce":"R2Rra24fVm5xa2Mg", "timestampMs":1571708929141
}
```

Here, the value of the **basicIntegrity** field in the check result is **false**. This means the system was corrupted. The app can notify the user of any potential risks if necessary.

The membership purchase API of the Pet Store app calls the **SysIntegrity** API to check whether the payment environment is secure and notifies the user if any risks are detected. This ensures that the user can make an informed decision about whether or not to proceed with the purchase, as shown in Figure 10.7.

Now that we've implemented code related to the **SysIntegrity** API, let's move on to AppsCheck development.

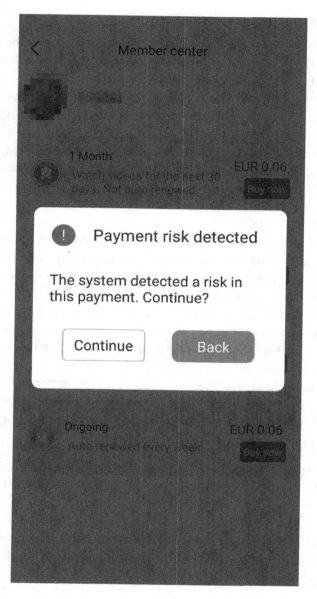

FIGURE 10.7   Payment risk reminder.

10.4 APPSCHECK

This section describes the AppsCheck feature. Let's understand its working principles, how to integrate it, and how to call the **AppsCheck** API to obtain a list of malicious apps on a user's device.

Our Pet Store app has not integrated AppsCheck. If you are developing an app that needs high security, such as for finance or banking, AppsCheck would be necessary. With AppsCheck, you'll detect possible risks when a user performs a critical operation like entering their password, transferring money, or making a payment, so as to ensure their privacy and app security.

10.4.1 Service Process

AppsCheck gives you a list of malicious apps installed on a user's device, allowing you to determine whether to restrict your app's behavior based on risks (from risky apps/viral apps). It detects over ten types of malicious apps and potential threats. The AppsCheck feature is simple – it neither requires you to send the check result to the TSMS server for signing nor verifies any signature. AppsCheck works as shown in Figure 10.8.

NOTE

Here, we'll use a common code snippet for integrating the AppsCheck feature.

1. Your app integrated with the Safety Detect SDK calls the **AppsCheck** API to request a list of malicious apps.

2. The **AppsCheck** API sends back a list of risky apps and viral apps. If the list is empty, it means that no risk or virus was detected.

10.4.2 Coding Practice

Call the **getClient** method in the **SafetyDetectClient** class to initialize the Safety Detect SDK, and then call the **getMaliciousAppsList()** method to obtain a list of malicious apps installed on the device.

```
private void invokeGetMaliciousApps() {
SafetyDetectClient AppsCheckClient = SafetyDetect.
getClient(MainAct.this);
// Call the getMaliciousAppsList() method in the
SafetyDetectClient class.
```

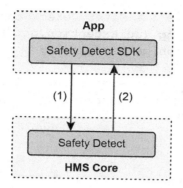

FIGURE 10.8   AppsCheck service process.

```
Task task = AppsCheckClient.getMaliciousAppsList();
task.addOnSuccessListener(new OnSuccessListener<Malici
ousAppsListResp>() {
@Override
public void onSuccess(MaliciousAppsListResp resp) {
// The app security check is successful.
if (resp.getRtnCode() == CommonCode.OK) {
List<MaliciousAppsData> appsDataList = resp.
getMaliciousAppsList(); if (!appsDataList.isEmpty()) {
// If any malicious app is found, obtain the details
about the malicious app.
getMaliciousAppInfo(appsDataList);
}
} else {
// The app security check fails. Obtain the failure
information.
Log.e(TAG, "Failed: " + resp.getErrorReason());
}
}
}).addOnFailureListener(new OnFailureListener() { @
Override
public void onFailure(Exception e) {
// If Safety Detect fails to respond, an ApiException
may occur.
if (e instanceof ApiException) {
ApiException apiException = (ApiException) e;
// Obtain the result code and its description.
```

```
Log.e(TAG, "Error: " + SafetyDetectStatusCodes.
getStatusCodeString (apiException.getStatusCode()) +
": " + apiException.getMessage());
} else {
// Throw an unknown exception and call getMessage() to
obtain the exception information.
Log.e(TAG, "ERROR: " + e.getMessage());
}
}
});
}
```

Use the method provided by **MaliciousAppsData** to obtain details about each malicious app on the returned list, including the app's package name, threat type, and SHA-256 value. The sample code is as follows:

```
private void getMaliciousAppInfo(List
<MaliciousAppsData> appsDataList) { Log.i(TAG,
"Potentially malicious apps are installed!");
// Read the details about each malicious app on the
returned list.
for (MaliciousAppsData maliciousApp : appsDataList) {
Log.i(TAG, "Information about a malicious app:");
// Call getApkPackageName() to obtain the package name
of a malicious app.
Log.i(TAG, "APK: " + maliciousApp.
getApkPackageName());
// Call getApkSha256() to obtain the SHA-256 value of
a malicious app.
Log.i(TAG, "SHA-256: " + maliciousApp.getApkSha256());
// Call getApkCategory() to check whether a malicious
app is a risky or viral app.
if (AppsCheckConstants.VIRUS_LEVEL_VIRUS ==
maliciousApp.getApkCategory()) {
// The malicious app is a viral app.
} else {
// The malicious app is a risky app.
}
}
}
```

The AppsCheck feature is relatively simple to use, as you do not need to report the check result to the TSMS server for signing. Instead, you only need to call the API provided by the Safety Detect SDK to obtain a list of malicious apps and their details.

10.5 URLCHECK

This section describes the functions and development procedure of the URLCheck feature, which detects malicious URLs.

10.5.1 Service Process

URLCheck enables you to identify malicious URLs such as those with phishing or Trojan horses, and classify them by threat type. Its process is shown in Figure 10.9.

NOTE

Here, we'll use a common code snippet for integrating the URLCheck feature.

1. Your app integrated with the Safety Detect SDK calls the **URLCheck** API to check a specific URL.

2. The Safety Detect SDK sends a URL check request to the URLCheck server. The URLCheck server then returns the check result to your app.

3. Your app obtains the check result and determines whether to allow access to the URL, notify the user of risks, or block the URL.

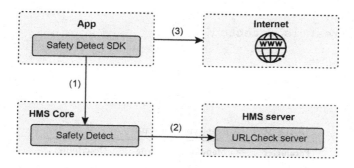

FIGURE 10.9   URLCheck service process.

10.5.2 Coding Practice

Call the **initUrlCheck()** method for initialization.

```
SafetyDetectClient client = SafetyDetect.getClient
(getActivity()); client.initUrlCheck();
```

Pass in the threat types you are concerned about as an input parameter for the check. Currently, supported threat types are defined in the **UrlCheckThreat** class of the Safety Detect SDK, as described in Table 10.1.

After initialization is completed, your app will be able to send a URL check request. The URL to check should contain the protocol, host, path, and query parameter name. Delete query parameter values, if any. For example, if the URL to check is **http://www.example.com/query?id= 123&name=bob**, change it to **http://www.example.com/query?id=&name=**. Here's the code:

```
// URL to check.
String url = "https://developer.huawei.
com/consumer/en/";
// Call the URLCheck API, pass the URL to check, app
ID, and threat type, and add a callback function.
SafetyDetect.getClient(this).urlCheck(url, appid,
UrlCheckThreat.MALWARE, UrlCheckThreat.PHISHING)
.addOnSuccessListener(this, new OnSuccessListener<UrlC
heckResponse>() { @Override
public void onSuccess(UrlCheckResponse urlResponse) {
if (urlResponse.getUrlCheckResponse().isEmpty()) {
// No threat is detected.
} else {
// A threat is detected.
}
}
})
```

TABLE 10.1   Threat Type Constant

Parameter	Mandatory	Type	Description
countryCode	Yes	Integer	Threat type. **1**: malware **3**: phishing

```
.addOnFailureListener(this, new OnFailureListener() {
@Override
public void onFailure(@NonNull Exception e) {
// An error occurred during communication with the
service.
if (e instanceof ApiException) {
// Obtain the HMS Core (APK) error code and its
description.
ApiException apiException = (ApiException) e; Log.d(-
TAG, "Error: " + CommonStatusCodes
.getStatusCodeString(apiException.getStatusCode()));
} else {
// An unknown exception occurs.
Log.d(TAG, "Error: " + e.getMessage());
}
}
});
```

If the result code **SafetyDetectStatusCode.CHECK_WITHOUT_INIT** is returned, there can be two possibilities – the app has not called the **initUrlCheck()** method, or an internal error occurred during initialization. Call the **initUrlCheck()** method again to complete initialization.

Process the **URLCheckResponse** object as follows:

```
List<UrlCheckThreat> list = urlCheckResponse.
getUrlCheckResponse(); if (list.isEmpty()) {
// If the list is empty, no threat is detected.
} else {
for (UrlCheckThreat threat : list) {
// type indicates the type of the detected threat.
int type = threat.getUrlCheckResult();
// Perform further processing based on the threat
type.
}
}
```

Once processed, close the session with the **shutdownUrlCheck()** method if the API will not be called anytime soon:

```
SafetyDetect.getClient(this).shitdownUrlCheck();
```

Table 10.2 describes the result codes returned during URL check.

TABLE 10.2   Result Codes for URL Check

Code	Error	Description
19401	APPS_CHECK_INTERNAL_ERROR	An internal error occurred during app security check.
19601	CHECK_WITHOUT_INIT	The **initUrlCheck** API is not called before calling the **URLCheck** API.
19602	URL_CHECK_THREAT_TYPE_INVALID	The **URLCheck** API does not support the passed URL categories. Currently, Safety Detect can only identify phishing and malware URLs.
19603	URL_CHECK_REQUEST_PARAM_INVALID	Invalid parameters for calling **URLCheck**.
19604	URL_CHECK_REQUEST_APPID_INVALID	The app ID passed for calling **URLCheck** is invalid.

10.6 USERCHECK

UserDetect identifies fake users by screen touch and sensor behavior. This is crucial to preventing spam registrations, credential stuffing attacks, bonus hunting, and content crawling. In addition to being more secure than traditional verification codes, UserDetect identifies both environmental and behavioral risks. Such risks, if detected, are submitted to the on-cloud risk analysis engine so suspicious users can be identified and then assigned to different security levels. UserDetect works in three ways:

- Environmental risk identification: identifies a fake device by device signature, or a rooted device, simulator, changer, or anonymous IP address.

- Behavior risk identification: identifies programmed operations based on the user behavior exhibited on the touchscreen and detected by the motion sensor.

- Captcha verification: increases the difficulty for a program to crack a verification code by adding semantic reasoning.

Let's learn how UserDetect works and how to integrate it.

> **NOTE**
>
> Code verification using the **UserCheck** API is unavailable in the Chinese mainland.

10.6.1 Service Process

As shown in Figure 10.10, UserDetect works in this way:

1. Your app calls the Safety Detect SDK to send a user check request to Safety Detect.

2. Safety Detect instructs UserDetect to evaluate the risks of the device environment. If the risk is deemed medium or high, UserDetect instructs the user to complete verification and sends a response token to Safety Detect. Safety Detect then forwards the response token to your app.

3. Your app submits the response token to your app server.

4. Your app server sends the response token to UserDetect to obtain the check result.

10.6.2 Coding Practice

In our Pet Store app, UserDetect is integrated for user sign-in. Let's go into detail about using the **UserDetect** API.

1. Initialize UserDetect.

   In the Pet Store app, call the **initUserDetect** API in the **onfRe-sume** method of the **LoginAct.java** class as follows to complete initialization:

```
@Override
protected void onResume() { super.onResume();
```

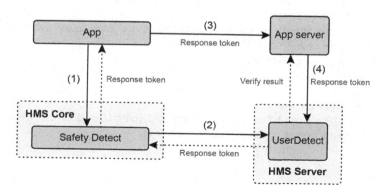

FIGURE 10.10   UserDetect service process.

```
// Initialize the UserDetect API.
SafetyDetect.getClient(this).initUserDetect();
}
```

2. Initiate a user check result.

A user check request is generally triggered when a user performs an operation (sign-in, registration, flash sale, or lottery drawing) or touches a UI component. After the check is successfully executed, the app will receive a response token.

In the **onLogin** method of the **LoginAct.java** class, call the **callUserDetect** method of **SafetyDetectUtil** to initiate a user check request. Before determining whether the user name and password are correct, the Pet Store app initiates a fake user detection request and obtains the check result through a callback. If the check result indicates that the user is real, your app will permit the user to sign in and continue to check the user name and password. Otherwise, your app will block the user and terminate the sign-in. The sample code is as follows:

```
private void onLogin() { final String name = ...
final String password = ... new Thread(new Runnable() {
@Override
public void run() {
// Call the UserDetect API with the current activity or
context and a callback specified.
SafetyDetectUtil.callUserDetect(LoginAct.this, new ICall
Back<Boolean>() { @Override
public void onSuccess(Boolean userVerified) {
// The fake user detection is successful.
if (userVerified){
// If the check result indicates that the user is real,
the user can continue the sign-in.
loginWithLocalUser(name, password);
} else {
// If the check result indicates that the user is fake,
the sign-in fails.
ToastUtil.getInstance().showShort(LoginAct.this,
R.string.toast _ userdetect _ error);
}
}
});
}
}).start();
}
```

The **callUserDetect** method in **SafetyDetectUtil.java** encapsulates key processes for fake user detection, such as obtaining the app ID and response token and sending the response token to the app server. The sample code is as follows:

```
public static void callUserDetect(final Activity activity, final ICallBack
<? super Boolean> callBack) { Log.i(TAG, "User detection start.");
// Read the app_id field from the agconnect-services.
json file in the app directory.
String appid = AGConnectServicesConfig.fromContext(-
activity). getString("client/app_id");
// Call the UserDetect API and add a callback for sub-
sequent asynchronous processing.
SafetyDetect.getClient(activity)
.userDetection(appid)
.addOnSuccessListener(new OnSuccessListener<UserDetect
Response>() { @Override
public void onSuccess(UserDetectResponse userDetectRe-
sponse) {
// If the fake user detection is successful, call the
getResponseToken method to obtain a response token.
String responseToken =userDetectResponse.getResponse
Token().
// Send the response token to the app server.
boolean verifyResult = verifyUserRisks(activity, respon-
seToken); callBack.onSuccess(verifyResult);
Log.i(TAG, "User detection onSuccess.");
}
})
}
```

Now, the app has obtained the response token through the **UserDetect** API of Safety Detect. Next, send the response token to your app server and call the **UserDetect** API on the app server to obtain the check result.

3. Obtain the check result.

Sign in to AppGallery Connect, click **My apps**, and find and click the app Pet Store.

Go to **Distribute > App information**, and obtain the app secret from the **App information** area on the right, as shown in Figure 10.11.

FIGURE 10.11   Obtaining the app secret.

Initiate a check result query request with the obtained app secret, app ID, and response token as follows:

```
public class UserRisksVerifyHandler {
private static final String APP_ID = "101778417"; pri-
vate static final String SECRET_KEY =
"79d84ac5ac404a88**********83b5b494fa3df03cf33aefd12e6
93da9"; public String handle(UserRisksVerifyReq user-
RisksVerifyReq) {
// Send the fake user detection result to the UserDetect
server to obtain the check result.
return HttpsUtil.sendRmsMessage(APP_ID, SECRET_KEY,
userRisksVerifyReq.getResponse());
}
}
```

The **sendRmsMessage** method in **HttpsUtil.java** obtains an access token from the Huawei OAuth server. Then, the app calls the check result query API of the UserDetect server based on the obtained access token:

1. Obtain an access token.

    Use the app ID and app secret to request an access token from the Huawei OAuth server. Here's the code:

```
private static String applyAccessToken(String appid,
String secretKey) {
// Construct an HTTP POST request object.
HttpPost httpPostRequest = new HttpPost("https://-
oauth-login.cloud.huawei. com/oauth2/v2/token");
```

```
// Set the content type.
httpPostRequest.setHeader("content-type",
"application/x-www-form-urlencoded");
// Construct the message body.
List<NameValuePair> entityData = new ArrayList<>();
entityData.add(new BasicNameValuePair("grant_type",
"client_credentials"));  entityData.add(new  Basic
NameValuePair("client_id", appid)); entityData.add(new
BasicNameValuePair("client_secret", secretKey)); UrlEn
codedFormEntity urlEncodedFormEntity = new UrlEncode
dFormEntity(entityData,
StandardCharsets.UTF_8); httpPostRequest.setEntity
(urlEncodedFormEntity);
// Execute the HTTP POST request.
String response = execute(httpPostRequest);
// Return the access token extracted from the
response body.
returnJSON.parseObject(response).get("access_token").
toString();
}
```

An example of the request is as follows:

```
POST  /oauth2/v2/token  HTTP/1.1  Host:  oauth-login.
cloud.huawei.com
Content-Type: application/x-www-form-urlencodedgrant_
type=client_credentials&client_
id=12345&client_secret=bKaZ0VE3EYrXaXCdCe3d2k9
few
```

2. Call the check result query API of the UserDetect server.

    Assemble the app ID, access token, and response token into a request and send the request to the UserDetect server.

```
public static String sendRmsMessage(String appid,
String appSecret, String responseToken) {
// 1. Construct an HTTP POST request object.
HttpPost httpPostRequest;
// 1.1 Concatenate the URI of the UserDetect server.
URI uri = buildUri(appid);
httpPostRequest = new HttpPost(uri); httpPostRequest.
addHeader("content-type", "application/json"); String
Entity entityData;
try {
```

```
// 1.2 Construct the message body.
JSONObject messageObject = new JSONObject();
// 1.2.1 Obtain the access token and add it to the
query message body.
messageObject.put("accessToken",    applyAccessToken(-
appid, appSecret));
// 1.2.2 Add the response token to the message body.
messageObject.put("response", responseToken);
entityData    =    new    StringEntity(messageObject.
toString());
} catch (UnsupportedEncodingException e) { Log.
catching(e);
return "";
}
httpPostRequest.setEntity(entityData);
// 2. Execute the HTTP POST request.
return execute(httpPostRequest);
}
// URI builder.
private static URI buildUri(String appid) { URIBuilder
uriBuilder;
URI uri = null;
try {
// URI of the UserDetect server API.
uriBuilder = new URIBuilder("https://rms-drcn.plat-
form.dbankcloud.com/ rms/v1/userRisks/verify");
// Add the app ID to the URI.
uriBuilder.addParameter("appid", appid); uri = uri-
Builder.build();
} catch (URISyntaxException e) { Log.catching(e);
}
return uri;
}
```

An example of a check result query request is as follows:

```
POST https://hirms.cloud.huawei.com/rms/v1/userRisks/
verify?appId=101294943
{
"accessToken":"CV7Qxu7U0aqtFYxj9FIw2LcOaFp
jsHBSHUz8lrGuTipIB2VJNUkBK630+WMCLxzti5xL
PxjYB6slP49sbc3vPY53XjM5", "response":"1 _ 76deea6daf1
ce20995e2b55e4651a8d6f2ffa8a7a6dfe5ce _ 15907"
}
```

An example of a response sent by the UserDetect server is as follows:

```
Content-Type: application/json
{
"success": true,
"challenge _ ts":" 2020-05-29T15:32:53+0800"
"apk _ package _ name":"com.example.mockthirdapp"
}
```

Return the obtained check result to your app directly through your app server. In the check result, **true** indicates a real user, and **false** indicates a fake user. Use this result to set a specific app reaction. During fake user detection, both your app and app server interact with HMS components. Our sample code only demonstrates key implementations. To learn about the implementation details in complete code, visit the URL provided in the appendix of this book.

4. Stop UserCheck.

After the false user is detected, disable the UserCheck feature promptly to free up resources. To do this, call the **shutdownUser-Detect** method in the **onPause** method of the **LoginAct.java** class in your app.

```
@Override
protected void onPause() { super.onPause();
// Disable the UserCheck API.
SafetyDetect.getClient(this).shutdownUserDetect();
}
```

That is the complete process of detecting fake users for the Pet Store app. Figure 10.12 shows relevant log information.

```
2020-08-10 21:47:22.468 6391-6681/com.huawei.hmspetstore I/SafetyDetectUtil: User detection start.
2020-08-10 21:47:46.163 6391-6391/com.huawei.hmspetstore I/SafetyDetectUtil: User detection succeed,
response=7_a060fc7f86374fd090caca88cc2e43bb51df508b61dfd152_1597067241697
2020-08-10 21:47:46.873 6391-6759/com.huawei.hmspetstore I/SafetyDetectUtil: verifyUserRisks:
result={"error-codes":"missing-input-response","success":false},
response=7_a060fc7f86374fd090caca88cc2e43bb51df508b61dfd152_1597067241697
```

FIGURE 10.12   Obtaining the check result from your app server.

10.7 SUMMARY

This chapter focused on the principles and practice behind Safety Detect. With the Pet Store app as illustration, we've described the SysIntegrity, URLCheck, AppsCheck, and UserDetect features. We learned how your app's payment function is protected by SysIntegrity and how user sign-ins are protected by UserDetect. Now, you're armed with the knowledge to build an app secured by Safety Detect. The next chapter will introduce how to integrate HUAWEI FIDO into the Pet Store app.

CHAPTER 11

FIDO

11.1 ABOUT THE SERVICE

HUAWEI FIDO arms apps with FIDO2, which is based on web authentication (WebAuthn[1]), and facilitates the construction of a user-friendly path to password-free authentication. Under this framework, users are authenticated by roaming authenticators (USB, NFC, and Bluetooth authenticators) and platform authenticators (fingerprint and 3D facial authenticators). HUAWEI FIDO also equips apps with powerful local BioAuthn capabilities, including both fingerprint authentication and 3D facial authentication.

FIDO2 is ideal for adding online identity verification to online services. Here are some of the specific ways that it implements password-free authentication:

- Fingerprint and 3D facial-based sign-in

- Fingerprint and 3D facial-based transactions

- 2FA transactions, with a password and a FIDO-capable Huawei phone as the hardware security key

BioAuthn is useful when the user's identity is confirmed on the phone itself, rather than on the server. The most common usage case involves the user unlocking their phone with their fingerprint or via facial recognition. BioAuthn is also ideal for apps that place a high threshold on privacy, for

DOI: 10.1201/9781003206699-11

App server   FIDO server

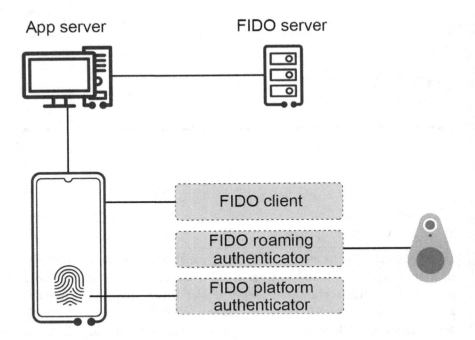

FIGURE 11.1   FIDO authentication process.

example those that require fingerprint or facial authentication to complete transactions or sign in.

Now let's take a look at how FIDO2 and BioAuthn work in practice.

11.1.1 Principles Behind FIDO2

FIDO is the technical architecture that supports online identity verification, and FIDO2 is the latest version of the standards. This architecture encompasses the app and app server, as well as the FIDO authenticator, FIDO client, and FIDO server. Figure 11.1 illustrates the FIDO authentication process.

1. FIDO authenticator: A mechanism or device used for local authentication. There are two kinds of FIDO authenticators, or security keys: platform authenticators and roaming authenticators.

    • Platform authenticator: An authenticator integrated into a FIDO-enabled device, such as one using the fingerprint sensor in a mobile phone or laptop.

- Roaming authenticator: An authenticator connected to a FIDO-enabled device via Bluetooth, NFC, or a USB cable. Some roaming authenticators take the appearance of USB keys or dynamic tokens.

2. FIDO client: This client is integrated into the platform to provide SDKs, or instead, integrated into the browser to provide JavaScript APIs. Supported platforms include Windows, MacOS, and Android with HMS Core (APK); supported browsers include Chrome, Firefox, and Huawei Browser. The FIDO client serves as a bridge for the app in calling the FIDO server and FIDO authenticator to complete authentication.

3. FIDO server: This server generates an authentication request in compliance with the FIDO specification and sends it to the app server to initiate FIDO authentication. Once the FIDO authenticator completes local authentication, the FIDO server will receive and verify a FIDO authentication response from the app server.

There are two main steps for FIDO: registration and authentication. In sign-in scenarios for example, registration involves enabling the fingerprint or 3D facial sign-in function, while authentication involves completing sign-in via fingerprint or 3D facial authentication.

Figure 11.2 illustrates the registration process, using an app that we've integrated the FIDO2 client SDK with.

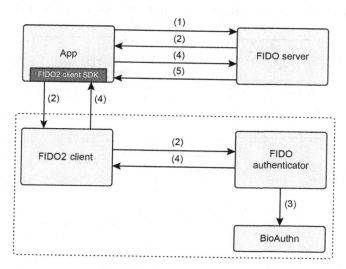

FIGURE 11.2 Registration process.

1. The app sends a registration request to the FIDO server.

2. The FIDO server generates a random challenge value and sends it to the app, which then forwards it to the FIDO2 client. The client connects to the FIDO authenticator and initiates registration.

3. After verifying the request, the FIDO authenticator generates a pair of public and private keys. The private key is saved to the local device and also used to sign the public key and challenge value to generate a signature.

4. The FIDO authenticator sends the signature to the FIDO2 client to be forwarded to the app, which receives and forwards it to the FIDO server for registration.

5. The FIDO server verifies the signature, saves the public key, and sends the handling result back to the app.

Figure 11.3 outlines the authentication process. You'll notice how it differs from the registration process.

1. The app sends an authentication request to the FIDO server.

2. The FIDO server generates a random challenge value and sends it to the app, which then forwards it to the FIDO2 client. The client connects to the FIDO authenticator and initiates authentication.

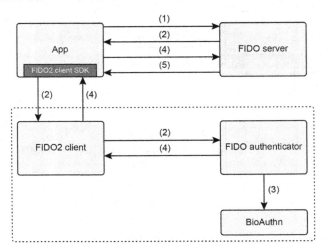

FIGURE 11.3   Authentication process.

3. After authentication is successful, the FIDO authenticator uses the saved private key to sign the challenge value to generate a signature.

4. The FIDO authenticator sends the signature to the FIDO2 client to be forwarded to the app, which receives and forwards it to the FIDO server for authentication.

5. The FIDO server verifies the signature, saves the public key, and sends the handling result back to the app.

11.1.2 Principles Behind BioAuthn

BioAuthn enhances security using native Android capabilities as a springboard, including local fingerprint authentication and biometric authentication. The improvement is in the following two areas:

1. System integrity check becomes the prerequisite for using BioAuthn. When the user uses BioAuthn on an insecure device, the app will recognize that the device is insecure, and halt biometric authentication. For more details about system integrity check, please refer to Chapter 10.

2. Cryptographic key verification is applied to ensure the reliability of authentication. A key object that is associated during biometric authentication can be set to be available, only following successful authentication. Huawei phones that run EMUI 9.1 or later store and use keys in a TEE to prevent tampering. This means that you'll only be able to encrypt data by using an associated key after authentication, and that the encryption won't work, even if a failed authentication appears successful in the Rich Execution Environment (REE).

With system integrity check and cryptographic key verification, you'll be able to place your complete trust in the local biometric authentication results.

Figure 11.4 shows the local biometric authentication process for an app with the FIDO SDK.

1. The app calls the BioAuthn API.

2. BioAuthn calls Safety Detect to check system integrity.

3. The app prompts the user to authenticate biometrically.

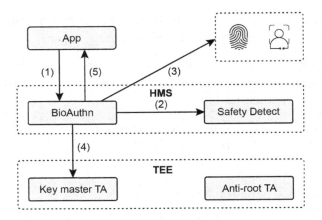

FIGURE 11.4 Local authentication process.

FIGURE 11.5 Selecting the Pet Store app.

4. BioAuthn verifies the authentication result.

5. BioAuthn returns the authentication result to the app.

11.2 PREPARATIONS

Before starting development, enable FIDO and integrate the FIDO SDK. To do this, you'll need to have registered as a Huawei developer, created a Pet Store app in AppGallery Connect, and configured the signing certificate fingerprint for the app.

1. Enable FIDO.

   1. Sign in to AppGallery Connect, click **My projects**, and select the Pet Store app, as shown in Figure 11.5.

   2. Go to **Manage APIs** and toggle on **FIDO**, as shown in Figure 11.6.

2. Integrate the FIDO SDK.

   First, download the **agconnect-services.json** file from AppGallery Connect, and add the file to the **app** directory for your project. Then

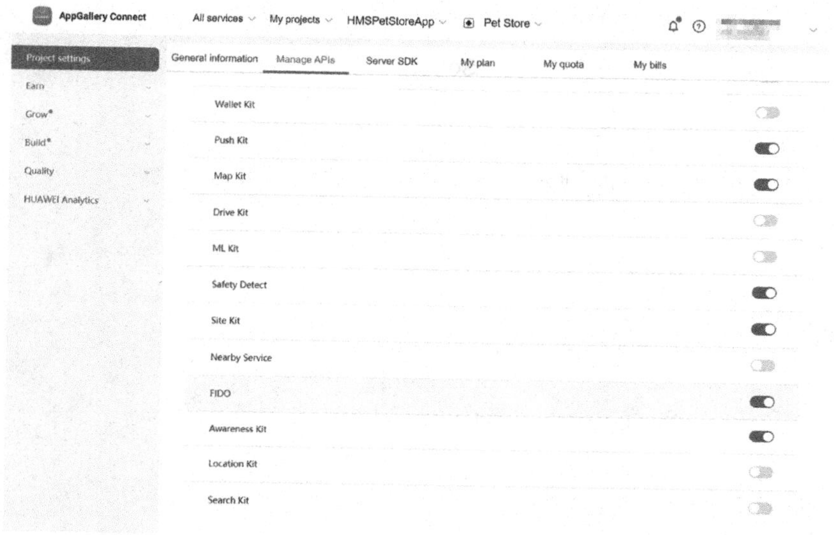

FIGURE 11.6   Enabling FIDO.

open the **build.gradle** file in the same directory, and add build dependencies on the FIDO SDK.

```
dependencies {
    implementation 'com.huawei.hms:fido-fido2:4.0.3.300'
    implementation 'com.huawei.hms:fido-bioauthn-
androidx:4.0.3.300'
    implementation 'com.huawei.hms:fido-bioauthn:4.0.3.300'
    // Select either fido-bioauthn-androidx or fido-
bioauthn. For details on which one to use, please refer
to section 11.4.
}
```

Here we've used the 4.0.3.300 version as an example, but you'll want to obtain the latest available version of the SDK on the HUAWEI Developers website. Click **Sync Now** in the upper right corner of Android Studio and wait for the synchronization to complete. Now that we've finished all of the necessary preparations, let's integrate the FIDO2 client.

11.3 FIDO2

Our goal is to integrate the FIDO SDK into the Pet Store app to implement fingerprint sign-in. When the user toggles on the fingerprint sign-in

FIGURE 11.7   Enabling fingerprint sign-in.

setting, as shown within the app settings in Figure 11.7, the FIDO2 registration API is called. After the registration process is completed, and the user touches **Sign in** on the sign-in screen, the FIDO2 fingerprint authentication API is called to instruct them how to use their fingerprint, as illustrated in Figure 11.8.

FIGURE 11.8   Fingerprint sign-in.

FIDO2-related processing is encapsulated in the **Fido2Handler.java** file within the Pet Store app project. Enabling the fingerprint function calls the **onRegistration** method of the **Fido2Handler** class to initiate FIDO registration. When registration is complete, the **onLogin()** method calls the **onAuthentication** method of the **Fido2Handler** class to complete sign-in authentication.

Let's now take a look at the code for processing logic in **Fido2Handler.java**. We'll learn how to receive the registration/authentication result returned by the FIDO2 client, by overriding the **onActivityResult** method of **Activity** and performing subsequent processing.

We'll show how this process works with the Pet Store app, which doesn't connect to a FIDO server. Instead, our sample code simulates FIDO server APIs that comply with the FIDO2 specification. It's important to remember to connect your app to an actual FIDO server – obtain the specifications, and then contact a FIDO server vendor for the API reference.

11.3.1 Initializing the FIDO2 Client

Perform the following steps:

1. Implement a single-parameter constructor in the **Fido2Handler.java** file, call the factory method **getFido2Client** provided in the FIDO SDK, and pass an **Activity** instance to initialize and obtain a **Fido2Client** object. This gets you a result returned by the FIDO2 client, which is received and processed in the **onActivityResult** method of the passed **Activity** instance.

```
public class Fido2Handler {
public Fido2Handler(Activity activity) {
    // Initialize the FIDO client.
    fido2Client = Fido2.getFido2Client(activity);
  }
}
```

2. Add the **Fido2Handler** object to the **SettingAct.java** and **LoginAct.java** files, and initialize the object.

```
public class SettingAct extends AppCompatActivity {
   // FIDO2-related processing
private Fido2Handler fido2Handler;
   @Override
```

```
protected void onCreate(@Nullable Bundle savedInstan-
ceState) {
    ...
    fido2Handler = new Fido2Handler(SettingAct.this);
}
}
```

11.3.2 Initiating the Registration Process

Add a switch component named **SwitchCompat** to the **SettingAct.java** file, and add a status change listener to call the **onRegistration** method of the **Fido2Handler** object. This initiates FIDO2 registration once the user has enabled fingerprint sign-in in your app's settings.

```
public class SettingAct extends AppCompatActivity {
  // Add a fingerprint sign-in switch.
  private SwitchCompat mSwitchCompatFingerPrintLogin;
  @Override
  protected void onCreate(@Nullable Bundle
savedInstanceState) {
    ...
    // Initialize the view.
    initView();
  }

  private void initFido() {
    mSwitchCompatFingerPrintLogin = findViewById(R.
id.setting_fingerprint);
    mSwitchCompatFingerPrintLogin.
setOnCheckedChangeListener(new
      CompoundButton.OnCheckedChangeListener() {
      @Override
      public void onCheckedChanged(CompoundButton
buttonView, boolean
        isChecked) {
        if (isChecked) {
          String username = ...
            fido2Handler.onRegistration(username, new
ICallBack() {
              @Override
              public void onSuccess(Object bean) {
                // Record the registration result.
```

```
              . . .
            }
          });
        }
      }
    });
  }
}
```

Now let's call the **onRegistration** method in the **Fido2Handler.java** file to learn how related code called by the method is processed.

1. Check whether FIDO2 is supported. In the **onRegistration** method of the **Fido2Handler.java** file, call the **isSupported** method of the FIDO2 client.

```
if (!fido2Client.isSupported()) {
  callBack.onError("onRegistration:FIDO2 is not
supported.");
  return;
}
```

2. Obtain the challenge value and related policy from the FIDO server.

```
// Assemble the request message of the FIDO server.
ServerPublicKeyCredentialCreationOptionsRequest
request = ...
// Obtain the challenge value and related policy from
the FIDO server.
ServerCreationOptionsResp response = fidoServerClient.
getAttestationOptions(request);
if (!ServerStatus.OK.equals(response.getStatus())) {
  callBack.onError("onRegistration: get attestation
options fail.");
  return;
}
```

3. Call the **getCreationOptions** method to assemble the registration request message, based on such data as the challenge value returned by the FIDO server.

```
public static PublicKeyCredentialCreationOptions
getCreationOptions(ServerCreationOptionsResp resp) {
  PublicKeyCredentialCreationOptions.Builder builder =
new PublicKeyCredentialCreationOptions.Builder();
```

```
    // Set PublicKeyCredentialRpEntity.
    setPublicKeyCredentialRp(resp, builder);
    // Set PublicKeyCredentialUserEntity.
    setPublicKeyCredentialUser(resp, builder);
    // Set the challenge value.
    setChallenge(resp, builder);
    // Set the supported algorithm.
    setPublicKeyCredParams(resp, builder);
    // Set the exclusion list.
    setExcludeList(resp, builder);
    // Set the authenticator selection criteria.
    setAuthenticatorSelection(resp, builder);
    // Set the credential preference.
    setAttestation(resp, builder);
    setExtensions(resp, builder);
    builder.setTimeoutSeconds(resp.getTimeout());
    return builder.build();
}
```

4. Use the **reg2Fido2Client** method to send a registration request to the FIDO2 client. First, call the **getRegistrationIntent** method of the FIDO2 client to obtain a **Fido2Intent** instance. Then call the **launchFido2Activity** method of the **Fido2Intent** object, and pass the parent activity and registration request code **Fido2Client. REGISTRATION_REQUEST** to start the FIDO2 client and register the activity. The registration request code here was specified by the FIDO SDK.

```
private void reg2Fido2Client(PublicKeyCredentialCreati
onOptions
    publicKeyCredentialCreationOptions, final ICallBack
callBack) {
  NativeFido2RegistrationOptions registrationOptions =
    NativeFido2RegistrationOptions.DEFAULT _ OPTIONS;
  Fido2RegistrationRequest registrationRequest =
    new Fido2RegistrationRequest(publicKeyCredentialCre
ationOptions, null);
    // Call Fido2Client.getRegistrationIntent to obtain a
Fido2Intent object.
    fido2Client.getRegistrationIntent(registrationRequest,
    registrationOptions, new Fido2IntentCallback() {
    @Override
    public void onSuccess(Fido2Intent fido2Intent) {
      // Call Fido2Client.REGISTRATION _ REQUEST to start
the FIDO2 client registration process.
```

```
       fido2Intent.launchFido2Activity(Fido2Handler.this.
   activity, Fido2Client.REGISTRATION _ REQUEST);
     }
     ...
   });
 }
```

11.3.3 Obtaining the Registration Result

Perform the following steps:

1. Obtain the result using the **onActivityResult** method in the **Setting Act.java** file. If the request code is **Fido2Client.REGISTRATION_ REQUEST**, which is specified by the FIDO SDK, call the **onRegister-ToServer** method of the **Fido2Handler** class to parse the result, and verify it on the FIDO server.

```
@Override
protected void onActivityResult(int requestCode, int
resultCode, @Nullable
    Intent data) {
  super.onActivityResult(requestCode, resultCode, data);
  ...
  if (requestCode == Fido2Client.REGISTRATION _ REQUEST) {
    // Verify the registration result on the FIDO server.
    final boolean registerResult = fido2Handler.
onRegisterToServer(data);
    // Set the fingerprint sign-in switch status.
    mSwitchCompatFingerPrintLogin.setChecked
(registerResult);
    SPUtil.put(SettingAct.this,        SPConstants.FINGER _
PRINT _ LOGIN _ SWITCH, registerResult);
  }
}
```

2. Parse the registration result and verify it on the FIDO server. In the **onRegisterToServer** method of the **Fido2Handler.java** file, call the **getFido2RegistrationResponse** method of the FIDO2 client to parse the registration result, and then send a result verification request to the FIDO server. Registration will complete upon success-ful verification.

```
public boolean onRegisterToServer(Intent data) {
    // Parse the registration result.
    Fido2RegistrationResponse fido2RegistrationResponse =
```

```
fido2Client.getFido2RegistrationResponse(data);

    // Access the FIDO server and verify the registration
result.
    return reg2Server(fido2RegistrationResponse);
}
```

11.3.4 Initiating the Authentication Process

In the **LoginAct.java** file, the **onLogin()** method calls the **onAuthentication** method of the **Fido2Handler** class. This initiates authentication once the user touches **Sign in** on the sign-in screen for the Pet Store app.

```
private void onLogin() {
  String username = ...
  fido2Handler.onAuthentication(username, new
ICallBack<Object>() {
    @Override
    public void onSuccess(Object bean) {
      // Record the sign-in status if fingerprint
sign-in is successful.
    }
    @Override
    public void onError(String errorMsg) {
      // Use a password to sign in if fingerprint
sign-in fails.
      loginUseNameAndPasswordWithUserDetect();
    }
  });
}
```

The FIDO2 authentication process is encapsulated in the **onAuthentication** method in the **Fido2Handler.java** file, with the following processing logic:

1. Check whether FIDO2 is supported. This process is similar to the registration process. You'll only need to call the **isSupported()** method of the FIDO2 client to do so.

   ```
   if (!fido2Client.isSupported()) {
     callBack.onError("onClickAuthentication:FIDO2 is not
   supported.");
   ```

```
    return;
}
```

2. Obtain the challenge value and related policy from the FIDO server.

```
// Assemble the request message of the FIDO server.
ServerPublicKeyCredentialCreationOptionsRequest
request =
  getAuthnServerPublicKeyCredentialCreationOptionsRequ
est(username);

// Obtain the challenge value and related policy from
the FIDO server.
ServerCreationOptionsResp response = fidoServerClient.
getAssertionOptions(request);
if (!ServerStatus.OK.equals(response.getStatus())) {
  callBack.onError("auth fail");
  return;
}
```

3. Call the **getCredentialRequestOptions** method to assemble the authentication request message, based on such data as the challenge value returned by the FIDO server.

```
public static PublicKeyCredentialRequestOptions
getCredentialRequestOptions(ServerCreationOptionsResp
response) {
  PublicKeyCredentialRequestOptions.Builder builder =
new PublicKeyCredentialRequestOptions.Builder();
  // Set the relying party (RP) ID.
  builder.setRpId(response.getRpId());
  // Set the challenge value.

builder.setChallenge(ByteUtils.base642Byte(response.
getChallenge()));
  // Set the trustlist.
  ServerPublicKeyCredentialDescriptor[] descriptors =
response.getAllowCredentials();
  if (descriptors != null) {
    List<PublicKeyCredentialDescriptor> descriptorList
= new ArrayList<>();
    for (ServerPublicKeyCredentialDescriptor descriptor
: descriptors) {
      ArrayList<AuthenticatorTransport> transports =
new ArrayList<>();
```

```
        if (descriptor.getTransports() != null) {
          try {

transports.add(AuthenticatorTransport.
fromValue(descriptor.
            getTransports()));
        } catch (Exception e) {
          Log.e(TAG, e.getMessage(), e);
        }
      }
      PublicKeyCredentialDescriptor desc = new
  PublicKeyCredentialDescriptor(
        PublicKeyCredentialType.PUBLIC _ KEY, ByteUtils.
          base642Byte(descriptor.getId()), transports);
      descriptorList.add(desc);
    }
    builder.setAllowList(descriptorList);
  }
  // Set extensions.
  if (response.getExtensions() != null) {
    builder.setExtensions(response.getExtensions());
  }
  // Set the timeout interval.
  builder.setTimeoutSeconds(response.getTimeout());
  return builder.build();
  }
```

4. Send an authentication request to the FIDO2 client. The request is
   encapsulated in the **authn2Fido2Client** method in the **Fido2Handler.
   java** file. First, call the **getAuthenticationIntent** method of the
   FIDO2 client to obtain a **Fido2Intent** instance. Then call the **launch-
   Fido2Activity** method of the **Fido2Intent** object, and pass the parent
   activity and **AUTHENTICATION_REQUEST**, the code specified
   by the FIDO SDK, to start FIDO2 client authentication.

```
private void authn2Fido2Client(PublicKeyCredentialRequ
estOptions
  publicKeyCredentialCreationOptions, final ICallBack
callBack) {
  NativeFido2AuthenticationOptions authentication
Options =
    NativeFido2AuthenticationOptions.DEFAULT _ OPTIONS;
  Fido2AuthenticationRequest authenticationRequest =
```

```
      new Fido2AuthenticationRequest(publicKeyCredential
CreationOptions, null);
      // Call Fido2Client.getAuthenticationIntent to obtain
a Fido2Intent object and
      // start the FIDO2 client authentication process.
      fido2Client.getAuthenticationIntent(authentication
Request, authenticationOptions,
        new Fido2IntentCallback() {
          @Override
          public void onSuccess(Fido2Intent fido2Intent) {
            // Call Fido2Client.AUTHENTICATION _ REQUEST to
start the FIDO2
            // client authentication process.
fido2Intent.launchFido2Activity(Fido2Handler.this.
activity,
            Fido2Client.AUTHENTICATION _ REQUEST);
          }
          ...
      });
    }
```

11.3.5 Obtaining the Authentication Result

Perform the following steps:

1. Call the **onActivityResult** method in **LoginAct.java** to obtain
   the authentication result. If the request code is **Fido2Client.
   AUTHENTICATION_REQUEST**, call the **onAuthToServer**
   method of the **Fido2Handler** class to enable parsing of the result,
   and verify it on the FIDO server.

```
protected void onActivityResult(int requestCode, int
resultCode, @Nullable
  Intent data) {
  super.onActivityResult(requestCode, resultCode, data);
  if (requestCode == Fido2Client.AUTHENTICATION _
REQUEST) {
    // Enable verification of the authentication result
on the FIDO server.
    final boolean authToServerResult = fido2Handler.
onAuthToServer(data);
    if(authToServerResult){
      ...
  } ...
}
```

2. Parse the authentication result and verify it on the FIDO server. In the **onAuthToServer** method of the **Fido2Handler.java** file, call the **getFido2AuthenticationResponse** method of the FIDO2 client to parse the authentication result, and then send a verification request to the FIDO server. Authentication will complete upon successful verification.

```
public boolean onAuthToServer(Intent data) {
    // Parse the authentication result.
    Fido2AuthenticationResponse fido2AuthenticationRe-
sponse =
        fido2Client.getFido2AuthenticationResponse(data);

    // Request the FIDO server to verify the authentication
result.
        return auth2Server(fido2AuthenticationResponse);
}
```

Thus far, we have integrated the FIDO2 client into the Pet Store app and used FIDO2 capabilities to implement fingerprint sign-in. Next, let's move on to BioAuthn integration.

11.4 BIOAUTHN

In this section, we'll learn how to use the BioAuthn-AndroidX SDK to implement both fingerprint and facial authentication. Although BioAuthn was not integrated into the Pet Store app, fingerprint authentication and facial authentication are both commonly-used functions, so we'll provide the reference sample code here.

Fingerprint authentication is based on **androidx.biometric:biometric: 1.0.0**. If you have used Android Support Library, you'll want to use the BioAuthn SDK for fingerprint and facial authentication to ensure compatibility. Here we'll use the BioAuthn-AndroidX SDK to integrate the fingerprint and facial authentication capabilities individually.

11.4.1 Fingerprint Authentication

Perform the following steps:

1. Initialize **BioAuthnManager** in **Activity**, and call **canAuth()** to check whether fingerprint authentication is supported.

```
// Specify whether fingerprint authentication is
supported.
```

```
BioAuthnManager bio
AuthnManager = new
BioAuthnManager(this);
int errorCode = bio
AuthnManager.canAuth();
if (errorCode != 0) {
  // Fingerprint
authentication is not
supported.
  return;
}
```

> **NOTE**
> Fingerprint authentication is only supported on devices that run Android 6.0 (API Level 23) or later. In addition, the device itself will need to support fingerprint authentication.

2. Construct the callback method **BioAuthnCallback** to process events such as authentication success and failure.

```
// Construct the callback method.
BioAuthnCallback callback = new BioAuthnCallback() {
  @Override
  public void onAuthError(int errMsgId, CharSequence
errString) {
    // Authentication error.
  }
  @Override
  public void onAuthSucceeded(BioAuthnResult result) {
    // Authentication success.
  }
  @Override
  public void onAuthFailed() {
    // Authentication failure.
  }
};
```

If the system encounters any security issues, the callback method **BioAuthnCallback.onAuthError()** will return an error code. For the list of codes, please refer to the HUAWEI Developers website.

If the system is secure, fingerprint authentication will proceed.

3. Construct a **BioAuthnPrompt** instance to display message prompts.

```
// Construct a prompt.
BioAuthnPrompt.PromptInfo.Builder builder = new
BioAuthnPrompt.PromptInfo.Builder()
.setTitle("This is the title.")
.setSubtitle("This is the subtitle")
.setDescription("This is the description");
```

```
// Prompt the user to use their fingerprint for authen-
tication, and also provide options for the user to use
the PIN, lock screen pattern, or lock screen password
for authentication.
// If the parameter is set to true here,
setNegativeButtonText(CharSequence) will not be
supported.
builder.setDeviceCredentialAllowed(true);
// Set the text of the authentication cancellation
button. If this parameter is set, setDevice
CredentialAllowed(true) will not be supported.
builder.setNegativeButtonText("This is the 'Cancel'
button.");
BioAuthnPrompt.PromptInfo info = builder.build();
```

When you create **PromptInfo** using **PromptInfo.Builder,** you'll only be able to select either **setDeviceCredentialAllowed(true)** or **setNegativeButtonText().** setDeviceCredentialAllowed(true) allows for fingerprint authentication to be changed to another authentication mode, such as lock screen password.

Please take note that **BioAuthnPrompt.PromptInfo.Builder. setDeviceCredentialAllowed(true)** cannot be used on devices that have an in-screen fingerprint sensor and run EMUI 9.x. This includes the Huawei Mate 20 Pro, P30, P30 Pro, and Magic 2 smartphone models. On such devices, authentication will fail immediately upon the user attempting to change the authentication mode to lock screen password. In addition, EMUI 9.x and earlier versions might restrict the number of fingerprint authentication attempts. To resolve this issue, you can apply one of the following methods:

- Not creating the **BioAuthnPrompt** object for the activity more than once.

- Calling the **Activity.recreate()** method to re-create the UI, after the authentication is complete.

- Closing and reopening the activity.

4. Call the **auth()** method for authentication.

```
BioAuthnPrompt bioAuthnPrompt = new BioAuthnPrompt(this,
   ContextCompat.getMainExecutor(this), callback);
bioAuthnPrompt.auth(info);
```

Now that we've configured fingerprint authentication, let's do the same for 3D facial authentication.

11.4.2 3D Facial Authentication

If the system encounters any security issues, the callback method **BioAuthn Callback.onAuthError()** will return an error code. For the list of codes, please refer to the HUAWEI Developers website. The procedure for integrating 3D facial authentication is as follows:

1. Initialize **FaceManager** in **Activity**, and call **canAuth()** to check whether 3D facial authentication is supported.

```
FaceManager faceManager = new FaceManager(this);
    int errorCode = faceManager.canAuth();
    if (errorCode != 0) { // Not supported.
     return; }
```

2. Construct the callback method **BioAuthnCallback** to process events such as authentication success and failure.

```
BioAuthnCallback callback = new BioAuthnCallback() {
    @Override
    public void onAuthError(int errMsgId, CharSequence
errString)
        { // Authentication error. }
    @Override
    public void onAuthHelp(int helpMsgId, CharSequence
helpString)
        { // Help. }
@Override
    public void onAuthSucceeded(BioAuthnResult result) {
// Authentication success. }
    @Override
    public void onAuthFailed() { // Authentication
failure.
    }
    };
```

3. Call the **auth()** method for authentication.

```
// Create a cancellation signal.
CancellationSignal cancellationSignal = new
CancellationSignal();
FaceManager faceManager = new FaceManager(this);
```

```
// Flags.
int flags = 0;
// Set the authentication message handler.
Handler handler = null;
// Pass the value false to KeyGenParameterSpec.
Builder.setUserAuthenticationRequired().
// (Recommended) Set CryptoObject to null.
CryptoObject crypto = null;
// Perform 3D facial authentication.
faceManager.auth(crypto, cancellationSignal, flags,
callback, handler);
```

11.5 SUMMARY

In this chapter, we've learned the two main features associated with the FIDO service: FIDO2 and BioAuthn. Our sample code shows you how to integrate the FIDO2 client and BioAuthn, as well as how to use the FIDO2 fingerprint authentication capability in the Pet Store app. In doing so, we've now concluded the development process.

Looking back, in Chapters 4–11, we integrated the Account Kit, IAP, Push Kit, Location Kit, Site Kit, Map Kit, Safety Detect, and FIDO services provided by HMS Core and implemented a range of basic functions for the Pet Store app, including account registration, sign-in, and personal center settings. In addition, we've also added a function for browsing nearby pet stores and pushing messages to attract more customers and set up a membership framework to garner revenue from pet videos.

Now that we've built our Pet Store app, let's turn our attention to debugging it and bringing it online.

NOTE

1 To learn more about WebAuthn, please refer to https://www.w3.org/TR/webauthn/#webauthn-client.

CHAPTER 12

Testing and Release

12.1 DIGIX LAB TEST SERVICES

DIGIX Lab Test Services, which consists of Cloud Testing and Cloud Debugging, is a Huawei-developed app testing platform designed to help you test apps integrated with Huawei's open capabilities on a wide selection of Huawei devices.

Cloud Testing takes care of compatibility, stability, performance, and power consumption, detecting exceptions such as crashes, unexpected exits, and black/white screens that occur when you install, launch, run, or uninstall the app. It also collects performance and power consumption indicators while your app is running, helping you precisely locate problems and make the necessary adjustments prior to releasing the app. Cloud Debugging enables you to remotely debug an app on the latest and most popular Huawei devices from any location in the world, as if you were running the app on your own device. The service also provides different levels of logs for you to locate and fix issues efficiently.

To access the DIGIX Lab Test Services, sign in to the HUAWEI Developers console with your registered HUAWEI ID and click **Customize console** in the upper right corner, as shown in Figure 12.1.

On the **App services** tab, select **Cloud Testing** and **Cloud Debugging** in the **Testing** area, as shown in Figure 12.2. Then click **Close**.

After that, click **App services** in the navigation tree on the left. The **Cloud Testing** and **Cloud Debugging** service cards are displayed in the **Testing** area, as shown in Figure 12.3. Click either card to open the corresponding service page. Now, we'll run these services on our Pet Store app.

DOI: 10.1201/9781003206699-12

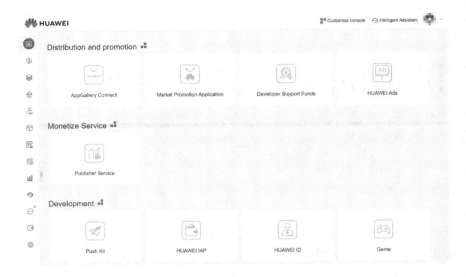

FIGURE 12.1   HUAWEI Developers console.

FIGURE 12.2   Customizing the console.

12.1.1 Cloud Testing

Cloud Testing is a one-stop service intended for testing mobile apps in an efficient yet cost-effective way, relieving you from the cost, technology, and efficiency challenges that come with app development and testing.

NOTE

For details, please refer to the Cloud Testing introduction and operation guide at https://developer.huawei.com/consumer/en/doc/development/Tools-Guides/introduction-0000001073380536.

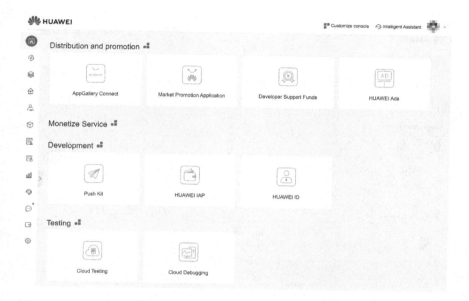

FIGURE 12.3 Cloud Testing and Cloud Debugging service cards.

NOTICE

Cloud Testing currently does not support testing for account sign-in or signed-in functions.

Sign in to the HUAWEI Developers console and click **App services** in the navigation tree on the left. Scroll down to the **Testing** area and click the **Cloud Testing** card. If this is your first time there, you'll see the page for creating a test. Otherwise, you'll see a list of tests. To create a test, click **New test** in the upper right corner, as shown in Figure 12.4.

Now let's take a look at how to test the compatibility, stability, performance, and power consumption of the app.

12.1.1.1 Compatibility Testing

This checks to see if your app behaves as expected across the full range of devices through which your users will access the app. A compatibility test covers the following items:

- Initial installation: checks whether the app is properly installed for the first time after being downloaded.

(a)

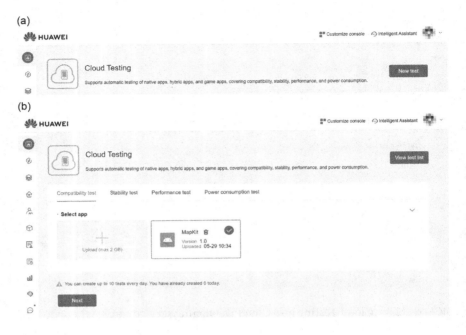

(b)

FIGURE 12.4   Creating a test.

- Reinstallation: checks whether the app is properly reinstalled after being deleted.

- Startup: checks whether the app properly displays its home screen when launched.

- Crash: checks whether the app crashes while running.

- ANR (Application Not Responding): checks whether the app fails to respond to user inputs.

- Unexpected exit: checks whether the app exits unexpectedly.

- Running error: checks whether an operation goes wrong while the app is running.

- UI error: checks whether there is a UI error, such as a page not completely displayed.

- Black/White screen: checks whether the screen goes black or white.

FIGURE 12.5 Creating a compatibility test.

- Exit failure: checks whether the app, or one of its screens, fails to exit, causing the app to be forcibly stopped.

- Uninstallation: checks whether the app is properly uninstalled, and whether residual data still exists after uninstallation.

Now, let's create a compatibility test:

1. Click the **Compatibility test** tab, click **Upload**, and upload the Pet Store APK. Figure 12.5 shows the uploaded APK.

2. Click **Next**. In the **Filter criteria** area, you can filter devices by device brand and Android version, as shown in Figure 12.6.

3. Select one or more device models and click **OK**. The dialog box shown in Figure 12.7 will display, indicating that the test has been successfully submitted.

4. Click **View test list** to see if the newly created test exists, as shown in Figure 12.8.

5. After the test is complete, click **View** to view the test report, where you'll see such items as the pass rate, number of different issues detected, and test result of each device model, as shown in Figure 12.9.

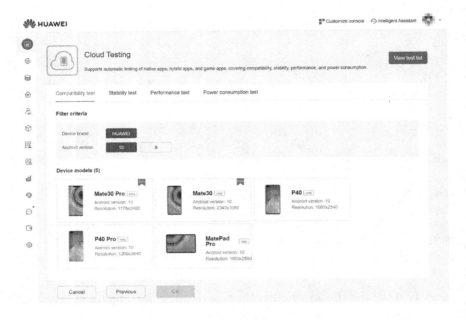

FIGURE 12.6   Filter criteria.

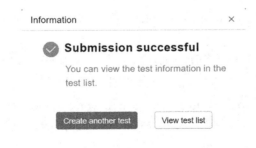

FIGURE 12.7   Successful test submission.

FIGURE 12.8   New test on the list.

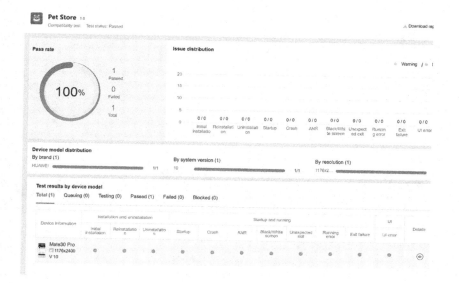

FIGURE 12.9   Compatibility test report.

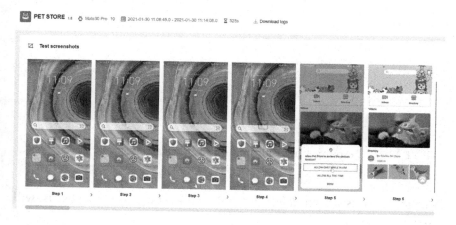

FIGURE 12.10   Test screenshots.

6. To view the test result details for a device model, click the ⊚ icon in the **Details** column. Figure 12.10 shows screenshots captured during testing.

Also available for viewing is the resource trace information, which includes the CPU usage, memory usage, and battery temperature, as well

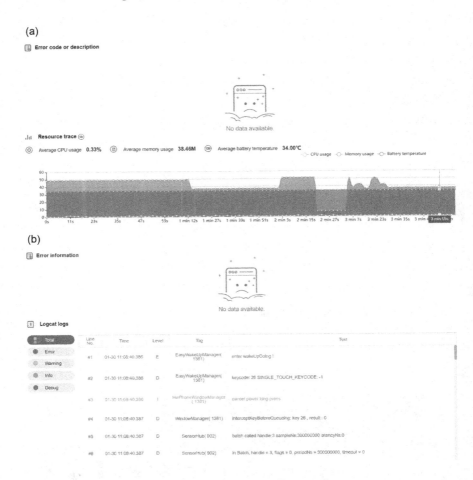

FIGURE 12.11   Resource trace information and Logcat logs.

as Logcat logs, as shown in Figure 12.11. Error information, if it exists, will also be displayed.

12.1.1.2 Stability Testing

Stability testing falls into long-term traversal testing and random testing. It enables you to detect stability-related issues, such as memory leakage, memory overwriting, frozen display, and crashes on Huawei devices. The procedure for creating a stability test is similar to that for creating a compatibility test. The only difference is that we'll need to specify the stability test duration, as shown in Figure 12.12.

FIGURE 12.12   Creating a stability test.

A stability test report shows the number of crashes, ANR errors, native crashes, and leaks detected, as shown in Figure 12.13. Your app will be deemed to have failed the stability test if the number of issues found for a single test item exceeds 10.

12.1.1.3 Performance Testing

Performance testing collects app performance data such as CPU and memory usage. The procedure for creating a performance test is also similar to that for creating a compatibility test task. The only difference is that you'll need to specify the app category when creating a performance test, as shown in Figure 12.14. Some test items in the test result may vary by category. For example, the pass requirements for the frame rate test are different for game and non-game apps.

A performance test report shows the cold start duration, warm start duration, frame rate, memory usage, and CPU usage, as shown in Figure 12.15.

12.1.1.4 Power Consumption Testing

Power consumption testing allows you to check your app's key indicators and determine how much power your app draws from different devices. The procedure for creating a power consumption test is similar to that for creating a compatibility test, except that you'll also need to set the

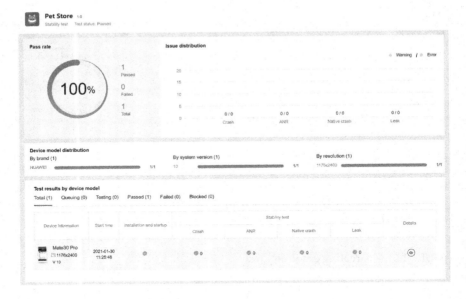

FIGURE 12.13   Stability test report.

FIGURE 12.14   Creating a performance test.

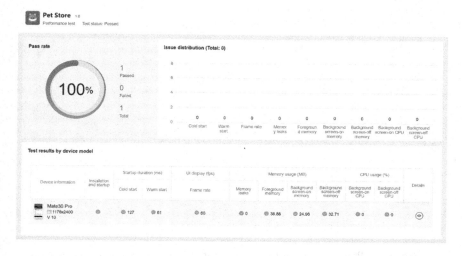

FIGURE 12.15 Performance test report.

FIGURE 12.16 Creating a power consumption test.

app category, as shown in Figure 12.16. Some test items in the test result may vary by category. For example, the evaluation standards for the audio usage duration test are different for audiovisual as opposed to other apps.

The test collects resource usage data including wakelock duration, screen usage duration, WLAN usage duration, and audio usage duration, as well as behavioral data such as the number of wakeup alarms per hour.

FIGURE 12.17   Power consumption test report.

The test report will provide you with a clear picture of your app's power consumption, as shown in Figure 12.17.

12.1.2 Cloud Debugging

Cloud Debugging is an efficient solution for debugging apps remotely on Huawei devices, which spares you from having to account for different device models and management challenges. In this section, we'll learn how to use the Cloud Debugging service on the Pet Store app.

NOTE

For details, please refer to the Cloud Debugging introduction and operation guide at https://developer.huawei.com/consumer/en/doc/development/Tools-Guides/introduction-0000001073540136.

12.1.2.1 Performing Remote Debugging in Real Time

1. Sign in to the HUAWEI Developers console and click **App services** in the navigation tree on the left. Scroll down to the **Testing** area and click the **Cloud Debugging** card to display the page shown in Figure 12.18.

2. Filter devices by region, series, operating system, and type. Then move the cursor to a device model in **Available** state and click **Start debugging**, as shown in Figure 12.19.

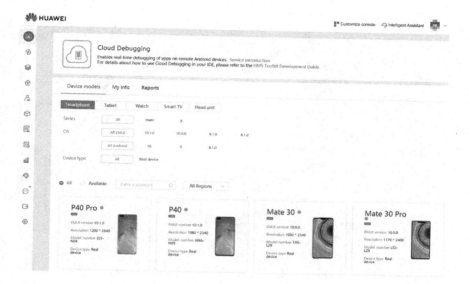

FIGURE 12.18   Cloud Debugging page.

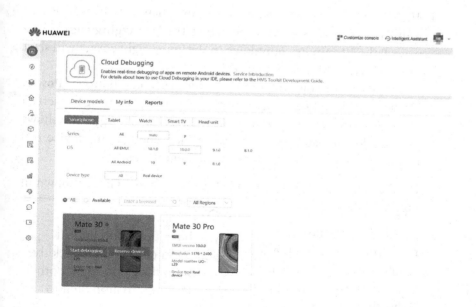

FIGURE 12.19   Filtering devices.

FIGURE 12.20   Applying for a device model.

3. Set the debug duration to 30 minutes, 1 hour, or 2 hours, and click **OK**. Here, we'll use a 30-minute duration, as shown in Figure 12.20.

4. The system allocates a device to you and then initializes it. Please wait for this process to complete. Once the **Debugging** page is displayed, the 30-minute countdown in the upper right corner will start immediately, as shown in Figure 12.21.

   The left side shows the device screen with four buttons (**Power, Home, Menu**, and **Back**), a drop-down list box for setting the screen resolution, and an icon for rotating the screen. The right side shows the tabs for uploading app or theme files, configuring device settings, taking screenshots, and viewing Logcat logs.

5. On the **Apps** tab, upload an APK (no more than 2 GB), as shown in Figure 12.22.

6. Check the APK upload progress. Once complete, the app is automatically installed.

   A message will appear indicating that the installation is successful. The app

> **NOTE**
>
> If you have uploaded an APK before, you can directly click the ⟳ icon in the upper right corner of the app information area to install the app.

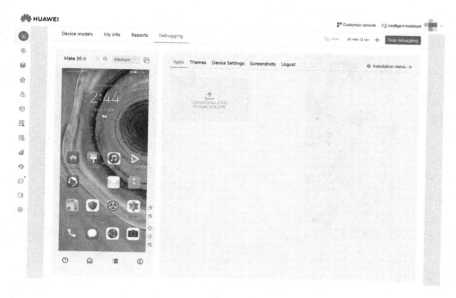

FIGURE 12.21   Debugging page.

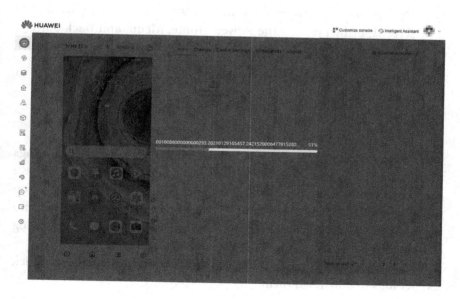

FIGURE 12.22   Uploading the APK.

FIGURE 12.23   Successful app installation.

version and type are displayed on the **Apps** tab page, as shown in Figure 12.23.

7. Operate the device by moving your cursor on or touching the device screens, or by pressing the **Power, Home, Menu,** and **Back** buttons remotely.

8. Go to **My info** to view your debugging information, as shown in Figure 12.24.

12.1.2.2 Remotely Viewing System Logs

On the **Debugging** page, click the **Logcat** tab and then click **Obtain logs** to show logs generated in real time during the debugging. Once you have clicked this button, its name will change to **Stop**. Click it again to stop showing logs. Figure 12.25 shows the **Logcat** tab. Logs are classified into the following levels: verbose, debug, info, warn, error, and assert. Each log contains the generation time, PID, log level, tag, and text.

The figure shows a partial log list. To view all generated logs, click **Export logs** to download them.

FIGURE 12.24   My info page.

FIGURE 12.25   Obtaining logs.

12.1.2.3 Rotating the Screen

On the **Debugging** page, click the ⬚ icon to rotate the screen to land-scape or portrait mode, as shown in Figure 12.26. However, it's important to note that a screen that does not support landscape mode will remain in portrait mode, with a displayed message informing you of this.

12.1.2.4 Viewing Device Details

To view details about a device that is being used for debugging, click the ② icon next to the device model on the **Debugging** page, as shown in Figure 12.27.

FIGURE 12.26   Rotating the screen.

Model number	TAS-L29
Build number	TAS-L29 10.0.0.191(C636E8R8P1)
Manufacturer	huawei
Screen width	1080
Screen height	2340
EMUI version	10.0.0
CPU version	arm64-v8a

FIGURE 12.27   Viewing device details.

12.2 APP RELEASE

Once the app has passed all testing items, it will be ready for release to HUAWEI AppGallery, an app distribution platform that secures apps through developer identity verification and four-layer protection. The following sections will walk you through the process of releasing an app to HUAWEI AppGallery, as outlined in Figure 12.28.

12.2.1 Signing In and Creating an App

As detailed in Chapter 4, the app has already been created.

12.2.2 Configuring Basic App Information

Basic app information includes the app introduction and icon. To configure the basic app information:

1. Sign in to the HUAWEI Developers console and go to HUAWEI AppGallery Connect. For more details, please refer to Section 4.2.2

2. Click **My apps** and then click the Pet Store app from the app list. On the displayed **App information** page, select compatible devices, as shown in Figure 12.29.

FIGURE 12.28 App release process.

FIGURE 12.29 App information page.

FIGURE 12.30   Adding a language.

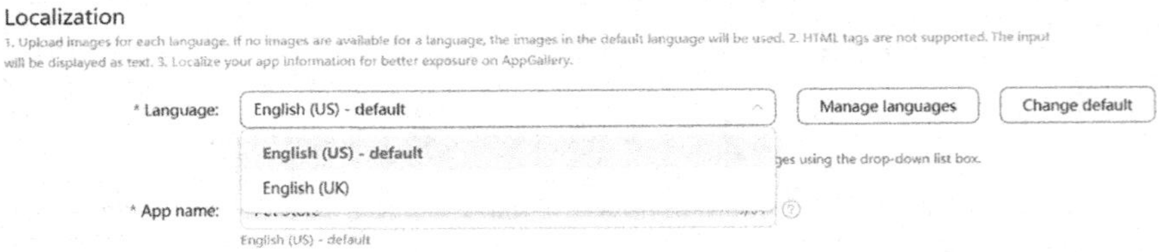

Localization
1. Upload images for each language. If no images are available for a language, the images in the default language will be used. 2. HTML tags are not supported. The input
will be displayed as text. 3. Localize your app information for better exposure on AppGallery.

* Language: English (US) - default   Manage languages   Change default

                English (US) - default   ges using the drop-down list box.
                English (UK)
* App name: ⑦

                English (US) - default

FIGURE 12.31   Selecting a language and setting the corresponding parameters.

3. Click **Manage languages** next to the **Language** parameter and
   select languages for which you wish to localize the app into, as
   shown in Figure 12.30. The system currently supports 78 different
   languages.

4. Select a language from the **Language** drop-down list box and set
   the corresponding parameters for the language, including the full
   description, brief introduction, app icon, and screenshots, as shown
   in Figure 12.31.

5. Configure all required information and click **Save**, as shown in
   Figure 12.32.

App information
This information will be displayed on HUAWEI AppGallery. Any changes will be released with the next version of the app.

[Save]

FIGURE 12.32   Saving the app information.

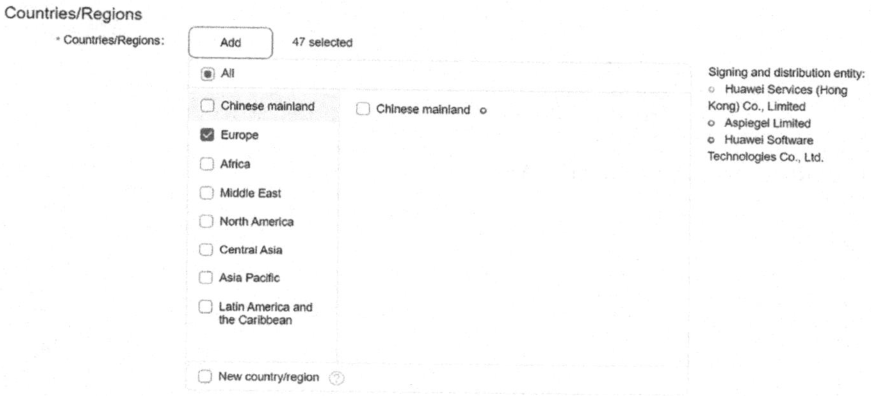

Countries/Regions

· Countries/Regions: [Add]   47 selected

◉ All   Signing and distribution entity:
                                                   ○ Huawei Services (Hong
☐ Chinese mainland   ☐ Chinese mainland ○   Kong) Co., Limited
                                                   ○ Aspiegel Limited
☑ Europe   ○ Huawei Software
                                                   Technologies Co., Ltd.
☐ Africa

☐ Middle East

☐ North America

☐ Central Asia

☐ Asia Pacific

☐ Latin America and
  the Caribbean

☐ New country/region ⑦

FIGURE 12.33   Selecting countries and regions for app distribution.

12.2.3 Configuring Distribution Information

Distribution information includes the countries and regions where you want to distribute the app and the age-appropriateness of your app content. To configure the app distribution information:

1. Click **Draft** under **Version information**. On the displayed page, click **Add** next to the **Countries/Regions** parameter and select the countries and regions where you want to distribute the app, as shown in Figure 12.33.

2. Click **Software packages** in the **Software version** area and upload the APK to be released, as shown in Figure 12.34.

3. Set **Payment type** under **Payment information** and **Category** under **In-app purchase**, as shown in Figure 12.35.

4. Click **Apply Ratings** within the area shown in Figure 12.36, and specify which age groups the app is suitable for.

5. Enter the privacy policy URL and configure copyright information by uploading any necessary supporting documents, as shown in Figure 12.37.

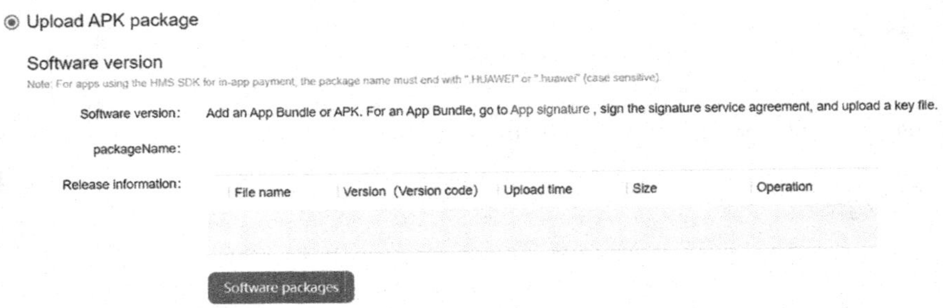

⦿ Upload APK package

Software version

Note: For apps using the HMS SDK for in-app payment, the package name must end with ".HUAWEI" or ".huawei" (case sensitive)

Software version:	Add an App Bundle or APK. For an App Bundle, go to App signature , sign the signature service agreement, and upload a key file.
packageName:	
Release information:	File name Version (Version code) Upload time Size Operation

Software packages

FIGURE 12.34   Uploading the APK.

Payment information

・ Payment type: ⦿ Free   ◯ Pay per download

In-app purchase

Category: ☐ Activation   ☐ Items   ☐ Unlocking game content   ☐ Virtual coins

☐ Paid chapters (reading app)   ☐ Paid courses   ☐ Membership   ☐ Other

(For apps using the HMS SDK for in-app payment, the package name must end with ".HUAWEI" or ".huawei" (case sensitive).)

FIGURE 12.35   Setting the payment and in-app purchase parameters.

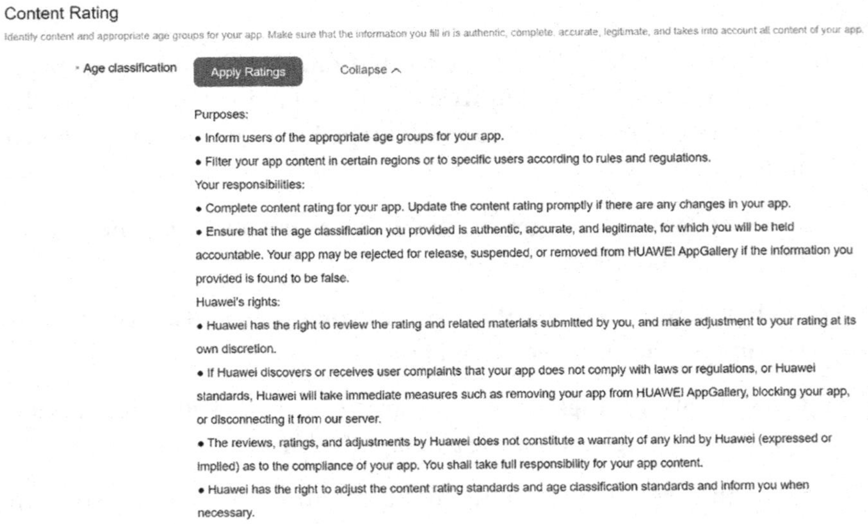

Content Rating

Identify content and appropriate age groups for your app. Make sure that the information you fill in is authentic, complete, accurate, legitimate, and takes into account all content of your app.

・ Age classification   Apply Ratings   Collapse ∧

Purposes:

• Inform users of the appropriate age groups for your app.

• Filter your app content in certain regions or to specific users according to rules and regulations.

Your responsibilities:

• Complete content rating for your app. Update the content rating promptly if there are any changes in your app.

• Ensure that the age classification you provided is authentic, accurate, and legitimate, for which you will be held accountable. Your app may be rejected for release, suspended, or removed from HUAWEI AppGallery if the information you provided is found to be false.

Huawei's rights:

• Huawei has the right to review the rating and related materials submitted by you, and make adjustment to your rating at its own discretion.

• If Huawei discovers or receives user complaints that your app does not comply with laws or regulations, or Huawei standards, Huawei will take immediate measures such as removing your app from HUAWEI AppGallery, blocking your app, or disconnecting it from our server.

• The reviews, ratings, and adjustments by Huawei does not constitute a warranty of any kind by Huawei (expressed or implied) as to the compliance of your app. You shall take full responsibility for your app content.

• Huawei has the right to adjust the content rating standards and age classification standards and inform you when necessary.

FIGURE 12.36   Configuring content rating.

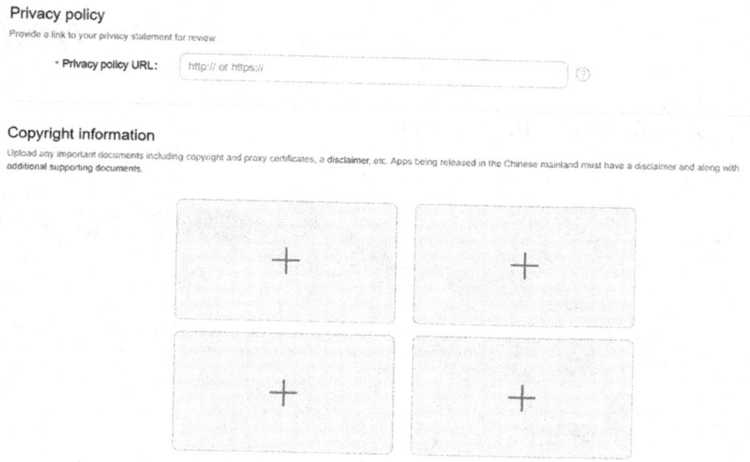

Privacy policy

Provide a link to your privacy statement for review.

‑ **Privacy policy URL:**   http:// or https://

Copyright information

Upload any important documents including copyright and proxy certificates, a disclaimer, etc. Apps being released in the Chinese mainland must have a disclaimer and along with additional supporting documents.

FIGURE 12.37   Configuring the privacy policy URL and copyright information.

Review information

Provide a test account and password in case we need to use some of your app functions that require user authentication, such as sign in, in-app content viewing, and in-app purchases. The account will be used by our reviewer to verify these functions.

☐ Login required

Notes:

0/300

Family sharing

Family sharing: ○ Yes   ◉ No

After you enable this function, up to 6 family members can use the app free of charge. This function only applies to apps released in the Chinese mainland. Family members cannot share in-app purchases.

Release schedule

‑ **Release date:**   ○ Upon approval   ○ On specific date

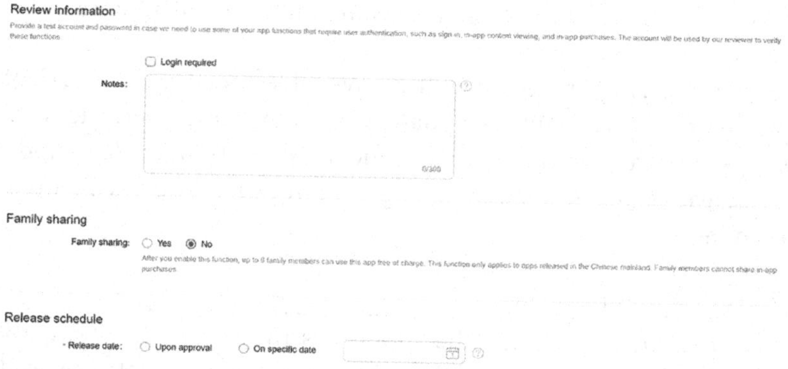

FIGURE 12.38   Configuring review information, family sharing, and release time.

6. Fill in the review information, set the family sharing function, and specify when you would like the app to go live, as shown in Figure 12.38.

12.2.4 Submitting the App for Release

After configuring all required information, submit the app for review.

1. Click **Submit**, as shown in Figure 12.39.

2. Check the app status. Once submitted successfully, the app will be placed under review, as shown in Figure 12.40.

FIGURE 12.39 Submitting the app for review.

FIGURE 12.40 App status.

3. Huawei will complete the review process as soon as possible. Please wait for the results to be sent to your contact email address.

Once the app is approved, it will be available for access on HUAWEI AppGallery. If you want to update your app, please refer to https://developer.huawei.com/consumer/en/doc/distribution/app/agc-update_app. Navigate to any other app management topics as you like if you want to learn more.

12.3 SUMMARY

In this chapter, we detailed the Cloud Testing service for compatibility, stability, performance, and power consumption tests, as well as the Cloud Debugging service for remote debugging on a wide range of Huawei devices. We also learned how to release an app to HUAWEI AppGallery.

We've now gone through the entire process associated with mobile app development and learned how to integrate several key open capabilities into the app. Now that you're familiar with the HMS ecosystem, you'll be able to take full advantage of a wide array of cutting-edge technologies, which can give you a leg up in this fast-paced mobile Internet era.

The HMS ecosystem is not limited to the key capabilities introduced in this book, and you're encouraged to stay tuned for more HMS capabilities, encompassing every stage of development, distribution, and monetization.

We hope that this book has given a glimpse into how Huawei's solutions can help you build high-quality apps and provide your users with next-level digital services. Let's explore and create a better future and bring digital to every person, home, and organization for a fully connected, intelligent world.

Appendix: HMS Ecosystem Concepts

BELOW ARE BRIEF SUMMARIES of HMS ecosystem-related concepts and terms that were mentioned in the book.

1. HMS Core

HMS Core is a collection of open capabilities created under Huawei's chip-device-cloud framework. In addition to the eight kits detailed in this book, ML Kit, Scan Kit, WisePlay DRM, and Ads Kit were released on January 15, 2020, as part of HMS Core 4.0. A few months later on June 29, 2020, Huawei released HMS Core 5.0, which encompasses enhanced open capabilities and 20 new functions, related to graphics, media, and a range of other fields, to address rapidly changing and varying needs of global developers. Please refer to the HUAWEI Developers website for information on the latest HMS Core open capabilities and support materials for how to use them.

2. HUAWEI Developers

The HUAWEI Developers official website serves as a bridge connecting Huawei with the developers throughout its ecosystem. As a platform that aims to facilitate the creation of an open, intelligent, and mutually beneficial ecosystem for users and developers alike, HUAWEI Developers has been crucial to nurturing all-scenario innovations. There you can enjoy access to a wide range of services, including ecosystem-wide initiatives, developer communities, technical support, and developer relationship management, which are global in scope and backed by high-level expertise. The service profile for HUAWEI Developers is shown below.

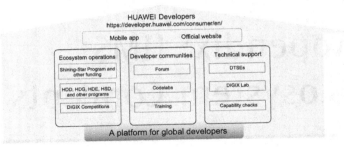

FIGURE A.1   HUAWEI Developers service profile.

3. Ecosystem-Wide Initiatives

The HMS ecosystem offers a myriad of different activities and initiatives, including incentive schemes, developer programs, and competitions, which are designed to facilitate greater engagement and nurture groundbreaking innovation.

(1) Incentive Schemes

Huawei has invested heavily in collaborative building of the HMS ecosystem, as indicated by the Shining-Star Program, first launched in November 2017, offering a US$1 billion developer-oriented incentive scheme for talented global developers. The initiative distributes innovation grants, marketing resources, and a range of other benefits to eligible developers, with the goal of giving them the support they need to succeed in today's fast-paced market.

(2) Programs

HUAWEI Developers strives to facilitate engagement and open exchange between developers and experts in the field, by offering a broad portfolio of events and support programs.

a. HUAWEI Developer Day (HDD)

HDD events are developer-centric gatherings dedicated to showcasing Huawei's latest open capabilities and services, and take the form of seminars, technical workshops, and leadership talks on cutting-edge innovations, technologies, and best practices in app development. As of the end of 2019, HDD events had been held in 46 cities around the world.

b. HUAWEI Developer Groups (HDG)

HDG is a non-profit program that assists developers who are passionate about Huawei services and capabilities in building communities for like-minded local developers. Developers who join an HDG group have the opportunity to meet fellow developers in their area, exchange ideas, and acquire new skills via in-person training sessions, technical salons, and other activities. The program also gathers technical experts and industry leaders to discuss the practical applications of HMS capabilities and share the latest technologies in various business fields. For more information about HDG and about how to become an HDG organizer, please visit https://developer.huawei.com/consumer/en/programs/hdg.

c. HUAWEI Developer Experts (HDE)

HDE is a worldwide program that recognizes individuals who demonstrate expertise in specific Huawei-related technologies and have made outstanding contributions to developer communities. Certified experts are given the opportunity to develop HMS-related courses and enjoy widespread exposure, by sharing their experience and knowledge at leading industry conferences. For more information about HDE and about how to become an expert, please visit https://developer.huawei.com/consumer/en/programs/hde.

d. HUAWEI Student Developers (HSD)

As its name suggests, HSD is focused on building a peer-to-peer learning environment for aspiring student developers. As of the end of 2020, 100 universities in China had already joined the HSD network, benefiting approximately 300,000 students. HSD activities range from campus ambassadorships and technical salons, to codelabs and DIGIX competitions, and are all dedicated to nurturing innovation and personal growth. For more information about HSD, please visit https://developer.huawei.com/consumer/en/programs/hsd.

(3) DIGIX Competitions

DIGIX is a series of competitions that aims to nurture groundbreaking product innovation, by showcasing Huawei's cutting-edge open capabilities and services. In addition to distributing awards in recognition of talented developers, the initiative also offers technical support ranging from capability integration to product marketing, and a range of easy-to-access resources. As of July 2020, over US$1.5 million in awards had been distributed at a dozen competitions, in recognition of more than 3000 achievements. To learn more about these competitions, please visit https://developer. huawei.com/consumer/en/activity/.

4. Developer Communities

HMS communities bring together developers from around the world and offer the chance to learn from and grow with your peers, wherever they may be.

(1) Forum

HUAWEI Developer Forum serves as a hub of discussion and exchange on Huawei open capabilities and services, with hundreds of Huawei technical experts and external key opinion leaders (KOLs) providing guidance and instruction. To join in, please visit https://forums.developer.huawei.com/forumPortal/en.

(2) Codelabs

A codelab is a guided tutorial offering step-by-step instructions on how to integrate Huawei open capabilities, with the goal of streamlining the app development and release processes. To benefit from such hands-on coding experience, please visit https://developer.huawei.com/consumer/ en/codelabsPortal/index.

(3) Training

This online learning portal provides educational resources and certification exams. HMS, Developer Zone, Tech Talk, and many other online resources are tailored to beginners and experienced developers alike. Since the platform's rollout at the beginning of 2020, nearly 200 courses have been held, helping hundreds of thousands of learners obtain expertise in new fields. Once you've finished certain courses, demonstrate your proficiency on the exams and get certified. For more details, please visit https://developer.huawei.com/consumer/-en/training. The following shows an example of our course certificates.

FIGURE A.2   Course certificate.

5. Technical Support

HUAWEI Developers provides a diverse range of technical support channels for its global developer community.

Notably, there are more than 300 developer technical support engineers (DTSEs) spread across the globe, who are trained to provide on-location guidance at each stage for developers to join the HMS ecosystem. Or alternatively, come chat with our intelligent assistant, contact our website customer service, or email devConnect@huawei.com for high-level service and troubleshooting.

Furthermore, we also offer DIGIX Lab Test Services, which consists of Cloud Testing and Cloud Debugging, and enables you to try out features for yourself on real Huawei devices. You can visit any one of seven DIGIX labs in Russia, Germany, Ireland, Singapore, Mexico, South Africa, and the UAE, to experience the future of app innovation firsthand, by testing out your apps, participating in activities, and meeting Huawei DTSEs in-person.

And let's not forget the vast array of documents and videos on the HUAWEI Developers website, which can be browsed at your convenience.

6. HUAWEI Developers App

This mobile app will keep you up to date on the latest news, competitions, and training videos. You can also use it to keep tabs on your products, account balances, operational reports, and other related data. The app can be found and downloaded on mainstream Android app stores.

7. Pet Store App Code and APK

To view the server and client sample code for the Pet Store app, please visit GitHub at https://github.com/huaweicodelabs/PetStore, or scan the following QR code with your phone's browser to download the APK:, see Figure A.3.

FIGURE A.3   QR code of Pet Store APK.

Printed in the United States
by Baker & Taylor Publisher Services